WHAT OTHERS ARE SAYING . . .

Unlike many Christian authors who are quick to pen their latest insights and experiences, Jim has been a practitioner of prophecy for many, many years. What really qualifies him to write this book, however, is that he is not only highly gifted in the prophetic, but even more importantly, he is a man after God's heart. The essential message the Church needs to understand today is that "the messenger is the message, and the prophet is the prophecy." Jim not only has a message; he is a living epistle of the whole art of intimacy with God, and of devotion with simplicity to the Person of Christ Jesus!

Marc A. Dupont
Mantle of Praise Ministries
Fort Wayne, Indiana

This is must reading for all Christians who want to hear what Christ is presently saying to His Church. Jim not only gives a scriptural presentation, but he prophetically reveals the heart of God and mind of Christ for this day and hour. The reader will be greatly enlightened and inspired to fulfill Peter's command (2 Peter 1:12) to be established in the present truth, especially dealing with the prophetic and apostolic. God bless you, Jim, for blessing the Church with such a wonderful presentation of truth.

Dr. Bill Hamon
Founder, president, bishop, Christian International Ministries Network

Here is a book loaded with interesting material and told in fascinating down-home style. Jim Goll's true-life stories, his sincere heart prayers at the end of each chapter, his practical advice about the prophetic, his insightful applications of Scripture—all propelled by an intense zeal to help the Church rise to her finest hour—make this book a valuable contribution to the current literature on the renewal of prophecy in today's Church.

Ernest B. Gentile
Author, Your Sons and Daughters Shall Prophesy

Jim has done it again! This is one of those books that is written at the right time. I believe that God is ready to pour out an Elijah spirit upon the Church. It's time for the prophetic ministry to come forth to impact the nations. This book is a great, timely book for pastors and prophets alike, and especially good for every church to use as a study guide. It will help the Church embrace this next great move of the Spirit!

Pastor Bart Pierce
Rock City Church

The hard work of a researcher, the accurate reporting of a journalist, the wit of a humorist, the theological mind of a scholar, the clarity of a teacher, the burden of an intercessor, the fire of a preacher and the spiritual experience of a seer . . . somehow God has wonderfully enabled Jim Goll to take on these various roles and blend them into one as he informs us about what he calls "the coming prophetic revolution." This important book gives credibility to the idea that it is already underway!

Michael Sullivant, pastor, author, prophetic leader
Metro Christian Fellowship, Kansas City

I find this an absolute must for those with prophetic gifting. The Scriptures used and the applications given make this practically a manual for warriors in God's Kingdom.

Che Ahn, Senior Pastor
Harvest Rock Church, Pasadena

Jim Goll's extraordinary ability to think through crucial issues relating to current prophetic ministry, and his skill at expressing the solutions in terms that the average believer can understand, come through loud and clear in *The Coming Prophetic Revolution*. Don't miss it!

C. Peter Wagner, Chancellor
Wagner Leadership Institute

This is a book we recommend wholeheartedly and enthusiastically. It is food for the hungry, rich and deep in content, yet well organized and simple in style. It is a wake-up call for a slumbering Church to abandon religiosity and come alive, to love God passionately, to reach out to help others and to become passionate warriors for Christ. It wisely encourages identifying root sources of wounds and frustrations that block growth, and welcoming correction for mistaken identifications. It talks a great deal about the importance of the revelation of the Father's heart. It urges the reader to pursue intimacy with God, to rest in Him and to partake of the life of Jesus Christ. It also issues a call to corporateness and cross-pollination in the Body of Christ. This book offers a great deal of sound instruction concerning prophets—lessons for beginners and guidelines for the mature regarding humility, respect for authority, openness to correction, recognizing conditional clauses in biblical words of prophecy, learning to recognize a call, developing Christlike character and a great deal more.

John and Paula Sandford
Co-founders, Elijah House International

This book takes us on a prophetic journey, cleverly navigating our way through scriptural principles. Each page captures the heart of Jim Goll, whose undying passion is for believers to receive and walk in the revelation knowledge of Jesus Christ. *The Coming Prophetic Revolution* is a must-read. I foresee it changing lives and preparing generations. Allow it to change and prepare you!

Dr. Kingsley A. Fletcher, Senior Pastor
Life Community Church
Research Triangle Park, North Carolina

The Coming
Prophetic
Revolution

The Coming Prophetic Revolution

A CALL FOR PASSIONATE,
CONSECRATED WARRIORS

JIM W. GOLL

FOREWORD BY DR. MICHAEL L. BROWN

Chosen Books
A Division of Baker Book House Co
Grand Rapids, Michigan 49516

Published by Chosen Books
A division of Baker Book House Company
P.O. Box 6287, Grand Rapids, MI 49516-6287

Printed in the United States of America

Library of Congress Cataloging-in-Publication Data

Goll, Jim W.
    The coming prophetic revolution : a call for passionate, consecrated
warriors / Jim W. Goll.
        p.   cm.
    Includes bibliographical references and index.
    ISBN 0-8007-9283-1 (pbk.)
    1. Prophecy—Christianity. I. Title.
BR115.P8 G65   2001
234'.13—dc21   2001028464

For current information about all releases from Baker Book House, visit our web site:
http://www.bakerbooks.com

This book is dedicated to my four miracle children—Justin, GraceAnn, Tyler and Rachel. This book is about something that is coming—something on the horizon, something not yet fully here. You will see; it will be your generation that will fully come into the contents written in this book. My prayer is that you will be right in the middle of the greatest revolutionary move of God that has ever hit planet earth.

Thank you guys for sharing and releasing me to the nations and believing in your good old dad. You have sacrificed much. Thank you for your prayers and patience with me. You make my heart giad. May you each be the unique vessel that God has created you to be. I love each one of you soooo much!

Your cheerleading dad

CONTENTS

FOREWORD

There can be no revolution without words. A revolution must be driven by concepts, by messages, by themes, by goals. It is the same with God's revolution. It requires His words, His concepts, His messages, His themes, His goals. Or, to say it another way, God's revolution requires prophets! Who else will receive and articulate the "now" word from the Lord?

Without prophetic voices there will be no Jesus revolution, no fresh wave from heaven overthrowing the status quo of sin and dead religion, no counterculture movement born from above and driven by the wind of the Spirit. The movement must have messengers. The trumpet must sound; otherwise the troops will not muster for battle. How we need clear words today, clarion calls from the throne, definite direction from the Master, specific strategies from the Lord! Without these we flounder.

Thankfully God is raising up a small army of prophetic servants in this generation, and the gifts of prophecy are being released afresh throughout the Body around the world. That is wonderful news! Unfortunately, much confusion remains about the nature and function of prophetic ministry, and many of the books written on the subject deal with the message more than the messenger, the exercise of the charismatic gift more than the development of the prophet's character.

Jim Goll's thorough, practical, edifying study addresses these crucial needs, calling us to the cross—again and again, until our flesh feels the sting—and pointing us to the Author and Finisher of our faith rather than to words and anointings alone. At the same time Jim offers dozens of ways to explore God's prophetic purposes for our lives. In that sense the book is an invitation—one Jim is uniquely qualified to write. He is a man of the Word. (You will be inundated with Scripture as you read the following pages.) He is a man of proven character. He is a man of the Spirit, highly trusted in his ability to hear the voice of the Lord and to convey accurate messages. He knows that of which he speaks and writes.

I was challenged personally to crucify my flesh as I studied the pages of this important manual. I was encouraged to believe God for a greater manifestation of the Spirit of revelation in my own life and service. I experienced the fear of the Lord when considering the consequences of taking sin lightly. All in all I found *The Coming Prophetic Revolution* a rich reading experience. And when I came to the end of the book—the call to "Prophesy Life!"—I felt faith rising within me, and I was ready to prophesy to the dead bones of this city, "You will live!"

It is time for the army to arise.

With passion Jim has written, "We were born to be revolutionaries. You were born again for this task. I was called from my mother's womb to help change the spiritual equilibrium of the Church—to unsettle her from her temporary state of lethargy and call forth a generation of passionate, consecrated warriors. Nothing short of a global, prophetic awakening in the Church will ever satisfy my soul, this side of heaven. *Come, Lord!*"

I believe the Lord *is* coming—to empower, to transform, to equip, to spark and to deepen the revolution. For all those who say, "Count me in, Lord," this book is for you. Read it and catch the prophetic spirit. Then go and change the world. It is your destiny!

Dr. Michael L. Brown, president
F.I.R.E. School of Ministry
Pensacola, Florida

A WORD
OF EXPLANATION

The Coming Prophetic Revolution is written for the hungry of heart and those with a gleam in their eye for something new and fresh to break forth on the scene of Christianity. Isaiah 42:9 depicts this wonderfully for us: "Behold, the former things have come to pass, now I declare new things; before they spring forth I proclaim them to you." This poignant verse accurately describes the content of the book you hold in your hands. New things will break forth as we cultivate the grace to sense, feel and tell them through relational intimacy with our Lord. This will result in a godly revolution in the Church.

As you begin your journey with me, you will find that not only does this book have some revolutionary ideas and concepts, but it is formatted uniquely. It is divided into four "tracks," each emphasizing a distinct element of the call to radical change. Track 1 is called "A Revolution of Lifestyle," followed by Track 2, "Enlisting in a Revolutionary Army." The pivotal Track 3 calls us to "A Revolution of Wisdom," and we close out with Track 4 on "The Revolutionary Vision." Each chapter ends with a prayer of invitation into this progressive journey, a "Pop Quiz" for discussion and to keep you on your toes, and a few books you might like to delve into "For More, Lord!"

There is another book within this book. Each track opens with a fascinating "Setup" or introduction penned from an aspect of the life of John, the beloved disciple of Jesus. By presenting a character sketch at the beginning of each track, I am attempting to build a relatable bridge to help carry the cargo contained in that track. I hope you enjoy this unique style, and benefit from these bridges constructed just for you.

The end of the book contains complementary appendix materials to aid you in your study and growth, and "Defining Our Terms: A Contemporary Glossary" on p. 290 to help you keep pace with my writing style and the lingo I use that you might not be familiar with.

Blessings on you as you read this call for passionate, consecrated warriors to arise—and may you respond to God's call!

A REVOLUTION IN LIFESTYLE

THE
SETUP

John at the Cross

He said to the disciple, "Behold, your mother!" From that hour the disciple took her into his own household.

John 19:27

Did you realize that John, the son of Zebedee, was the only disciple of the Twelve specifically named as having been at the crucifixion of our Lord Jesus Christ? We know Simon of Cyrene helped to carry His cross, and that a group of women followers of the Messiah were present (Luke 23:26–27). It is also well documented that Mary, the mother of Jesus, was looking on, accompanied by her sister, Mary the wife of Clopas, and Mary Magdalene (John 19:25). I wonder where the others were?

But John, the beloved, the friend of Jesus, was there. No wonder he speaks so much in his writings about the lavish love and forgiveness of God. This John actually saw the crucifixion. He witnessed the effects of the crown of thorns piercing the brow of the Savior. He saw the face of Jesus marred. He saw the results of the 39 lashes on His lacerated, raw back. John witnessed firsthand the nails piercing His hands and feet. He heard the desperate cries of the Son of Man, the only Son of God, for help. The sound of Christ Jesus' words from the cross probably echoed in John's heart and mind all his life. He could never get away from the cross.

According to John 21:20, this was "the disciple whom Jesus loved . . . the one who also had leaned back on His bosom at the supper and said, 'Lord, who is the one who betrays You?'" Remember? This same John who was at the cross is the same John who had laid his head on the breast of the Messiah. I wonder what he heard when his ear was laid upon the chest of Jesus?

Strange path, this one called Yochanan (Hebrew for *John*) walked on. It seems that his journey with his Lord took a different turn than that of the others. Think, ponder, reflect with me. John laid his head on the chest of the Creator of the universe. This same John later stuck through the excruciating ordeal of the criminal death of an innocent Man. Not only was John at the cross, but he was given an amazing stewardship—the ongoing care of Yeshua's mother, Miryam (Mary).

You know, I would give the care of my mother only into the very best hands. Don't you think that is exactly what Jesus did? I wonder what Yeshua saw in this man called Yochanan? Why did He give the care of His mother into this man's hands? What was different in him? Did he have an uncommon love for his Master?

Later in life this same disciple spoke of simple things. He groomed the next generation, and generations to come, whetting their taste buds by penning his epistles with words of love. I wonder why?

Don't you think it is time for radical change in the expression of Christianity? Why not look more closely at the life of John, the beloved disciple, to find some keys to a revolution of lifestyle? Keys like intimacy, devotion, faithfulness and friendship with God.

Perhaps one key to a prophetic revolution would be sticking close to the cross. Want to volunteer to walk in a cross-current pattern to the ways of the world? Then read on, and whet your appetite for intimacy with God by choosing the path less traveled—the way of the cross.

1

A REVOLUTION
OF INTIMACY

Let's dream together. What will it take for radical, revolutionary Christianity to emerge? What will it take for a holy, abandoned, authentically empowered Church to explode in the twenty-first century? If you dare to dream with me, yet tolerate my being pragmatic at the same time, I will venture to ask two more gut-level questions: Do we in the Western world even know what authentic Christianity looks like? And what are the outstanding characteristics of the faith needed to make a lasting change in the third millennium?

I might not have all the right technical answers, but this I know: Before you can have the right solutions, you must first be asking the right questions. As I travel across the earth, I have the privilege of sampling many divergent expressions of the global Body of Christ, and also of hearing the growing pains that come from being stretched. From this vantage point I see, hear and feel a common sound—yes, a cry from a new level of hunger. What is this ache in the heart, this hunger pain rolling around in our bellies?

As I put my listening ear to this sound, I will tell you how I interpret it: *We are on the verge of a prophetic revolution.*

Yes, a revolution is coming—a dramatic shift or change. Watch out, world! Watch out, slumbering Church! This sleepy bridal giant is about to shake off her passivity, arise and be all that God has destined her to be. A clarion call to change and intimacy is ringing across the stage of time. Draft notices are being sent out from heaven: *Wanted—Passionate, Consecrated Warriors.*

A battle is being waged in our day—an end-time battle of passions, an unprecedented competition between the altars of fire. The spirit of this world is out of control and vying for the attention of any half-interested soul. Many are being captured through the vices of sin that yell, "Taste me, feel me, eat this, do that!" We have more glitzy "Hollywood" in the Church than we do "holy goods."

But good news is on the horizon. While the battle is reaching a boiling point, the war is not lost. This fierce fight of the ages will escalate as waves of God's irresistible love wash over us and the constraints of stale religiosity are replaced by passionate, fiery, relatable Christianity. A revolution of intimacy is coming in the Church. Isn't that what your heart is aching for? Like John, the beloved disciple of Jesus, we, too, shall learn to lean our heads on our Master's chest and rest in the sound of His heart beating in the rhythm of love (John 21:20). Indeed, a revolution of intimacy is coming to the Church.

A Revolution in the Prophetic

There are different ways we can approach the prophetic. We might be talking about the parcel some refer to as the office of prophet as a foundation of the Church (Ephesians 2:20; 4:11). Or you can define it in terms of the ministry of prophecy that some regard as the consistent or even residential operation of this grace (Romans 12:6; 1 Corinthians 12:28). You can identify the gift of prophecy that can be considered the occasional or circumstantial manifestation of the Holy Spirit given to edify, comfort and exhort the listener (1 Corinthians 12:10; 14:3). You can elaborate on what Scripture calls the seven Spirits of God (Revelation 1:4; 3:1; 5:6), including the Spirit of the Lord and the spirits of wisdom, understanding, counsel, strength, knowledge and fear of the Lord (Isaiah 11:1–3).

Or we could even take time to expound on the diversity of what I call the revelatory "gracelet" (1 Corinthians 12:4–6)—a grace package of God—as demonstrated in Anna, the prophetic intercessor; David, the prophetic psalmist of the Lord; Gad, the seer; Joseph, the prophetic administrator; and as many other unique expressions as there are snowflakes that fall from the sky. Another appropriate approach emphasizes the heart or spirit of prophecy as recorded in Revelation 19:10: "Worship God. For the testimony of Jesus is the spirit of prophecy."

I would love to take you on a romp through Church history and demonstrate to you that these prophetic and other spiritual gifts never truly ceased in operation. Rather, they went into seasons of hibernation, and then often reemerged dramatically, like tidal waves crashing in on the shore. I will touch on some of these reemergences along the way, but in this book I want to tack in a bit different manner. (There are many good books already written, to which I refer you to in "Referral Reading for More Good Stuff," p. 298.)

Again, remember, a message is truly prophetic only if it comes from the heart of God, magnifies the Lord Jesus Christ and draws the listener into greater love and obedience to Jesus Christ, our glorious Master and Lord (Revelation 19:10).

Here is my opening poignant statement that underscores all that this book is about: *If there is to be a revolution in the prophetic, then there must be a prophetic revolution in the Church. And if there is a prophetic revolution in the Church, there will be the greatest global awakening of authentic Christianity that this world has ever seen.*

But how, O Lord, can these kinds of course alterations occur? How will such desperately needed cataclysmic changes ever take place? That is what this book will attempt to answer. We need another global paradigm shift in the Body of Christ. It is time for a divine confrontation!

And right at the outset of this book, let me give you a sneak preview of how this coming prophetic revolution will take place in you and me and in the collective entity we call the Church. It will happen by the breath of almighty God Himself.

The Intimate Breath of God

As we begin our journey, let me share with you some thoughts and principles drawn from the book of beginnings on the relationship between intimacy and the prophetic.

Genesis 2:7 grants some awesome relational insights. "The LORD God formed man of dust from the ground, and breathed into his nostrils the breath of life; and man became a living being." What a beginning! All mankind took on life by the very breath of God's mouth. Talk about an intimate exchange! Ponder this for a while. In some manner God blew into the lump of clay that He had fashioned, and Adam's body took on an added dimension. Man became a living being.

That is what the prophetic life and ministry are all about—human beings being filled with the breath of God, and then in turn exhaling onto others the breath of life they have received from their Creator. This is what our Messiah did as well. After His resurrection He appeared to His disciples, who were hiding for fear. He said, "As the Father has sent Me, I also send you" (John 20:21). Then Jesus breathed on them and said, "Receive the Holy Spirit" (verse 22).

At the Last Supper of Jesus with His trainees, John leaned back on the Lord's breast (John 13:25). What do you think he heard? Yes, probably the pulsating heart of the Savior, but he also would have heard something else: the Messiah's very breath as He inhaled and exhaled. Imagine being so close to the Lord that you hear Him breathing!

Some of the writers of the past knew something of this intimacy. Consider the inspired four stanzas of an old hymn penned in 1878, "Breathe on Me, Breath of God" by Edwin Hatch:

> Breathe on me, Breath of God,
> Fill me with life anew,
> That I may love what thou dost love,
> And do what thou wouldst do.
>
> Breathe on me, Breath of God,
> Until my heart is pure,
> Until with thee I will one will,
> To do and to endure.
>
> Breathe on me, Breath of God,
> Till I am wholly thine,
> Till all this earthly part of me
> Glows with thy fire divine.

> Breathe on me, Breath of God,
> So shall I never die,
> But live with thee the perfect life
> Of thine eternity.[1]

Yes, man became a living being. Adam was not some zombie walking around with no purpose or expression of affection or emotion. Nor was he bored with the ordinary paces of life. How did man become a living soul? What changed the ordinary into the extraordinary? The intimate breath of almighty God blown into Adam's lungs. So it was that he became a transporter of God's presence, a contagious carrier of the infectious Spirit of God.

God's Original Design

God's original intent was for all of us to be carriers of His presence. Today the Lord is looking for vessels He can breathe into once again. He seeks some that He can put His mouth upon, as it were, and blow into them His Spirit, so that their lungs, their hearts, their souls, their bodies, their temples will be filled with the very breath of the Almighty. He wants us to be carriers of His most brilliant presence. What could be greater?

That was the Lord's original intent. And we know what followed: "For this reason a man shall leave his father and his mother, and be joined to his wife; and they shall become one flesh. And the man and his wife were both naked and were not ashamed" (Genesis 2:24–25). Here we are given a graphic picture of what things look like when a man or woman is filled with the brilliance of God's presence. When we are filled with His *pneuma* (the Greek word for "breath"), we are not self-absorbed and fearful but walking with God and others in transparent love.

Adam and Eve were not ashamed. They were not overcome by guilt, nor were they driven by condemnation. They were not hiding behind whatever leaves they could find. They were naked; they were walking in honesty; they were enjoying intimate communion with God; and they "knew" each other.

That is God's design for marriage, which is the picture of the union He plans for us as the bride of Jesus Christ (Ephesians

5:22–32), our incredible, glorious Husbandman. This Master of ours wins our hearts with one glance of His eye (Song of Solomon 4:9). And the amazing thing is, one glance of our own eyes shining back into His undoes His heart as well. What a profound mystery! The revelation of this truth alone would create a revolution of intimacy among God's people. It is awesome, and it is pictured right here in the Garden of Eden, at the beginning of all things.

Adam and Eve were hiding behind nothing. Their hearts were beating with love for one another, and they were not ashamed. There were no barriers to intimacy.

The Problem

You know what happened:

> [The serpent] said to the woman, "Indeed, has God said, 'You shall not eat from any tree of the garden'?" The woman said to the serpent, "From the fruit of the trees of the garden we may eat; but from the fruit of the tree which is in the middle of the garden, God has said, 'You shall not eat from it or touch it, or you will die.'"
>
> Genesis 3:1–3

God did not say they could not touch it—rather, that they could not eat it. So we see the enemy's tactic of exaggeration beginning already.

> The serpent said to the woman, "You surely will not die! For God knows that in the day you eat from it your eyes will be opened, and you will be like God, knowing good and evil." When the woman saw that the tree was good for food, and that it was a delight to the eyes, and that the tree was desirable to make one wise, she took from its fruit and ate; and she gave also to her husband with her, and he ate. Then the eyes of both of them were opened, and they knew that they were naked; and they sewed fig leaves together and made themselves loin coverings.
>
> verses 4–7

The deceiver acted out of His nature. Eve and Adam were deceived. Thus did sin and a cover-up plan come into being. Deception entered the world. Enticement drew the man and woman away from fellowship with their Maker. How I wonder what the heart of God felt at that moment! The crown of His creation had now rejected their Creator for a bit of false knowledge from a forbidden piece of fruit. How that must have grieved Him!

Previously all Adam and Eve had known was communion with God and with each other. All they had experienced was intimacy—relational love without fear of rejection. They would hear the Lord walking in the Garden (Genesis 3:10) and walk and talk with Him. How marvelous! This is what they were created for—to commune with their Creator.

In the Garden with Our Beloved

In the little country Methodist church in the heartland where I grew up, we sang a marvelous hymn that shaped the course of my life, "I Come to the Garden Alone" by C. Austin Miles. This song, along with "What a Friend We Have In Jesus," "Sweet Hour of Prayer," "Have Thine Own Way, Lord" and a few others, marked my heart at an early age for life.

> I come to the garden alone,
> While the dew is still on the roses,
> And the voice I hear, falling on my ear,
> The Son of God discloses.
>
> [Refrain]
> And He walks with me, and He talks with me,
> And He tells me I am His own
> And the joy we share as we tarry there
> None other has ever known.
>
> He speaks, and the sound of His voice
> Is so sweet the birds hush their singing,
> And the melody that He gave to me,
> Within my heart is ringing.
>
> I'd stay in the garden with Him
> Though the night around me be falling,
> But He bids me go; through the voice of woe,
> His voice to me is calling.[2]

This old hymn depicts a beautiful communal relationship with our Beloved. That is the way it was in the beginning. But instead of "I come to the garden alone," God came into the Garden seeking fellowship with man. Imagine, they could actually hear Him walking! I wonder what the sound of God's footsteps sounded like.

I constantly ask God questions like this. I say, "Lord, what did that sound like? What was it like to hear You walking in the Garden? What did it sound like to hear Your voice on the wind?" I believe His walking with Adam and Eve in the Garden is not some old story in a dusty, antiquated book from yesterday. It is reality. In fact, the spiritual realm is more real than this earthly realm.

God walks with me and He talks with me. This is what I was born for. And it is what *you* were made for, too—to walk and talk with our Master in the garden of His love. This is intimacy. If you and I would radically return to the arms of His intimate love, I am convinced there would be a prophetic revolution across the Body of Christ and we would be awakened by the kisses of His love (Song of Solomon 1:2).

With the right set of lenses on, you can see that this is all about a living relationship, can't you? Hearing God. Seeing God. Following His lead. Sniffing out His trail. If only I could hear the echo of His footsteps. . . .

That is the heart of the prophetic. We are called to be a prophetic generation, a prophetic Church, a people leaning against Jesus with His heart pounding in our ears. Intimacy is the convergence of two hearts, His and ours, coming into rhythm together, so that there is only one sound. The writers of old, the desert fathers and the Christian mystics called this "greater union with Christ." Today, once again, the Lord is breathing these themes into life.

The Four Big Questions

Here were Adam and Eve, in transparent honesty and intimate communion with God. All of a sudden—uh-oh! Things changed. With their dignified coverings in place, Adam and Eve started playing hide-and-seek with God. When the Creator of the universe came on His daily stroll, the same as He had every other day, they heard the familiar sound they had previously cherished. Then the Lord God called to them, "Where are you?" (Genesis 3:9).

Did He who has a commanding view of all things suddenly get spiritual amnesia and misplace the crown of His creation? Had He forgotten their names or blanked out on their address? What was He doing? Didn't the omnipotent and omniscient One already know the answer?

Of course. But that was just one of four big questions the Lord asked of Adam and Eve—and He asks these questions of you and me!—as they hid behind the barriers of shame, guilt and fear of rejection. Let's list the questions with their corresponding answers:

Question #1: "Where are you?"

Response: "I heard the sound of You in the garden, and I was afraid because I was naked; so I hid myself."

Questions #2 and 3: "Who told you that you were naked? Have you eaten from the tree of which I commanded you not to eat?"

Response: "The woman whom You gave to be with me, she gave me from the tree, and I ate."

Question #4: "What is this you have done?"

Response: "The serpent deceived me, and I ate."

Listen to these penetrating words:

"Where are you?"

"Who told you?"

"Have you eaten?"

"What is this you have done?"

Once again, why did God ask these questions? Had He suddenly gone brain-dead? Ponder for a moment in your own life when the voice of God has asked *you* a question. Why does He do this? The amazing truth is that *every question God asks of us is an invitation to intimacy!* Questions are an invitation into dialogue, to communion, to "come now, and let us reason together" (Isaiah 1:18).

God wants to talk to you. He wants more than just the "right" answers so you can pass His tests. He wants to draw near to you. He is your adoring Father and He cherishes His kids! Questions from the Lord are an invitation to emerge from the place of hiding into transparent honesty and light.

The Leaves We Hide Behind

Can you imagine, after Adam and Eve had known God, and He knew them, how quickly the spiritual climate changed? As a result of their disobedience, they experienced instantaneous barriers to their intimacy with Him. Walls shot up. After their sin they plucked off leaves from the nearest bush as quickly as they could and sewed coverings for themselves. They were hiding from the Lord their Creator for the first time in their lives.

But God, in His passionate pursuit, was still drawing close. A new reaction stirred within them as He drew near. Previously they had run toward the sound of His footsteps. Now they ran in the other direction. Before, their response had been joy: "Oh, wow, it's Father!" Now it was dread and fear: "Oh, no, it's Father!" They were guilt-ridden. Never had they had such an emotional reaction or even such a thought before! They had not known condemnation or fear or shame. Now, as a result of their disobedience, they ran and hid from the voice of God (the prophetic, we could say).

Obviously these were real live leaves they picked and sewed together for their coverings. But we pick and choose covers and hiding places as well. And the moment we hide behind our defensive fig leaf mindsets from the revelatory voice of God, the heart of God, the acts of God and the power of God, it starts getting extremely complicated. Why? Because now we automatically filter the voice, presence and power of God through screens. If God's word does finally penetrate our hearts or minds, it seems as though it has become diluted due to our abundant rationalization, analytical skepticism, theological theories of cessationism or traditional emotional barriers. We might not sew actual fig leaves, but the obstructions to fellowship over our hearts and souls shield us just as effectively (or ineffectively) from God's approaching presence.

May I point out some of the leaves we hide behind? They are progressive; hiding behind one set leads to our concealment behind the next as well.

The Ditch of Guilty Feelings

The first set of leaves that many hide behind is guilt. Some seem to stay there all their lives, like a car that has been sideswiped and is still sitting in the ditch years later. Sinful acts or mistakes from the past or present loom in their faces, but instead of running to their loving Savior and admitting their fault, they sprint in the opposite direction and hide out in the darkness of guilt. This hiding place is the breeding ground for condemnation, accusation and other ugly attitudes. But all these can be avoided through old-fashioned confession of sin and cleansing by the blood of our Lord Jesus Christ.

There are various categories of guilt: *real guilt* due to real sin; *exaggerated guilt* due to the combination of real sin and the work of "the accuser of our brethren" (Revelation 12:10); and *false guilt* as a result of the voice of the destroyer, releasing condemning, lying spirits (1 Kings 22:21–23; John 8:44; 10:10). All these forms of guilt are very real in the realm of our emotions.

The cure is simple and direct. First John 1:7 gives us the remedy: "If we walk in the Light as He Himself is in the Light, we have fellowship with one another, and the blood of Jesus His Son cleanses us from all sin." Step into the light. That is where we find cleansing. So I have a "word from the Lord" for you: Climb out of the sleazeball ditch and run to the light of God's Word. "The truth will make you free" (John 8:32). Forgiveness, cleansing and healing love are waiting for you there.

The Masquerade of Hurts from the Past

The second layer of leaves that hides us from the love of God and keeps us from intimacy with Him is the religious masquerade, concealing deep-seated hurts from the past. Religious people wear masks quite well, pretending all is well with their souls while holding the Lord, the very Lover of their lives, at arm's length. Pretenders we become, masquerading in the parade of hypocritical churchianity.

But the real Jesus came to heal the brokenhearted and set at liberty those who are bruised (Isaiah 61:1; Luke 4:18–19). Jesus is our Healer. We must take off our masks and let Him dig deep at times, touching the very source of our pain. Let Him probe and even pierce through the festering wounds to allow the light of His unchanging love to penetrate your being. Expose it to the light. Surrender. Forgive. Sow blessings to others instead. This is the way out of the masquerade—remaining open-faced before God, releasing mercy and forgiveness for hurts from the past and letting Him do the same.

The Onlooker's Bench of Fear

Let's consider a third tier of camouflage. We want to be part of things, enjoy life, step out and be used by the Lord. But our woundedness, made more raw by the taunts of the enemy, keeps us on the bench looking on while others are enjoying being in the middle of the game. We become cautious observers afraid to run onto the playing field.

This is the area I have struggled with the most. What will I look like if I do this? What will others think of me? How well will I perform? But if we allow ourselves to be held back by the fear of rejection or the fear of authority or the opinions of others, eventually we will become people-pleasers, strangled by the anticipation of their opinions.

Hear me in this: If God can help *me* off the spectator's bench, He can help you, too. My mind was numbed by the belittling notions of what I expected others were thinking of me. Hogwash! Fear paralyzes us while authentic faith propels us forward. So trade in those fears; exchange them at the cross (Isaiah 8:12–13). Be bold like a lion for Jesus' sake. *Do something!* Jump off the bench, tread on those spirits of intimidation (Luke 10:19) and be more than a conqueror (Romans 8:37)!

Truly, the remedy is our Father's great love. Bask in the light of His unfathomable devotion—what the King James Version calls *lovingkindness*. Do a word study on it. Ask for a revelation of it.

Soak in the reality that "if God is for us, who is against us?" (Romans 8:31). He does not just tolerate you. You were not an accident waiting to happen. You were created in His image and for His pleasure (Revelation 4:11). You are the object of His consuming love. That is hot stuff! It is revolutionary!

Prune-Faced Criticism

There is a fourth layer of fig leaves that we can use to protect our image. Before you know it, you are not only a spectator sitting on the bench; you are the judge of the games. First you develop an old, wrinkled-up prune face; then you begin operating out of a religious spirit called criticism. You have your ten points by which you judge everything around you. Like the judges at the Olympics, you even give scores to the participants of the games. You leave a particular gathering or event and say, "Well, it could have been better, if only. . . ." But you offered nothing to help it to be better. Why should you? You have already been there, done that and even gotten the T-shirt.

Sorry, but these are the has-beens of yesterday's moves of God. They stopped moving forward and now they hold the job of negative, critical overseers of the playing field of today.

Some of you might have just said, "Ouch!" Or maybe you said, "You sound as though you're spitting nails." But it takes the penetrating light of truth to blast away our protective shields. Truth may hurt for the moment, but when it is prayed and spoken with the motivation of love, it cleanses and sets free. I might be speaking a bit pointedly, but honestly, I want us to be delivered from all entanglements so that God can usher in the coming prophetic revolution. I know you do, too.

The Stronghold of Imposed Limitations

This brings us to the fifth layer of leaves we hide behind—that of imposed limitations. In this stage we start believing the ridiculous, idiotic lies of the devil about ourselves, and those lies become negative strongholds of the mind (2 Corinthians 10:4–6). Words not in alignment with the will and Word of God are transmitted from the enemy's camp to attack our minds. At times those thoughts are even planted by people in authority. Their effect is to confine us in boxes with low ceilings and false expectations. As we believe those evil reports or actual word curses spoken against us as "the way it will always be," we are shut into cramped, dark boxes. Proverbs 23:7 reminds us of the promise and the problem: "As [a man] thinketh in his heart, so is he" (KJV).

Ed Silvoso, in his marvelous book *That None Should Perish*, has given us a good working definition of such spiritual strongholds. They represent "a mindset impregnated with hopelessness that causes us to accept as unchangeable situations that we know are contrary to the will of God."[3]

As we acknowledge as hopeless what God declares is changeable, we have come into alignment, at least in part, with the devil's thought processes and plans for us. In this fifth stage, we go way past the realms of guilt, woundedness, fear and criticism. We no longer want to step out into the light. We flat-out don't even think He accepts us, loves us or has any plan for us—even a leftover plan.

But the light of God brings with it an invitation to honesty and humility. "Oh, yeah," you say. "You mean so I can look ugly, like a mess in front of everybody." No, not at all. If you demonstrate honesty and humility, you won't look ugly; you will look beautiful, particularly before God. He loves the humble and afflicted, and shines His grace upon them (Proverbs 3:34; 1 Peter 5:5). Nothing is more beautiful than the grace of God. As you let Him shine His grace on you, you will look beautiful, too.

Now realize this: God also likes a fighter. In fact, God loves a fighter. You need to know that there are times you will have to wage war with the name and blood of Jesus to break out of your box of imposed limitations and stinky thinking. But there *is* a way out. The gateway is the cross of our lovely Lord Jesus!

Opportunities and Temptations

As we back up in the book of Genesis, we hear the serpent telling Adam and Eve, "God knows that in the day you eat from [the fruit] your eyes will be opened, and you will be like God . . ." (Genesis

3:5). So what did Eve do? "When the woman saw that the tree was good for food, and that it was a delight to the eyes, and that the tree was desirable to make one wise" (verse 6), she partook.

There are three statements here that represent both opportunities and temptations: *The forbidden tree was good for food; it was a delight to the eyes; and it was desirable to make one wise.*

We find similar enticements in 1 John 2:16–17: "All that is in the world, the lust of the flesh and the lust of the eyes and the boastful pride of life, is not from the Father, but is from the world. The world is passing away, and also its lusts; but the one who does the will of God lives forever." The original temptation is still centered in these very things: the lust of the eyes, the lust of the flesh and the boastful pride of life. As we yield to these false motivates, we start erecting barriers around our eyes and our hands—the very tools God wants to use as receptacles for His great presence.

1. The Lust of the Eyes

God wants our vision to be clear and single. He wants His eyes to burn brightly through our own (Ephesians 1:17–19; Revelation 1:14). But when we give our eyes away to the enemy's camp, they become filled with vain images and other distractions. What we are doing is allowing tainted filters and visual obstacles to block the prophetic presence. We are hiding, and the revelatory seer dimension in which the Lord wants us to walk—for example, through dreams, visions and angelic visitations—becomes hindered. As we give ourselves to the lust of the eyes, the seer realm starts getting cloudy. It gets smeared, jumbled and filled with distorted images, because the lenses through which we are looking are not pure.

"Blessed are the pure in heart, for they shall see God," Jesus taught in the Sermon of the Mount (Matthew 5:8). This it why it is imperative that we guard the "eye gate" and keep the eyes of our heart clean and pure. This is why the god of this world (John 14:30; 2 Corinthians 4:4) is sending a barrage of filth for the eyes of the world to behold. A battle is raging, the battle of passions. Will we let our eyes get filled with junk and poke out the prophetic gift of the seer in our midst? It will and does do that. But if we keep pure eyes, a realm of visionary revelation will open up with greater clarity for us.

I am not trying to present a work ethic or advocate earning God's grace and gifts. We cannot earn a present. But we must keep ourselves clean from the lust of the eyes in order to gracefully receive what the Father has to offer.

2. The Lust of the Flesh

The second tempter mentioned is the lust of the flesh. Oh, the impulses and temptations that this body creeps up and speaks to each of us! We must go through the cleansing and crucifying of the lust of the flesh. Do you know why? Because God wants His power to move through human vessels. He wants our hands to be clean and our hearts to be pure, as Psalm 24:3–4 describes: "Who may ascend into the hill of the LORD? And who may stand in His holy place? He who has clean hands and a pure heart. . . ."

When the eyes of our hearts are pure, we can behold Him; and as we do, His presence can move and work through our clean hands. We need to be a people cleansed of the lust of the eyes and purged from the lust of the flesh. What these temptations accomplish is getting us into a whole lot of wrong places, seeing wrong things and motivating us to do bad stuff!

Romans 6:13 exhorts us not to "go on presenting the members of your body to sin as instruments of unrighteousness; but present yourselves to God as those alive from the dead, and your members as instruments of righteousness to God." The issue becomes one of presentation. To whom you present your members, they become a slave. If unto the Lord, then they become a slave to the Holy Spirit; if unto sin, they become slaves to sin. What a promise! What a warning!

Yes, what a promise! God wants to use our little hands to impart the power of His great presence. Isn't that crazy?—your hands and mine used to release the power of His presence!

Romans 6:19 urges us to "present your members as slaves to righteousness, resulting in sanctification." Awesome! But that is God's way. As we present the members of our fleshly bodies to the Lord, He does a miracle: He sanctifies them. That means these feet, hands, eyes, mouths and hearts become set apart for the Lord's glory and purposes. As we present, He sanctifies. What He sanctifies, He empowers. Then, like Isaiah, as we are touched by authentic fire, He will touch others through our lives with His miraculous fire. It doesn't get much better than that.

3. The Boastful Pride of Life

Then there is the boastful pride of life. Who gets the credit? Who receives the glory? In many ways boastful pride deals with false worship. Eve saw that the fruit was desirable to make one wise. But wise in whose eyes? Wise in comparison to ourselves, yes, and wise in comparison to others, but not wise in comparison to God.

The boastful pride of life, then, is actually a realm characterized by false worship. If you are walking in the boastful pride of life, ultimately it is an issue of self-exaltation. The basic meaning of *worship* in the Hebrew language means "to bow down in prostration before." Pride is the antithesis of worship. Worship exalts another, while pride sits on its own self-appointed throne.

I think I can hear the wheels of your mind grinding: "O.K., but what in the world does this have to do with the prophetic ministry?" My response: Everything! God has an address; it is called *p-r-a-i-s-e*. He is enthroned on the praises of His people (Psalm 22:3). Wherever Jesus is praised and magnified with holy abandonment in worship, love and adoration, a throne in the heavenlies is set up over that person, that home, that congregation or that city. Then Someone named the Ancient of Days, the Lord of glory, comes and sits down on the throne. Daniel 7:9 remarkably describes such a scene: "I kept looking until thrones were set up, and the Ancient of Days took His seat." What happens when the Almighty takes His seat? He rules in the midst of His enemies.

The act of worship is one of our most powerful tools of spiritual warfare. It builds a throne in the heavenlies where Jesus' rule can be released and the demonic powers of darkness dismissed. Worship displaces darkness. So when you are walking in extravagant, passionate worship, guess what happens? Your passionate praise of our Lord pushes the throne of pride out of the way, and He comes to take His seat of honor. He draws near! Worship is prophetic action that releases the spirit opposite to the boastful pride of life.

I tell you the truth, as we enter into true worship, His presence comes. And in His presence we find *everything* (Psalm 16:11). In His presence we can hear Him, feel Him, touch Him, know Him, see Him, we might even smell Him—the beauty of His fragrance.

Praise has a whole lot to do, therefore, with prophetic life and ministry. It is connected with our giving God His rightful place in our lives, in our congregations and even in whole cities. In fact, extravagant praise is a key that unlocks His presence with us.

Cultivating Intimacy in the Prophetic

The realm of the prophetic—hearing God's voice, receiving visions, knowing His heart and so on—is extremely simple. At times we overly complicate this scene. It is a relational issue. Just hang out with Jesus; He likes talking to His friends. The focus of the prophetic is being with God and learning to lean our heads on our Beloved, as the disciple John did. It is showing up and being where God is. It is not hiding but relating. Bottom line, that is how all this wonderful activity takes place. Remember, it is not what you know but *who* you know!

Here are some keys I have been learning over the past 25-plus years of ministry in cultivating God's prophetic presence in my life. There are not seven effective steps to being a successful prophet—not that I know of, anyway! But here are seven helpful hints that have been mileage markers along my own journey of cultivating intimacy in the prophetic.

1. **Rest around the Ark.** Where did the voice of the Lord come to young Samuel (1 Samuel 3:3–4), who became the last of the judges and one of the greatest prophets ever? In the Temple near the Ark of God. Be like little boy Samuel and find your resting place near the Ark of His presence. Learn to rest in the presence of God.

2. **Love mercy.** Mercy is a quality of the heart. If we do not have it, we will judge by the externals and be moved by opinions rather than by the Spirit of God (1 Samuel 16:7; Titus 3:4–7). Let Micah 6:8 be your goal: "He has told you, O man, what is good; and what does

the LORD require of you but to do justice, to love kindness, and to walk humbly with your God?"

3. **Pray in the Spirit.** Fresh revelation will be released to you as you edify yourself and charge up your battery of faith by praying in the Holy Spirit (1 Corinthians 14:4). "[Build yourself] up on your most holy faith, praying in the Holy Spirit, keep [yourself] in the love of God" (Jude 20–21).

4. **Inquire of the Lord.** The key to learning is asking. The key to receiving is listening. The key to revelation is inquiring of the Lord (Psalm 27:4, 8–14). Keep looking, asking, searching and inquiring of the Lord for Him to reveal truth, revelation and insight. He will answer a seeking, teachable heart.

5. **Learn to hold a secret.** Everything you receive as revelation does not come with an automatic license to share it. God reveals His secrets "to His servants the prophets" (Amos 3:7), but learn to ask permission whether you are to communicate them or not. God is looking for close friends He can share His secrets with.

6. **Love the anointing.** If you want to grow in the giftings and gracelets of God, then love the manifested presence of the Lord (Exodus 33:15–16; 1 John 2:27). Cultivate His presence and anointing in your life by getting into the atmosphere where the Holy Spirit is moving. Some things are better caught than taught.

7. **Risk!** Fruit is borne out on the limb. Eventually we have to move out of our comfort zones and step out in faith. Remember, faith is always spelled *r-i-s-k*. Keep taking these progressive steps and you will grow (Romans 10:17; Hebrews 4:2; 11:6). Climb out of your boat and trust the Lord. He loves to go on adventures with His friends.

Take and Eat

As we close the opening chapter of this first track, "A Revolution in Lifestyle," let's return to Genesis, where the first "take-and-eat" is given in the Bible. "Take and eat" was first spoken by the enemy to Adam and Eve (Genesis 3:1–5). They disobeyed God and did as the sly serpent connived them into doing. Sin came, and with it, barriers to intimacy. But the next "take-and-eat" in the Bible is the remedy for us all: Jesus talking with His disciples.

Jesus said, giving them the bread, "Take it; this is my body" (Mark 14:22). The one great cure for all the barriers we hide behind is the take-and-eat of the cross of Jesus. It is "Take and eat" of the life of God's only Son. "Take and eat" of this glorious Man, Christ Jesus. He has already done it all. He gave His blood to purchase us all. As we revel in who Jesus is, God the Father wraps His arms around us, and we have this warm presence called passion within our hearts, and this thing called revelation that starts bubbling up and happening.

It will bring a revolution in the Church. Jesus' friends will draw close to His chest to hear His very heart beat. A revolution of intimacy is on its way, and it is available to you.

Let me pray for you right at the beginning of this book, to help set the hook so deeply that you will be drawn close to Jesus' bosom, just like John, the beloved disciple. After all, Jesus is looking for new recruits who will hear the passionate sound of His love beating through their beings. Want to lean your ear His way?

Father, I present this lovely person before You right now. You know his or her walk. You know who he is. You know where he has been. You know his name. You don't just tolerate him. You love him, and come passionately to draw close to encounter him. You know the leaves he hides behind, yet You come searching him out. Come, Lord, embrace Your beloved.

Father, I present this hungry soul to You. Even as You spoke to me some years ago, I now pray over him or her: "I will keep coming with waves of My presence upon you until I make you into all that I have destined you to be." God, I bring this person before You now and ask for waves of Your great love to flood his being. Open a door in the Spirit for him, Lord, and let the wind of Your Spirit blow across his life. May waves of Your presence wash over him and draw him close to You. In Christ's name I pray. Amen.

Whether you are from an evangelical, Third Wave, fundamentalist, Pentecostal, charismatic, liturgical, Orthodox, house church or unchurched orientation, or if you are from some other historical, traditional part of what we call the Church, know this: There will be a revolution of intimacy in the Church of the third millennium. A generation of passionate, consecrated warriors will arise, people who love the fruit of the Spirit as much as the gifts of the

Spirit, people of character to carry the gift. He will restore to us the centrality of the cross as our authentic prophetic lifestyle. The Lord is doing and will continue to do a great and mighty work to restore us to the position of leaning on our Beloved.

Want to be a part? I am hoping you are one of the thousands around the world who are crying, "More, Lord!" So be brave and keep on reading. I have penned this book with you in mind.

POP QUIZ—KEEPING YOU ON YOUR TOES!

1. What are the barriers to intimacy in your life—the leaves you hide behind?
2. Why does God ask man questions? Has God ever asked you a question? If so, what?
3. What are the three fleshly world motivating forces, according to 1 John 2:16?

FOR MORE, LORD!

Mike Bickle, *Passion for Jesus* (Lake Mary, Fla.: Creation House, 1993)

Jim W. Goll, *Wasted on Jesus* (Shippensburg, Pa.: Destiny Image, 2000)

Tommy Tenney, *The God Chasers: My Soul Follows Hard After Thee* (Shippensburg, Pa.: Destiny Image, 1998)

2

CHARACTERISTICS OF A PROPHETIC PEOPLE

If we plan to talk about characteristics of a prophetic people, we had better dig the trenches of cultivating genuine character. It takes character to carry the gift.

Most prophets I know are real characters, for sure! From my vantage point, you must have a bit of an adventure streak in you just to survive the rapids in this whitewater rafting ride. It also requires the character of endurance to leave a lasting impression in the Christian life. Remember, a river without banks is just runoff water. The *charismata* (Holy Spirit gifts) without character are a swamped raft just waiting to happen. But when character is shaped in the image of Christ Jesus, then the presence, power and authority of the Holy Spirit have an effective course through which to be channeled.

Leonard Ravenhill, the fabled British evangelist, stated, "The prophet comes to set up that which is upset. His work is to call into line those who are out of line! He is unpopular because he opposes the popular in morality and spirituality. In a day of faceless politicians and voiceless preachers, there is not a more urgent national need than our cry to God for a prophet!"[1] Indeed, upholding morality is the job of a prophet. But doing this kind of work takes tried and tested character to endure the storms that come.

A Wider Definition of the Prophetic

Let's consider some definitions concerning the prophetic from a variety of angles to help us grasp a wider view of our field. (Just a reminder here: Remember the section "Defining Our Terms: A Contemporary Glossary" on p. 290 in the back of the book, to help you with quick working definitions.) The more snapshots we can look at, the better our overall comprehension of the subject matter.

I have used the following simple definition for the last few years: *Whether it is preached truth, prayed burden or spontaneous utterance, a message is prophetic only if it brings its generation into the knowledge of the heart of God for that time.* The key issue is possessing revelatory knowledge of the heart of God for our time. This is what makes us relevant, up to date, fresh and not just drawing on yesterday's leftovers.

Let me give you a few other phrases or definitions to chew on.

First, *A prophetic person speaks the word of the Lord in the name of the Lord. He carries weight by virtue of the ethical, moral and spiritual urgency in his message.* The distinctive thought in this definition is "the urgency of the message." Does it contain something vibrant and passionate? Is there an imperative expressed in the content and probably by the one delivering it?

Let's take a glimpse through another lens: *A person is prophetic not by birth or by official designation, but by the power of his or her inner call and the response of the hearers.* Something happens in the presence of an authentic word. There is a weight, a glory that rests on the word of the Lord. And a sparking occurs within those who hear, creating faith or a call to action.

The single-most characteristic mark of a true prophetic person is the evidence that he or she has stood in the counsel of Jehovah and declared faithfully what he or she has heard from God's mouth. Wow! That states it well. The messenger has something to say because he or she has been with God and stood in His counsel. A related phrase, *the whole counsel of God,* will come up again and again in this book, and it comes from Paul's assurance to the Ephesian elders in Acts 20:27: "I have not shunned to declare to you the whole counsel of God" (NKJV).

Prophecy is the expressed thoughts of God spoken in a language that no one with a natural gift of speech could ever articulate. The substance and nature of prophecy exceed the limits of what the human mind is capable of thinking or imagining. Prophecy comes through the mouth, is written by the hand or demonstrated through the actions of human beings, but it comes from the heart and mind of God—spiritual thoughts in spiritual words. After several years of meditating on this subject, that is the best summation I have been able to come up with concerning the gift of prophecy.

Now let me build on this understanding and present to you, from my set of lenses, some characteristics of prophetic people. Allow the Holy Spirit to write freshly on the screen of your heart any additional views of what a prophetic man or woman might look like.

Developing New Images of Prophetic People

When we consider the stereotypical images of prophetic vessels, we might think of wrinkled old men with long, pointy fingers shouting vehemently outside the ranks of those whom they are addressing. Wearing ragged clothes, eating grasshoppers for meals, they pronounce their declarations of doom, then proceed on to the next village to do the same. They are rejected lone rangers who think they alone carry the pure, unadulterated word of the Lord. They come across as unapproachable men of the cloth who have never struggled with a worldly thought. Their job: to judge the Church and help God out in the process, just in case He does not do a good enough job. (Remember, this is a distorted view of the prophet!)

In contrast, Ernest Gentile, in his excellent book *Your Sons and Daughters Shall Prophesy*, lists six descriptive terms of an authentic prophet. These are: *friend of God; man of God; messenger of the Lord; servant of the Lord; watchman;* and *interpreter.*[2] He goes on to give us five sets of adjectives describing character traits of a genuine prophet: *devoted and loyal; committed, obedient and humble; holy, prayerful and compassionate; daring, bold and faith-filled;* and *studious and patriotic.*[3] Doesn't this sound like a higher and better way than the prophet in isolation, rejection and rebellion?

Here are four pictures of prophetic people.

1. They Are People of Genuine Faith

Consider Hebrews 11:8–10:

> By faith Abraham, when he was called, obeying by going out to a place which he was to receive for an inheritance; and he went out, not knowing where he was going. By faith he lived as an alien in the land of promise, as in a foreign land, dwelling in tents with Isaac and Jacob, fellow heirs of the same promise; for he was looking for the city which has foundations, whose architect and builder is God.

Now I am going to blow your circuits on what it means to be a faith person. How many of us know where we are going? How many of us know what the next five years hold for us? How many of us feel we are groping in the darkness? Take courage! You might just qualify to be prophetic.

Abraham was captivated by God with a vision and purpose. But the Scriptures indicate that he stepped out "not knowing where he was going." With that thought in mind, might you fit the image of a prophetic person of faith?

God gives us hints. He gives us directions. But believe me, we still have to walk by faith, one step at a time. God plays leapfrog in His spiritual alphabet with us, giving us just enough to get us going. He likes jumping onto the first lily pad in the pond of His purpose, the one marked *a*, *b* and *c*, and then jumping over to the pad with *l*, *m* and *n* posted on it. Next thing you know, the Holy Spirit's guidance reveals another hint to us of our divine destiny. Suddenly the goal of it all comes into view. Yes, we now see *x*, *y* and *z*. "Oh, boy," we exult, getting all cranked up. "Look at that. I see it now!" Then we hit *e*, *f* and *g*. "Huh? Whoa, baby, where is that next pad?"

This is reality. To me it sounds like the path Abraham took—the prophet, the friend of God, the father of our faith. Abraham had a vision, a calling. He was a man of covenant. Consider the following dialogue:

Look at the stars, Abram. See how many are out there. That's your destiny. Now go take another peek at your calling. Go on into the desert and see if you can count the grains of sand. Know what I'm going to do with your life? I am going to multiply your seed.

"Huh? Me? What do you mean? It's too late for me."

Keep looking up, Abram. You can't, but I can.

Along the way you step on one of those seemingly sturdy lily pads He led you to, and it folds beneath your feet. Down you sink into the water! But then you learn to get back up the very way you started. *Help!* Dependency on God is called faith.

Abraham was given profound vision and purpose. Hebrews 11 tells us that "he went out, not knowing where he was going." But while he was in the process of becoming that man of faith, taking progressive steps into the journey we call destiny, he kept looking because he had seen x, y and z. He had glimpsed something that was worth the cost of looking foolish and making mistakes along the way. He was willing to be a pioneer of faith to blaze a trail that others could follow.

Abraham was looking for something—actually, for Someone. Like all authentic prophetic pilgrims who came after him, he maintained his gaze upward. He kept looking for the city whose builder and architect was God.

With this set of lenses, you might see your circumstances differently and take courage. You might just qualify to be an authentic prophetic person—a man or woman of genuine faith.

2. They Are Pioneers Taking New Territory

Prophetic people are those who go before and open the way for others. They are called pioneers, forerunners or "breakers" in the spirit. They pay the price, often as intercessors, plowing up fallow ground so that others can follow in their trail as sowers, planters, waterers and eventually reapers. Micah 2:13 describes this activity: "The breaker goes up before them; they break out, pass through the gate and go out by it. So their king goes on before them, and the LORD at their head." Before there is a breakthrough, there must always come a breaker.

The world has its hit squads that do the dirty work. Send those guys in and get your job done. So it is with the prophetic. These commandos, armed with the tools of spiritual warfare, kick down the gates of the enemy so that spoils can be taken for the Kingdom of God. This image seems to fit the radical new breed of revolutionaries. The grace of a John the Baptist or an Elijah seems to be upon these warriors, and they, too, become forerunners, preparing the way for the release of the Lord's presence.

Michael Sullivant, in his excellent book *Prophetic Etiquette*, gives us his thoughts on the work of these pioneering ministries.

> Surely, if there was a "forerunner ministry" that served to prepare the way for the first coming of Christ, there will be a similar ministry raised up by God "in the spirit and power of Elijah" to prepare both the Church and the earth for the Second Coming—the culmination of God's purposes in human history. This is no mere theological "stretch"—it is simple, straightforward and clear.[4]

Pioneers they truly are. They love the task of plowing new territory, but they cannot wait till the next round of gifted laborers appears, relieving them of their temporary responsibilities. Bad settlers they were born to be; spiritual boredom sets in if they tend one field for too long. So they revel when another takes over the tasks they themselves began. Fresh grace seems to appear as a glint in their eyes over a new assignment revealed. These prophetic pioneers are paying the price as groundbreakers.

Know this for sure—if you are going to be a prophetic person, sooner or later you will be used with a plow in your hand.

3. They Are Messengers with a Clear Word

Prophetic people carry a living word of not being conformed to this world, and they wield this message masterfully like a sharp, two-edged sword. T. Austin Sparks states it this way: "Prophetic ministry under the Holy Spirit is a ministry through growing revelation. A prophet was a man who went back to God again and again, and did not come out to speak until God had shown him the next thing."[5] Messengers carry a word with them. Their job is to be mouthpieces on behalf of another. Anna's prophetic message, as recorded in Luke 2:38, was simple; she "continued to speak of [Jesus]." He is our message!

Here is a good image, then, to reflect on: True messengers speak and live the message of the cross. Ultimately the cross must be our passion (1 Corinthians 1:23; 2:2). We must preach Jesus Christ crucified and risen from the dead. That goes against the grain in a godless society. But there is no deeper life message than the simplicity and centrality of the cross.

The power of God rests not on the wisdom, articulation and education of men and women, but on the foolishness of the preaching of the cross. The Lord wants to bring us back into proper focus. We are to be people with a message. Is it possible that you could qualify for such a simple yet profound task?

4. They Are Members of a Servant Community

With our new set of lenses, let's look at one more picture of a prophetic people. In contrast to much Old Testament stereotyping, these radical warriors do not walk alone. They are not isolated individuals, though they often thrive on seclusion. They are a people knit together relationally as part of the greater Body of Christ. They are connected to the community of believers called the Church. They are members of a servant community.

The Church at large is to be a prophetic people. Remember the hot, piercing words of Moses: "Would that all the LORD's people were prophets, that the LORD would put His Spirit upon them!" (Numbers 11:29). How else will the slumbering giant awaken unless some revelatory dynamite is set off right in the middle of her?

We are all called by God. But we are not called to be lone rangers. Nor are there supposed to be a few elite, awesome superstars in the Church. We are *all* called to walk in the anointing of a word of knowledge or wisdom, His character and His power. We are called to do it together. First Peter 4:10 reminds us, "As each one has received a special gift, employ it in serving one another as good stewards of the manifold grace of God." This has the sound of a prophetic servant community to me!

When you study the armor of God in Ephesians, you will see that one area of your body is not protected. That is your hind side. Somebody else covers it for you, according to the book of Joel: "They run like mighty men, they climb the wall like soldiers; and they each march in line, nor do they deviate from their paths. They do not crowd each other, they march everyone in his path; when they burst through the defenses, they do not break ranks" (Joel 2:7–8).

If you are marching in an army, somebody is striding in front of you and someone behind you, watching your heels. In a sense, then, part of your armor is not just the shield of faith or the breastplate of righteousness, but the people you are in step with. That means *you* are part of the armor for someone else, too! You might be prophetic eyes for another soldier, to guard him, watch for him, pray for him, love and care for him, remind him, heal him, comfort him, even kick and prod him so he won't collapse. Others, in turn, are your rearguard and will spur you on as well. That is what it means to be part of a servant community of believers.

Yes, new lenses to look through for a new generation of revolutionaries. Images of pilgrims of faith, pioneers breaking open new territory, messengers with a clear word, and members of a servant community. Let's proceed and let the Holy Spirit lay hold of us and shake us, if necessary, out of our slumber.

Seven Signs of an Awakened Prophetic People

As I stated in the first chapter, the Lord is arousing His sleeping bride with the kisses of His intimate love. Consider the biblical analogy of being awakened from sleep. I wonder what an awakened warrior bride looks and acts like when she first gets up? Have you ever been rudely awakened by an alarm in the middle of the night that you did not set? You sit up in bed, eyes wide shut and ready for who knows what? Well, all I know is, it is time to wake up from our sleep.

In our search for authentic characteristics of prophetic people, let's take a peek at Romans 13:11–14:

> Do this, knowing the time, that it is already the hour for you to awaken from sleep; for now salvation is nearer to us than when we believed. The night is almost gone, and the day is near. Therefore let us lay aside the deeds of darkness and put on the armor of light. Let us behave properly as in the day, not in carousing and drunkenness, not in sexual promiscuity and sensuality, not in strife and

jealousy. But put on the Lord Jesus Christ, and make no provision for the flesh in regard to its lusts.

I want to give you seven signs of being an awakened prophetic people, based on this passage.

1. They Are Spiritually Alert

I know a prophetic minister who is wonderfully used by the Lord. Some months ago when this gentleman was on a personal retreat, an angel came with a shofar, according to his testimony, and stood at the end of his bed. The angel blew the shofar and said one word: "Awake!" The word to the Church is the same: *Awake!*

The prophetic ministry in particular is supposed to blow a trumpet in the ears of the Church and cause her to arise. The apostle Paul is saying this in the above passage: "It's time to wake up, Church!" *It is high time* is the way the King James Version translates this phrase in verse 11. I like that. It is high time for us to wake up out of sleep. If we are spiritually awake, then all our senses are alert and working. We are not dozing off on the job, but attentive and ready to respond. God will shake up this slumbering giant, if He has to, in order to awaken us to action.

2. They Cast Off Darkness

"Let us therefore cast off the works of darkness" is the way the King James Version puts verse 12. The NASB says we are to "lay aside the deeds of darkness." The issue is this: An authentic prophetic person is among those who cast off the works of darkness. We are to lay them aside. As Ephesians 5:7–10 remarks, "Do not be partakers with them; for you were formerly darkness, but now you are Light in the Lord; walk as children of Light (for the fruit of the Light consists in all goodness and righteousness and truth), trying to learn what is pleasing to the Lord."

If you are prophetic, that means you are going against the grain. It means you live a holy life, swimming against the current of mainstream society. That distinction means more than just your living up to a code of do's and don'ts. You have a Helper who not only supports you as you cast away the excess baggage, but He lives within you and will do it through you.

When God puts His presence on His people, it becomes the outstanding distinguishing characteristic that sets them apart from all others (Exodus 33:16). He makes us different because He is different. We can then cast off the deeds of darkness because, simply put, the Helper is helping out!

The phrase *cast off* has a particular action connotation to it. It is not displaying passivity, but showing an aggressive act on our side as well. When you cast something off, you take it and throw it as fast and as hard away from you as you can.

When I was a kid I saw a double-header baseball game in which Bob Gibson of the St. Louis Cardinals and Juan Marichal of the San Francisco Giants both pitched. That was a dream for me! At other times I have watched Nolan Ryan and other aces smoke the ball past the batter. I was never any good at the game myself, but I sure loved observing those great pitchers at their art. Imagine throwing a ball ninety to a hundred miles an hour. That is the picture I want you to see. Even if you don't follow baseball—wind up, Church! Cast off those deeds of darkness with a fast fling. We cannot afford to keep them around.

3. They Are an Army of Light

Because we are fighting in a real war, we are also to "put on the armor of light" (verse 12) and walk in the light. Put on this Man Christ Jesus (Galatians 3:27, KJV). He is the greatest warrior of all time, the original revolutionary activist.

In a class I took on public opinion and mass communication during my university days in the early 1970s, at the height of the Jesus People movement, we were to pick a historic revolutionary figure of the past, then devise a media campaign blitz for that person, as though he or she were still alive. As a Jesus person, I did not have a hard time choosing who my revolutionary figure would be. I came up with a campaign song, a chant declaration, display ads, the whole nine yards. More than 25 years later, I still believe Jesus is the most radical leader who ever lived. And He continues to lead an all-volunteer army.

He is really good at drafting people into that army. My wife, Michal Ann, was given a dream in which the Holy Spirit was looking for prophetic mentors—mothers and fathers in the Spirit. In this dream she was standing in line with a bunch of people, and the Holy Spirit was saying, "Whoever wants to volunteer to be a father or a mother in the prophetic, I want you to step forward." My wife continued to stand in the line, as everybody else took a step back. She continued standing there all alone, making it appear that she had stepped forward. The Holy Spirit said, "You volunteered!" She pondered, *I volunteered?* Then a wind came from behind and flung her forward. "Yes," God said, "you volunteered!"

Jesus wants us to constantly reenlist for the army of God (Psalm 110:3) and put on the armor of light. Displace darkness by walking in the light. What is the light? It is truth. Truth is not just correct doctrine; it is truthfulness worked into our innermost parts. We are a volunteer army and our effective weaponry is truth—not just by what we speak, but by what we live out.

Christ Jesus is still alive today and wants to live His radical life through like-minded desperadoes. Hey, be distinctly different! Arise! Shake off passivity and be a consecrated warrior for our Lord. Does He deserve anything less?

4. They Live Transparent and Honest Lives

The KJV puts Romans 13:13 like this: "Let us walk honestly, as in the day." The NASB renders it, "Let us behave properly as in the day." Do you know what the world is looking for? Definitely not Christians who say they have their acts together and then don't. No, the world would rather see a people who are in process and actually admit it. That builds a bridge from the Church to the world—a bridge called honesty and transparency. It is a span we need to build because the world is looking for people who are real. We can then direct seekers, in hope, to the One who is changing us.

True prophetic people are not just a bunch of faddish folks going along with the latest trend. Real Christians are not fakes. It is not always easy to be honest and transparent and open, but it is breathtakingly refreshing.

I am learning a principle dealing with the impartation of spiritual life. The more transparent and honest I am, the more life is imparted to others. Transparency builds hope in people. When I allow others to see my brokenness, struggles and process, they can relate to the pressures I am going through, yet see that I continue to walk on. That gives them hope that they, too, can continue on the journey of becoming. And something deeper than teaching occurs.

5. They Flee Carnality

"Not in rioting and drunkenness, not in chambering and wantonness, not in strife and envying" (Romans 13:13, KJV). "Not in carousing and drunkenness, not in sexual promiscuity and sensuality, not in strife and jealousy" (NASB). Isn't it intriguing that, right in the same group of sexual issues to be dealt with, we find strife and jealousy?

It is no coincidence. They are partners with spiritual adultery. Yes, you heard me—strife and jealousy cause divisions and breakups in ministries and churches. You become jealous of what someone else has in contrast to what you possess. You want that person's car, his house, his job, his physique, his spouse, his calling or ministry. Your envy arises out of insecurity over your own identity.

But let's not be sowers of strife and competition or motivated by selfish ambition. When I say to avoid carnal living, I am not referring just to the outward issues. I am including the attitudes of the heart: motivations, ambitions, lusts. We must cast off competition, ambition, jealousy and strife, as well as party spirit, sensuality and sexual promiscuity. Let's run as fast as we can in the opposite direction. Let's scurry to the Lord and cry, "Help!" May He purify our hearts so that our hands can be clean.

6. They Lean on Jesus

The next sign of an awakened prophetic people is probably the most strategic. The KJV aptly phrases it, "Put ye on the Lord Jesus Christ" (verse 14). He is our message. He is our life. Let's put on and demonstrate and exhibit this Man, our source and strength for living.

Notice once again the study in contrasts. When we admit our weaknesses, Jesus provides the remedy of His very own strength. He is our everything, and He loves for His people to be dependent on Him. Yes, we are weak but He is strong.

Remember John, the disciple of Jesus, who learned this in the process of becoming a true disciple. After a few years of life in the trenches of ministry, he leaned his head on the heart of Jesus. What do you think? Could you learn to do the same? Leaning on Jesus is the most prophetic thing that anyone can do, and it does not require a special gift.

Another old hymn goes buzzing through my head right now, "Leaning on the Everlasting Arms." Take a quick glance at these wonderful old words, simple yet true:

> What a fellowship, what a joy divine,
> Leaning on the everlasting arms;
> What a blessedness, what a peace is mine,
> Leaning on the everlasting arms.
>
> [Chorus]
> Leaning, leaning, safe and secure from all alarms;
> Leaning, leaning, leaning on the everlasting arms.
>
> Oh, how sweet to walk in this pilgrim way,
> Leaning on the everlasting arms;
> Oh, how bright the path grows from day to day,
> Leaning on the everlasting arms.
>
> What have I to dread, what have I to fear,
> Leaning on the everlasting arms?
> I have blessed peace with my Lord so near,
> Leaning on the everlasting arms.[6]

7. They Keep Their Priorities Right

"Make not provision for the flesh, to fulfil the lusts thereof" (verse 14, KJV). "Ouch!" you might respond, as the conviction of the Holy Spirit settles on your soul. Do you know what this has to do with? When nobody is watching. When you are on a trip. When you are in that hotel room alone. When you are away from your parents or at college. When you are home alone. I have a word for you: Keep your priorities right. After all, Someone is watching over your shoulder. Be the real thing. Have the real content in the can. Don't be a fake.

Here, then, is the issue: Be wise. Don't give the flesh or the devil an inch. He always tries to get extra mileage out of any deal. Don't let him. Any void or vacuum always gets filled up with something. If you squelch the prophetic nature of the Holy Spirit, then the opposites of these seven characteristics will come into play. This opens the door for the Jezebel spirit to romp through our midst.

This demonic spirit hates the prophetic and seeks to destroy God-ordained authority. It causes fear, debilitating discouragement, depression and immobilization (1 Kings 16:31; 18:4, 19; 19:1–4; 21:5–19, 25–27; 2 Kings 9:7–10; 22–37; Revelation 2:20–23). Perversions of many kinds will be the outcome.

So keep your priorities right and make no allowance for the flesh or the devil.

An Exhortation from the Heart

In rounding out this chapter, I want to share something with you from my heart. I am a man on a search. I am constantly looking for God. I seek fresh understanding and applications that relate to our day and time. And here is my tough conclusion on the characteristics of prophetic people.

We have been doing a bunch of practicing on one another for years—at conferences, seminars and Sunday morning meetings. For a long time I have been a trainer in many of these settings. But when are we going to really do the stuff? Isn't it time for us to stop using one another as guinea pigs and actually get out to the streets and do some good? I have an idea that the real, authentic fruit of prophetic people becomes available to be picked when we *Just Do It!*

So take your hands out of your pockets and lay them on someone. Step out. Just do something, for Jesus' sake. Open wide your mouth and let God fill it (Psalm 81:10).

Michael L. Brown, founder and president of the F.I.R.E. School of Ministry in Pensacola, Florida, echoes my own heart in his gut-wrenching book *Revolution! The Call to Holy War:*

> People are crying out for liberty. They are hurting and confused, not knowing which way to turn, not knowing who will lead them out. What will they do? Will we offer them true freedom, or will Satan beat us to the punch yet again, offering his destructive counterfeits? I say we take this revolution to the streets and proclaim liberty to the captives in Jesus' name. Freedom is the word for the hour! This was how the Son of God spent His life, as Peter spoke of "how God anointed Jesus of Nazareth with the Holy Spirit and power, and how he went around doing good and healing all who were under the power of the devil, because God was with him" (Acts 10:38). How clear this is! He sets captives free because God was with Him and the Spirit was on Him. What else could He do? And what else can we do?[7]

OUR INTERCESSORY CRY

Father, we want to be authentic prophetic people who talk the talk and walk the walk. Help us be pilgrims of faith, pioneers breaking open new territory, messengers with a clear word, members of a servant community. Help us to be spiritually awake, ready to cast off darkness as activists in Your army. Make us into real, transparent Christians who escape carnality by running into the safety of Your arms of love. Grant us grace to stay in the race for the long haul and not treat Your presence as if it were the latest fad. Help us keep our priorities right.

Lord, we want to be authentic prophetic people. We long for a prophetic revolution to take place in our lives and in the Church. Shake us up if You have to. We want to be all that You want us to be. In Jesus' great name and for His sake. Amen.

POP QUIZ—KEEPING YOU ON YOUR TOES!

1. What do you consider some of the authentic characteristics of prophetic people?

2. If you were to ask the Lord to strengthen you in one particular area, what would it be and why?
3. According to Romans 13:11–14, what are some of the characteristics of prophetic people?

FOR MORE, LORD!

David Blomgren, *Prophetic Gatherings in the Church: The Laying on of Hands and Prophecy* (Portland: BT Publishing, 1979)

T. Austin Sparks, *Prophetic Ministry* (Shippensburg, Pa.: Destiny Image, 2000)

Robert Stearns, *Preparing the Way* (Lake Mary, Fla.: Creation House, 1999)

3

THE CROSS AS OUR
PROPHETIC LIFESTYLE

Although receiving and releasing spiritual gifts is an important part of the package, the mature prophetic person has as his or her goal a lot more than being God's mailman or delivery boy. Being a prophet has to do first with friendship with God, with having a heart passionately on fire with the Lord Jesus Christ. And if we are going to be a friend of God, we must be lovers of the cross.

James 4:4 strongly admonishes us, "You adulteresses, do you not know that friendship with the world is hostility toward God? Therefore whoever wishes to be a friend of the world makes himself an enemy of God." There is no way you can be a friend of God if you are not also a friend of the cross.

What does it mean to be lovers of the cross? That is what we will explore in this chapter. Once again I turn to the writings of T. Austin Sparks:

> We cannot have the knowledge of the Lord—the most important thing in the mind of God for us—except on the ground of the continuous application of the Cross, and that will go right on to the end. Do not imagine that there will come a day when you have done with the Cross, when the principle of the Cross will no longer be neces-

sary and when you have graduated from the school where the Cross is the instrument of the Lord. Such a day never will be! If you are going on into greater fulness of knowledge—I mean spiritual knowledge of the Lord—and therefore greater fulness of usefulness to Him, you must take it as settled that the principle of the Cross is going to be applied more and more deeply as you go on.[1]

Friendship with God

Abraham is the first person identified in Scripture as a prophet (Genesis 20:7). We call him the father of faith, the first of the patriarchs, a man of the covenant and other noteworthy titles. But the Scriptures mention another important thing about this man: "Was not Abraham our father justified by works when he offered up Isaac his son on the altar? You see that faith was working with his works, and as a result of the works, faith was perfected; and the Scripture was fulfilled which says, 'AND ABRAHAM BELIEVED GOD, AND IT WAS RECKONED TO HIM AS RIGHTEOUSNESS,' and he was called the friend of God" (James 2:21–23; see also 2 Chronicles 20:7; Isaiah 41:8).

Abraham's friendship with God is borne out in Scripture by his many close encounters of an intimate kind. Isn't that what you want to see happen in your life, too? More than anything in my life, I want to be a friend of God. But if we are not friends of the cross, we are at enmity with God.

Now the one entity I truly want on my side is God Himself! I do not want to fight Him. When I choose the cross of Jesus, I am choosing friendship with God. Galatians 6:14 reminds us, "May it never be that I would boast, except in the cross of our Lord Jesus Christ, through which the world has been crucified to me, and I to the world." Paul is not speaking of a whimsical attitude toward the application of the cross in our lives; he is referring to the cross as our lifestyle.

Called to act in a spirit opposite to the spirit of this world by embracing Christ's cross as our own is the heart of the prophetic, the gate into greater friendship with our Creator and the Lover of our souls.

What do good friends do? They like hanging out with one another. They have a relationship that has become established over a period

of time. Two new friends are often melded together through sur-
viving the tensions of good times and bad. All significant relationships are tested through the trial of fire. Trust is not a spiritual gift;
it has to be built over time. But once trust has been nurtured, faithful friends enter another level in their relationship. They begin to
share their heart-kept secrets one with another.

So it is with the prophetic: "Surely the Lord GOD does nothing
unless He reveals His secret counsel to His servants the prophets"
(Amos 3:7). One of the great blessings in this life is to hear the Lord's
voice. Lean your ear His way and let Him share with you wonderful words of life! In his book *Prophetic Ministry* Rick Joyner elab-
orates on that verse in Amos: "The Lord does not want to do anything without sharing it with the prophets, because the prophets
are His friends. . . . The essence of prophetic ministry is to be the
special friend and confidant of God."[2]

May friendship with God be your aim, while you "earnestly desire
spiritual gifts, but especially that you may prophesy" (1 Corinthians
14:1). Usually this kind of relationship—walking in the shadow of
the cross as your prophetic lifestyle—takes some time to cultivate.
Crucified servants make no special claim to be heard, but they
speak, act and are content to leave the matter there, confident not
in themselves, but that they have heard from God and that every
word from the Lord will find fulfillment.

Now *that* deals with the mature package of the prophetic! The
problem is, most of us do not initially respond that way; we take it
personally if we feel our word has not been received. Then we end
up defensive, antagonistic and a little unfriendly in the process.

Our responsibility, however, is not whether a particular word is
received. It is standing in the counsel of God—listening to His voice
alone—and then bringing forth His heart with character, honoring
spiritual authority and relating in a manner of teachableness. We
can be confident that if it is His word, He will bear witness to it.
God's thoughts are not our thoughts; His ways are not our ways.
But when His word goes forth, it will not return void, but will
accomplish the purposes for which He sent it forth (Isaiah 55:8–11).
In one dimension, then, you have done your job. But afterward do
not shoot to kill, particularly your pastor! Be a friend of God by
being a servant friend to those in authority.

A Mouthful of Splinters

We can lay the foundation for all true believers in Christ, no matter what our gift or ministry, by looking at Hebrews 12:1–2 (NKJV):

> Since we are surrounded by so great a cloud of witnesses, let us lay aside every weight, and the sin which so easily ensnares us, and let us run with endurance the race that is set before us, looking unto Jesus, the author and finisher of our faith. . . .

Slow down; watch this next phrase now:

> . . . Who for the joy set before Him endured the cross, despising the shame and has sat down at the right hand of the throne of God.

I am thankful that this verse says Jesus *endured* the cross; it does not say it was fun or easy. It also gives us a hint of *how* He endured it. Jesus could see what was coming as a result of embracing the cross: "For the joy set before Him. . . ." Paul told us that *death works in us that life might work in others* (2 Corinthians 4:12). So look beyond the cross and see what lies on the other side. As you do, joy and strength will come, and you will be supernaturally enabled to bear your cross with joy.

Because there is a cross tailor-made for every one of us. It is shaped with just you in mind. (He knows how to make it fit, too!) The rich young ruler of Matthew 19 had a cross made specifically for him. Jesus said to no other person what He said to that wealthy young man: "You've done well. Now sell all that you have and give it to the poor."

The problem is, we tend to get legalistic and try to make a specific word from Jesus fit everyone else. Then we end up offering an admonition like, "You've got to sell everything and give it all to the poor." Believe me, we need a whole lot bigger heart of compassion for the poor. But that was a specific word to a specific person. The prophetic presence was being released through Jesus at that moment, exposing the idol in the young man's heart. It must have been the issue he struggled with the most: bowing down at the altar of mammon. Jesus was offering him the cross tailored just for him. But he turned away because it was too hard. He could not see beyond the cross to what lay ahead on the other side.

Jesus has a revelatory word that will cut right through to where you need it most. That sharp, piercing message will be different for you than for anybody else. What He asks you to give up and what He asks you to carry will not be exactly the same as for the next person.

Years ago I was deeply touched by a message calling us to have "A Mouthful of Splinters." Sounds terrible, doesn't it? But the Lord wants us to kiss the cross, to embrace the cross, to love the cross. It is your friend, not your enemy. It is true, body piercing saved our lives. So kiss the cross and get a mouthful of splinters.

I want to make sure in the opening section of this book that our aim is straight and our target clear. Our goal is not primarily becoming a prophetic servant community or even a revolutionary generation of passionate, consecrated warriors. Gifts are given by grace, but fruit is grown by kissing the cross. Our goal in this life, then, is to be changed into the image of Christ Jesus. It is about Him, not about us. It is all about You, Jesus. The focus of our lives must be the centrality of His cross in all things.

Each generation has different enemies released against it by the powers of darkness, which requires a fresh, prophetic application of God's Word so it can walk counter to the accepted but unbiblical norms of contemporary society. To be authentic revolutionary agents calling for change, we must carry our crosses. Otherwise you or I will be nothing more than "a noisy gong or a clanging cymbal" (1 Corinthians 13:1–3).

Classic Statements on the Cross

Now that we have clarified our target, let's look at some classic, vintage statements of forerunners already walking this pilgrim's path. Then I will list some old-fashioned, tried-and-true Scriptures to help us keep our focus on the cross.

Dr. Bill Hamon, founder of Christian International and author of several books, has years under his belt understanding the centrality of the cross in the life of the prophetic person. Let's take a look at what this pioneer has to say:

> The principal players in the biblical story—God, humanity, and the devil—are still the principal players today, and though we live under a new covenant, these characters have not changed. God still speaks through His prophets, people still resent and resist God's prophetic word, and the devil still does all he can to destroy the prophets. So persecution and suffering are all part of the prophet's cross to bear. Jesus said that unless we are willing to take up our crosses and deny ourselves, we cannot be disciples (Mt. 16:24). How much more does this principle apply to being prophets? Prophets must take up their ministry crosses joyfully, denying themselves all the fleshly indulgences of these prophetic pitfalls, weed seed attitudes and syndromes.[3]

Two other prophetic statesmen of our day are John and Paula Sandford, founders of Elijah House Ministries. Their book *The Elijah Task: A Call to Today's Prophets* is one of the classic texts that many in my generation cut our teeth on. Here is what this wise couple has to say about embracing the cross:

> End-time prophets must be thoroughly dead to themselves in our Lord and risen to perfect obedience. Their minds must be purely in Him, lest they cast water on fires God is building, or worse yet, call for fires of suffering out of their own hidden desires for vengeance. The necessity of discipline is thus heavy upon us. Any fire, spiritual or earthly, is most difficult to control. Yes, controlled fires have warmed our houses, cooked our food and driven our engines. Controlled spiritual fire is even more necessary and valuable. Men must learn, as Paul did, to let affliction work its weight of gold.[4]

Let's take a peek at what Ed Dufresne, in a lighter and yet convicting fashion, relates in his book *The Prophet: Friend of God:*

> I once asked myself, "What am I doing, living in a hotel room? I could be home with my wife and my son!" And the Spirit of the Lord rose up in my spirit and said, "Dead men don't gripe." You know what happens to a living sacrifice? It dies. Dead men never fight back, either. . . . Dead men never get even. . . . Prophets must give

up their bodies as a living sacrifice. Even today they throw stones at prophets. Some of you say, "Yes, I want the prophet's ministry." Will you still want it when things like this happen? Will you still be willing to "present your bodies a living sacrifice, holy, acceptable unto God, which is your reasonable service"?[5]

Last let's turn our ear to one of the voices God is raising up in this generation—Dr. Michael L. Brown, author, instructor and revivalist. This prophetic statesman is calling for a holy war on complacency in the Church:

> Our Savior made this perfectly clear, establishing two foundations for battle. The first foundation is, *Take up your cross.* The second foundation is, *Put down your sword.* We tend to get things reversed! We take up our sword, relying on human methods to change the world, and we put down our cross, despising God's method to change the world. God's method runs counter to the flesh. God's method seems weak and foolish. God's method flies in the face of established wisdom. God's method seems doomed to failure and defeat, yet it is the only way to succeed and win. God's method is the Cross![6]

Classic Scriptures on the Cross

Having looked at these in-your-face statements from some of our veterans, let's load our guns with the original ammunition, by way of Scripture statements from Jesus Himself and His apostolic follower Paul. Don't try to avoid getting nailed right now. As you read these verses, just lift up your hands, give up and surrender to the Commander-in-Chief:

> "Anyone who does not take his cross and follow me is not worthy of me."
>
> Matthew 10:38, NIV

> "If anyone wishes to come after Me, he must deny himself, and take up his cross and follow Me. For whoever wishes to save his life will lose it, but whoever loses his life for My sake and the gospel's will save it."
>
> Mark 8:34–35

We who are alive are always being given over to death for Jesus' sake, so that his life may be revealed in our mortal body. So then, death is at work in us, but life is at work in you.

2 Corinthians 4:11–12, NIV

May it never be that I would boast, except in the cross of our Lord Jesus Christ, through which the world has been crucified to me, and I to the world.

Galatians 6:14

Brethren, join in following my example, and observe those who walk according to the pattern you have in us. For many walk, of whom I often told you, and now tell you even weeping, that they are enemies of the cross of Christ, whose end is destruction, whose god is their appetite, and whose glory is in their shame, who set their minds on earthly things.

Philippians 3:17–19

Ouch!, *Amen!* and *Oh, me!* Nothing cuts and heals like the Word of God.

Now let's build on these understandings by turning to lessons from the last journey of Elijah and Elisha as recorded in 2 Kings. I have found it helpful in my walk to glean from the lives of others—lessons from characters in Scripture and other historic and contemporary heroes of the faith. Walk down the path with me now as we consider lessons from the life of the prophet Elijah as he is about to graduate to heaven and leave his work for the next generation to complete.

The Last Journey of Elijah and Elisha

With your imagination surrendered to the Lord, ponder with me what the settings must have looked like. I wonder what Elijah's emotions were doing and saying as he prepared to depart this life. And consider the turbulence Elisha must have been going through when he was told repeatedly—three separate times!—to stay behind.

It came about when the LORD was about to take up Elijah by a whirlwind to heaven, that Elijah went with Elisha from Gilgal. Elijah said

> to Elisha, "Stay here please, for the LORD has sent me as far as
> Bethel." But Elisha said, "As the LORD lives and as you yourself live,
> I will not leave you." So they went down to Bethel.
>
> 2 Kings 2:1–2

Elijah's imminent departure foreshadows the life of our Messiah,
when Jesus would soon be caught up into heaven and leave His
work in the hands of His followers. Continue to read these verses
with this understanding.

Training the Next Generation

> Then the sons of the prophets who were at Bethel came out to
> Elisha and said to him, "Do you know that the LORD will take away
> your master from over you today?" And he said, "Yes, I know; be
> still." Elijah said to him, "Elisha, please stay here, for the LORD has
> sent me to Jericho." But he said, "As the LORD lives, and as you your-
> self live, I will not leave you." So they came to Jericho. The sons of
> the prophets who were at Jericho approached Elisha and said to
> him, "Do you know that the LORD will take away your master from
> over you today?" And he answered, "Yes, I know; be still."
>
> verses 3–5

See, these curious prophetic types had been getting schooled in
the revelatory ways of God, and now they were picking up on what
was coming. The next generation in training, in both Bethel and
Jericho, was going to Elisha and saying, "Hey, listen, do you understand what's going on? Do you know that the Lord will take away
your master from over you today?" A multiplication of the revelatory presence was occurring.

But I imagine Elisha was having to deal with a bit of frustration
at this juncture. He was in his final rounds of being mentored, and
now the next generation under him was being zealous and con-
temptuous, as he had probably been in his earlier years. He
answered, "Yes, I know; be still." I wonder if he was thinking, *Oh,
no, you mean I'm going to have to put up with this, too?*

Crossing Over the Line

> Then Elijah said to him, "Please stay here, for the LORD has sent
> me to the Jordan." And he said, "As the LORD lives, and as you your-

self live, I will not leave you." So the two of them went on. Now fifty men of the sons of the prophets went and stood opposite them at a distance, while the two of them stood by the Jordan.

verses 6–7

You want to go. Your master has just said to stay. Are you going to follow your hunger pangs and push on, or are you going to submit and do what looks right? Others were watching Elisha's every move with great anticipation, fifty sons of the prophets in each location.

Ever feel as if you live in a public goldfish bowl and everyone is watching your every move? Welcome to the club. It is part of your training.

Elijah took his mantle and folded it together and struck the waters, and they were divided here and there, so that the two of them crossed over on dry ground.

verse 8

I love the English rendering of this passage. Notice the words carefully. The two of them *crossed over* on dry ground. It seems to me that the *cross* was being presented to Elisha at every crossroads. Who was he going to obey, God or man? Imagine the struggle as he searched for wisdom and proper discernment. Ponder the conflicting issues of honor and zeal. Was he going for it out of selfish ambition, or out of desperation for God's purposes to come forth and succeed? There was a cross tailor-made for Elisha, and it was being offered right now.

The Promise on the Other Side

When they had crossed over, Elijah said to Elisha, "Ask what I shall do for you before I am taken from you." And Elisha said, "Please, let a double portion of your spirit be upon me."

verse 9

Isn't it amazing that the hunger of a man or woman can determine the amount of God received? Could it be that Elisha's cry for a double portion was that of urgency for the next generation to come into its inheritance? He knew he would need more of God's grace and power for his ministry and to conquer his enemies.

> [Elijah] said, "You have asked a hard thing. Nevertheless, if you see me when I am taken from you, it shall be so for you; but if not, it shall not be so."
>
> verse 10

Time for another lesson in the prophetic. Wow! Talk about on-the-job training, critical last-minute lessons on your way out! "If you see me. . . ." It sounds to me as if "keep-your-eyes-open-at-all-times" must be a valuable lesson to learn.

> As they were going along and talking, behold, there appeared a chariot of fire and horses of fire which separated the two of them. And Elijah went up by a whirlwind to heaven. Elisha saw it and cried out, "My father, my father, the chariots of Israel and its horsemen!" And he saw Elijah no more. Then he took hold of his own clothes and tore them in two pieces.
>
> verses 11–12

What did Elisha see? Whom did he see? A transfer from one generation to the next was accomplished as the realm of fatherhood was illuminated to Elisha's eyes. The purpose of the cross is to lead us into a deeper revelation of the Father's heart. But something had to be taken away in order that something even greater could come. "And he saw Elijah no more." What a test! What a cost! What a cross!

Elisha Succeeds Elijah

> He also took up the mantle of Elijah that fell from him and returned and stood by the bank of the Jordan. He took the mantle of Elijah that fell from him and struck the waters and said, "Where is the LORD, the God of Elijah?" And when he also had struck the waters, they were divided here and there; and Elisha crossed over.
>
> verses 13–14

Notice Elisha's focus is no longer on his master; it is on *the* Master. "Where is the LORD, the God of Elijah?" There comes a point when each of us has to take the baton for ourselves. We can sit in the grandstands observing for only so long. After moving from my comfortable place in Kansas City to Nashville, some friends came up to me and said, "Step up to the plate. You're not the new kid on the block. Now step forward!" Eventually you have to do something for Jesus' sake. Hits and runs take place only when you pick up the bat—or the mantle—and go to the plate.

> Now when the sons of the prophets who were at Jericho opposite him saw him, they said, "The spirit of Elijah rests on Elisha." And they came to meet him and bowed themselves to the ground before him.
>
> verse 15

The next generation recognized that the passing of the torch had occurred. With honor and reverence they prostrated themselves in an act of submission to the new delegated authority. The baton had been passed—but the first test was just about to begin.

Tests for the New Generation

> They said to him, "Behold now, there are with your servants fifty strong men, please let them go and search for your master; perhaps the Spirit of the LORD has taken him up and cast him on some mountain or into some valley." And he said, "You shall not send." But when they urged him until he was ashamed, he said, "Send." They sent therefore fifty men; and they searched three days but did not find him. They returned to him while he was staying at Jericho; and he said to them, "Did I not say to you, 'Do not go'?"
>
> verses 16–18

When Elisha crossed back over the Jordan, he was met by the company of prophets who, although recognizing the Spirit of God on him, were still looking for the familiar. They were dialing back to yesterday's blessing.

Too often we miss what God is doing today because we are looking for a repeat performance of what He did yesterday. Beware of attitudes and religious spirits that cause us to seek contentment with yesterday's blessing and not reach forward in God, even if they recognize that the Spirit of God is on another. Religion in a negative sense ties up the mind into strongholds of skinny thinking and skepticism. Do not be doubtful and unbelieving, but cry out for God to give to His people the authentic double portion.

Our Biggest Test: The Success of the Past

Along the path are places where God reveals to us aspects of His covenant nature. These sites become places of "visitation" or "revelation" to us. Too often, though, we camp out at the last thing God revealed as though there are no more traits of His personality for Him to demonstrate. A protectionist mindset causes us to become squatters in the past instead of continuing to be pioneers. In my lifetime alone I have seen congregations, networks and whole denominations give so much of their energy to preserving the best of the past that they miss what the God of today is doing. As for me and my house, there must be more—more of His great, brilliant presence.

To get a more complete picture of "The Cross as our Prophetic Lifestyle," let's take a closer look at each of the locations where Elijah told Elisha to stay. Understanding what occurred at each of these historic sites will tighten our grasp of the cost that is often involved in going further with the Lord.

Gilgal: The Place of Cutting

According to Scriptures, many events transpired in this strategic place. A monumental passage took place at this site when a whole generation of Israelites miraculously crossed the Jordan River. A baton had been given prophetically once before, right here, from one generation to the next, from Moses to Joshua.

Then, in the place called Gilgal, God gave Joshua instructions for the whole group of warriors who had been born in the wilderness and never been circumcised. So, swallow hard! First things first. Gilgal is a place of the cutting away of the flesh.

Anybody want to volunteer to walk out the prophetic purposes for your generation? Guess where the first stop is? Gilgal. The name *Gilgal* means "wheel or rolling thing." What happened at Gilgal?

They sharpened up their flint knives at Gilgal, and the men who had never received physical circumcision were circumcised (Joshua 5:2–3). It was the place of the rolling back. It was the place of the removing of the flesh. It was the cross.

I have an idea that it hurt. But the cutting away of the flesh was an outward sign of Israel's being the covenant people of God (Genesis 17:9–14; Romans 2:29; Colossians 2:11).

Do you still want to be part of the next generation of prophetic people to emerge? Guess what? You have an appointment at Gilgal. Get circumcised in your heart.

Bethel: The House of God

After the appointment of the removal of the flesh, God knew exactly what He was doing. Elijah, one of the fathers of the faith, had been down this road before. A trap was now set, a tripwire, to see if the next generation would keep on following in the shadow of the cross.

Elijah said to Elisha, "Stay here please, for the LORD has sent me as far as Bethel" (2 Kings 2:2). He was saying, "Hey, I'm moving on now. But Elisha, you stay right here." Was that ever a test! A test of hunger. A test of passion. A test concerning being comfortable.

Let's be honest. Even after you get circumcised, the pain leaves after a while and you get used to your new territory. You might even begin triumphing over your enemy. You begin to settle into your comfort zone. And then the divine intruder shows up to unsettle your nest! Time to keep moving.

Do you remember some of the things that happened in Bethel? Bethel was the place where Jacob took a nap, was visited by angels in a dream and realized it was a place of divine visitation (Genesis 28). *Bethel* means "the house of God." It is the house of bread. Jacob woke up and exclaimed, "How awesome is this place! This is none other than the house of God, and this is the gate of heaven" (verse 17).

An appointment was now set in Bethel, and the next leg of the journey was beginning. This was a test of Elisha's tenacity, of his character. His foundation was being checked to see if, "for the joy set before him," he would endure the path to the cross. Elisha replied, "No way, buddy, are you leaving me out!" And he crossed on over with Elijah to the city called Bethel.

Crossing on over is what He wants us to do in our individual Christian journeys. He wants to take us from the place of the removal of the flesh into the house of God. He wants to make *us* into a house of God. And He has a passion to break forth through openings in the realm of the Spirit, and for His manifested presence to tumble on down. Oh, that we would love His presence more than we love this world!

On to Jericho

I would have liked to have camped out at Bethel. Bethel was awesome, and I would have been tempted to stay there. How about you? Imagine Elijah telling you, "Hey, do I have an opportunity for you! Maintain this place of His presence. I gotta go on to Jericho." I kind of think you, too, would have been a little tempted to stop moving forward and just settle in. But eventually you do not care what the cost is. Your cry becomes, *O Lord, no matter the cost, if there is anything more out there, I must have it. I must have You!*

If the Holy Spirit moves, the prophetic person has to keep moving, too. Surely He is still at Bethel. But there must be more. Do you see the pattern? You must cross over to the next truth, the next revelation, the next display of the progressive purposes of God for your generation. Jesus said, "A man shall leave his father and mother . . ." (Mark 10:7).

On to Jericho! But what could this mean?

In this place, remember, under the next generation of leadership, the walls came tumbling down (Joshua 6). The purpose of every Bethel is to receive God's presence to tear down walls. Some people just want to camp out and party at Bethel, but there is a higher plan. The true prophetic person realizes that God has allowed us to experience His breakthrough presence for a purpose—to tear down the walls that surround entire cities. There is a cross for every new level and purpose, a cost to leaving the best of yesterday to enter into the unknown of tomorrow.

So Elisha responded, "As the LORD lives, and as you yourself live, I will not leave you." The Lord and His progressive purposes won out once again.

Time to Cross the River Jordan

At Jericho we are delivered of our small-mindedness and gain a citywide vision. Elijah had an even bigger mission in mind, though: "The LORD has sent me to the Jordan." At this point you know Elisha's reaction. So the two of them traveled on down the road, with fifty of the next-generation school of the prophets watching in amazement.

There are people watching you as well. Congregations are watching. Cities are watching. We reach a place in our pilgrimage where we are no longer crossing over for our inheritance only. We realize that our sacrifice can make a difference, and we are working in order for our generation to enter in.

How did Elijah and Elisha cross the Jordan River? It would take a miracle to continue on, just as it had taken a miracle hundreds of years earlier when Joshua led the children of Israel into the Promised Land. But the further you go with God, the less there can be of you and the more there must be of Him. "Elijah took his mantle and folded it together and struck the waters, and they were divided here and there, so that the two of them crossed over on dry ground."

The word *Jordan* means "to cast down, to subdue, to take down like an enemy." It was now going to take the fullness of all Elijah had learned to cross over into the promises.

What lay beyond the Jordan? It represented the promise for the entire next generation—from Moses to Joshua and from Elijah to Elisha. The baton was about to be passed on. They had to press on to face the waters of the Jordan River where things are brought down, cast down, subdued, taken like an enemy.

Any one of these—Joshua, the children of Israel, or Elisha—could have said, "Isn't it good what we have achieved?" It truly *would* have been good, in a sense. And it would have been terribly sad. Passionate, revolutionary people cannot stop. Consecrated warriors are willing to continually embrace the cost of leaving behind what has been pioneered in order to plow up virgin territory, for Christ's sake; to go before others so that they, too, can cross over to the next level.

What happened? Elijah and Elisha crossed over, as we have seen, through miraculous intervention.

Time for Fathers and Mothers

Like Elisha, you will be given opportunities to stop. And indeed, there will be times that it is right and necessary for you to stop in your journey for a while. To sit down and count the cost. To sit down and catch your breath. To sit down and lick your wounds and let Jesus heal you. Remember, progressive death works in us so that progressive life will work in others.

Every new level has a cost, but every new level offers a new dimension of grace. And every new invitation of greater impartation requires a new level of embracing the lifestyle of the cross. Every time you go through the eye of the needle, you leave behind the successes and failures you just experienced in the last leg of your journey. You can either hold onto what you have, or you can give what you have and watch it be multiplied into the lives of others. You get the privilege of coming forth naked in this life in order to go clothed into the next place.

That is necessary for you (like Michal Ann in her dream) to become a father or mother in the Lord. The impartation of life begets life. Whether in the prophetic realm, the pastoral realm, the spirit of prayer, or whatever Kingdom dimension into which you have been called, increase comes by grace, by faithfulness, by counting the cost and by receiving a revelation of the great heart of the Father.

So it happened. Elisha insisted. Elijah was taken up. Elisha saw and received the double portion.

I doubt that Elisha was asking for a double portion for the sake of his personal ministry. I firmly believe that he saw part of the cost in front of him, and that his tenacity was a heart cry of absolute desperation. He yearned for what God intended for his generation. Elisha had to have more.

And an amazing thing occurred. The Scriptures record twice the number of miracles occurring through Elisha's life as through Elijah's. Imagine that! The presence of God increased in an awesome dimension from one generation to the next.

Moravians

*24 hr 7.
PRAYER*

It's Your Turn!

Gifts can be imparted, but you must embrace the cross for yourself. No one else can do it for you. Embracing the cross involves dying to what is good in order that something better can come forth. This is the pattern of the prophetic lifestyle and the test for all who long for the progressive purposes of God. Death works in us that life might work in others.

The Lord is not looking for two or three awesomely gifted people with detailed words of knowledge to wow the crowds. The Holy Spirit is searching for people who will spend intimate time with their Father and waste their lives on Him. I would love to increase in many prophetic arenas, but that is not my major goal anymore. My aim is to be a friend of God, to lean my head on Jesus' bosom, to love the cross, to have a mouthful of splinters.

I also long to see a revolutionary, passionate, consecrated generation of warriors of the cross—servant believers who are enflamed with love for their Messiah, who walk cross-current with society, who release His fragrance of life and presence in whatever they do and wherever they go.

Some years ago, having gone through a difficult time of trials and emotional bruising, I had a dream in which different figures from Church history came and stood before me—people like John Huss, Martin Luther and Count Nicolaus Ludwig von Zinzendorf, benefactor of the Moravians. Then the scene changed to modern times and a well-known prophet of our day faced me. His words pierced my being: "The glory of the cross is to bear your pain without defending yourself." I woke up stunned, not condemned but inspired, knowing what the Lord required of me in that season. I was grateful. I was shocked. I was relieved. And I was shown the way out of my dilemma—the way of the cross.

Let me wrap up Track 1 of this book in the majestic words of the first verse of another great hymn, *Must Jesus Bear the Cross Alone?* It needs no explanation!

> Must Jesus bear the cross alone,
> And all the world go free?
> No, there's a cross for everyone,
> And there's a cross for me.[7]

OUR INTERCESSORY CRY

Father, in Jesus' name I pray over the words of this chapter, that they will not return void but that they will find personal, practical applications for each one who reads. Whether old or young, experienced or inexperienced, profoundly gifted or in a place of new beginnings, may each see the vision of the cross clearly.

God, I ask for the grace that was on Elijah to be released to this generation. I ask for the double portion, Lord! And with each test that comes of "Let's stay here," may something rise up within this one that says, "I shall yet pursue. I shall go on, no matter what the cost." Help this one to deny self, take up his or her cross and live. May the cross truly be this person's prophetic lifestyle, in Jesus' holy name. Amen.

POP QUIZ—KEEPING YOU ON YOUR TOES!

1. What was the cross Elisha had to bear in order to continue his pursuit of his destiny in God?
2. What does it mean to you, practically speaking, to deny self, pick up your cross and follow Jesus?
3. What does "going for the double" mean to you?

FOR MORE, LORD!

Michael L. Brown, *The Revolution: The Call to Holy War* (Ventura, Calif.: Renew, 2000)

David Ravenhill, *For God's Sake Grow Up!* (Shippensburg, Pa.: Destiny Image, 1998)

Leonard Ravenhill, *Why Revival Tarries* (Minneapolis: Bethany, 1959, 1982)

ENLISTING IN
A REVOLUTIONARY
ARMY

THE
SETUP

John's Radical Surrender

> Going on from there He saw two other brothers, James the son of
> Zebedee, and John his brother, in the boat with Zebedee their father,
> mending their nets; and He called them. Immediately they left the
> boat and their father, and followed Him.
>
> Matthew 4:21–22

In this Scripture we see the cost of enlisting in a revolutionary army. John, who was transformed into a passionate lover
of God, had lost everything he knew in order to come into that
which he did not yet know. Oh, the cost of authentic discipleship!
Now muse with me for a while. . . .

Zebedee was raising his family to be God-fearers. Like other good
fathers, he was also teaching his sons a trade that they, too, would
be expected to pass on to their sons. Zebedee, a Jewish man, had
probably studied the Torah and the prophets and been taught that
one day that the Messiah would come. He would also have read in
Isaiah that there would come a forerunner calling for every crooked
way to be made straight.

Then some strange man wearing a coat of camel's hair emerged
from the wilderness. He had a peculiar diet and an even stranger
demeanor. Word was already circulating for the Jews to be leery

of this on-the-fringes prophet called John the Baptist who was paving and pointing the way toward another whom he said was greater than he. He was preparing the way, so the Baptist said, for the Messiah. The whole region was in an uproar. Zebedee probably felt he needed to steady the boat a bit, as people were getting into a frenzy.

Then the old man's worst dream came true. The One the prophet was pointing toward came and pointed His finger into the heart of Zebedee's life. Yeshua was on a pilgrimage to pick His own group of men to disciple. Sure enough, the young thirty-year-old appeared on the Galilean shores, came straight toward Zebedee's boat and did not even ask permission to speak to his two sons. Bypassing authority, the young zealot spoke right to the hearts of the young men: "Follow Me, and I will make you fishers of men" (Matthew 4:19). Immediately James and John jumped from the boat, left their father and started off on a new trek—the process of becoming a disciple.

Do you realize the cost they paid when they surrendered to their new Lord? No money, no job, no understandable future. They had just hurt the one person they had been trained all their lives to honor and whom they never wanted to bruise—their father. They left him to finish the fishing. They left him with no inheritance. But something in their hearts said, "Go." So they left all they knew to become something that their minds could not comprehend.

James and John understood fishing for fish. But what was fishing for men? What kind of bait do you use to do that? Sounds like a setup for a wrong interpretation of words of revelation; for misunderstanding what the Nazarene was really saying. Do you think there was the potential for false expectations?

Nonetheless off they went. And off went John in radical surrender to join an emerging new army of radical men who would jostle for position and misinterpret the sayings of their Leader. Mercy! Think John ever wanted to turn back and go home? I imagine so. But when you have been bitten by the bug, there is no turning back.

So it is today with the emerging prophetic revolutionary army our Lord is calling forth. Jesus said that no man can put his hand to the plow and look back (Luke 9:62). You must keep looking forward. That is what John did. That is what you must do as well.

Think you will make a few mistakes in learning how to use your new arsenal, and even shoot at a wrong target? Probably. But remember, disciples are made, not born. The passionate, consecrated group of warriors that the Holy Spirit is preparing today will not only receive a revelatory message to deliver; they will become revolutionary messengers along the way.

Like John, get ready to jump out of your comfortable boat, make a radical surrender and become a catcher of men!

4

SURRENDERING TO THE COMMANDER

I'm in the army now! I signed my life over to the Commander-in-Chief years ago and have no intention of taking it back. My life is no longer my own. In one sense I am not even looking to reenlist. I am what you call career military. You see, I have been bought with a price and my life is now hidden with Christ in God (Colossians 3:3). When I search for my life apart from Him, I cannot find it. He took me up on the deal, hid my life in Himself years ago, and any attempt I make to find it elsewhere ends up in a lonely, pathetic side alley.

Often we start out with great zeal mixed with unperceived, zealous ambition propelling us forward to the frontlines of service. God allows this. He even hooks us and draws us in to His purposes. He loves passionate people! He would rather have a piece of rock to chisel than some passive blob.

I remember the day and place I prayed as a young man in the Jesus People movement in the early 1970s: "Here I am, Lord. I sign up to be on the frontlines of what You are doing across the earth. If You are moving, I want in on it! Here I am. I surrender to You, Lord, the Commander-in-Chief."

Another ageless hymn contains the content of what I am attempting to convey. Remember, we surrender first to the Person and then to the purpose. Let's review the piercing words of "I Surrender All" penned by J. W. Van Deventer in 1896:

All to Jesus I surrender,
All to him I freely give;
I will ever love and trust him,
In his presence daily live.

[Refrain]
I surrender all, I surrender all,
All to thee, my blessed Savior,
I surrender all.

All to Jesus I surrender;
Humbly at his feet I bow,
Worldly pleasures all forsaken;
Take me, Jesus, take me now.

All to Jesus I surrender;
Make me, Savior, wholly thine;
Fill me with thy love and power;
Truly know that thou art mine.

All to Jesus I surrender;
Lord, I give myself to thee;
Fill me with thy love and power,
Let thy blessing fall on me.

All to Jesus I surrender;
Now I feel the sacred flame.
O the joy of full salvation!
Glory, glory, to his name![1]

Guess what? I just got you (or rather, He did)! When you read that hymn, I believe you made it into a prayer. He heard that prayer. But be warned—He remembers everything and will come collecting. He has been taking me up on my early prayer ever since.

But to be honest with you, when I threw my hands into the air and said something like, "I surrender!", I think He had a gun stuck in the middle of my back. In any case, I surrendered to the Commander-in-Chief of the Lord's revolutionary army and enlisted. I hope you have, too.

His Unfolding Plans

Do you ache for change, and are you willing to surrender all, as young David was on the day he confronted Goliath? When we consider the giants of our own generation, the Lord asks us a question, much as David inquired of his brother: "Is there not a cause?" (1 Samuel 17:29, NKJV). Is there not a purpose and a destiny for us to fulfill as well? When your brothers stand around looking intimidated, should we not arouse ourselves and others and say, "Get up, there *is* a cause in the land!"

It has always been the same. Every revolution is birthed on the altar of sacrifice and dedication. Michael Brown writes, "Why is this dedication to a cause—this passionate, often selfless, sometimes murderous, always fanatical dedication—characteristic of revolutionary movements? It is because the revolutionary has an unshakable conviction that something is terribly wrong with society, that something very important is missing, that something major needs to change, indeed, that it *must* change, and that it must change *now*."[2] Desperate times require desperate measures. Just open your eyes and look around. These are the times in which we live. Is there not a cause?

We were born to be revolutionaries. I was purchased through the blood of Jesus to be a Kingdom-shaker. So were you. You say, "Who, me?" Yes, I am talking right to you. Otherwise your heart would not be beating so fast right now and spiritual adrenaline rushing through your veins. You would not be reading this crazy book, for another thing. Yes, you were born again for this task.

It has been years since I first prayed that dangerous prayer of surrender to God's call and cause on my life. There have been times along the journey that I was tempted to take that prayer back. Why? Because pioneers on the frontlines get shot at. (I have a few scars to prove it.) But already I have been graced to live one incredible life in God, and I am hooked on Jesus. So, like Caleb (Numbers 14:24), I have a gleam in my eye and look with eager anticipation to what lies ahead of this revolutionary army God is raising up.

I was called from my mother's womb to help change the spiritual equilibrium of the Church—to unsettle her from her temporary state of lethargy and call forth a generation of passionate, consecrated warriors. Nothing short of a global, prophetic awakening in the Church will ever satisfy my soul, this side of heaven.

Come, Lord! Join zeal, character and wisdom as a three-cord strand in each of our lives. Then come and pour out Your golden anointing on us so that, with power, we can do the works of Christ Jesus.

No two flowers unfold exactly the same. Even when they open similarly, some are appointed with longer staying power; some display more brilliant colors; some have only a short while to release their distinctive fragrance in their day in the sun. The flower does not determine its fragrance or appearance. It just keeps looking up to the sun for daily strength and letting its roots go down deep to drink of the nutrients needed for its vitality.

In the same way, the Son is in charge of our callings and giftings. No person can give you a calling in this life. Gifts are His alone for the giving. A purpose or destiny is His to distribute. The call of when, what and with whom is not about us; it is up to Him.

Ephesians 1:18 spells it out very plainly for us: "I pray that the eyes of your heart may be enlightened, so that you will know what is the hope of His calling." I like that. It is not the hope of my calling"; it is His calling. That sets me free. I do not have to sweat something up. He has a plan, and is more committed to working out that plan than even I am. I then become a steward of the gift, cause, calling or grace of God. I sure want to be a good one! (I will share more on our part of the equation in chapter 11, "Seizing Your Prophetic Destiny," so let's just leave it at that for now and continue on.)

The ways of God with man are a wonder to behold. While biblical principles apply to us all, His ways and means are distinct with each one of His kids. Being a father of four children, I am definitely learning that what works with one does not necessarily work with another. There is no cookie-cutter parenting, and it sure seems that God does no carbon-copying in His approach to us, either. After all, He is a real Father and we really are His individual, "fearfully and wonderfully made" kids!

As with any office or ministry gift, three principles always apply: *called, trained* and *commissioned.* These steps are not just a one-time series of events, but are often repeated several times in an individual's life. Gifts and callings are not stagnant but progressive in nature. Let's consider each of these progressive steps, then, with reference to nurturing the calling of God on our lives.

1. The Way God Calls

How does the prophetic call come? As we compare scriptural examples as well as contemporary life experiences, we find a variety of times, styles and ways people have been called into prophetic ministry. Some seem to be born with a gift. Others are born again with a gift, or baptized in the Spirit with a gift. Still other callings are gradual and emerge later in life, even though the person was called sovereignly before he or she was born.

Following are a few biblical examples of people called in diverse ways to prophesy:

Samuel: called as a child (1 Samuel 3:1–14)

Elisha: called as a man while plowing a field (1 Kings 19:19–21)

Jeremiah: called before he was conceived (Jeremiah 1:4–19)

Amos: called while he was a herdsman and grower of figs (Amos 1:1; 7:12–14)

John the Baptist: called in the womb (Luke 1:41)

How Do I Know If I Am Called?

The next logical question is, What about me? How do I know if I have a specialized prophetic gift or ministry (1 Peter 4:10–11) beyond the weaponry given out to each conscript (oops, I mean *volunteer*)? Here are a few signals to look for in your or another person's life:

- You encounter supernatural events, visitation of angels or Jesus (1 Samuel 3:1–14; Isaiah 6:1–13; Jeremiah 1:4–19)
- People begin to tell you (1 Samuel 3:9, 20)
- Leadership recognizes it (Proverbs 18:16)
- You receive an initial prophecy about the future (like Samuel, Isaiah, Jeremiah, Zechariah)

- The gifts of the Spirit through others call you forth (Acts 13:1–3; 2 Timothy 1:6)
- God confirms His word (2 Corinthians 13:1)
- Fruit is borne (Mark 16:20)

My Own Calling Experience

Even though my mother was never barren, she did miscarry a little boy who had been in her womb five months. She lifted a prayer on that day—July 3, 1951—that God heard. "Lord, if You will give me another son," she said, "I will dedicate him to Christ's service." One year later, to the exact date, my parents were overjoyed to greet their third child and only son into the world, Jimmy Wayne.

I think I must have come out of the womb waving my hands and shouting, "Hallelujah!" All I have ever known in this life is Jesus. All I have ever wanted to do is know and love Him. He is my passion. Apart from Him I have no breath, no meaning, no life.

As I grew up it seemed that I was kept on a short leash. I just could not do the things a lot of kids did. One reason was the haunting prayers of my mother. The youngest of four children, she had parents who feared the Lord—the "give-me-that-old-time-religion" kind of stuff. As I compose this, her brother, my Uncle Arnold, just celebrated his ninetieth birthday. He has served in the United Methodist ministry more than sixty years! Many felt that I was pegged to follow in his footsteps.

I remember as a child sitting at the feet of my Great-Grandmother Hall's rocking chair. This godly lady, my dad's grandmother, looked down at me and said something like this: "He has a good, straight back. He'll make a good preacher someday." I also recall my eighth-grade teacher, who said, "He'll either be a preacher or a lawyer. He can argue with a fencepost and win!" I do not know if they were prophesying or not. All I know is, I remember what they said and it stuck with me.

Years passed with many wonderful experiences with God, church and long walks on which I poured my heart out to the Lover of my soul. Then, around the age of twenty, I ran square-dab into the Jesus People movement. It was as though I instantly found home, destiny and purpose. Gifts exploded as I became filled with the Holy Spirit. I started prophesying and have never stopped.

Thereafter, for the next ten years, I prayed almost daily for the school of the prophets to come forth, like the school under the prophet Samuel (1 Samuel 19:20). I really did not know what I was asking for. All I knew was that as I delighted myself in Jesus, He put His desires for my life into my heart. My heart was now beating in unison with His. And remember, when two hearts beat as one, heaven's ladder will come down.

I could tell you many wonderful stories, but the truth is, prophesying is His calling. Not mine, not yours. When you try in your own strength to bring something into being, it is frustrating at best; but when He is your primary focus, you both will succeed.

2. Getting Your Training Wheels

Do you ever have the feeling that some mysterious flakes have been given their driver's licenses without having gone through driver's education classes? Having a son who just got his driver's license, I know the value firsthand of driver's ed: The insurance is cheaper! Well, I am afraid some folks today are trying to do advanced techniques in public prophetic acrobatics when they have not even had experience with training wheels in their local church! This is a vital issue today. Help, Lord! And, yes, He is coming to our aid.

In the past there has been a release of modern models of the pastor, teacher and evangelist. We have had teaching concerning apostolic builders and their significant role. But, for the most part, there has been poor "father modeling" for those desiring to nurture the prophetic call.

When I began more than 25 years ago, I had two books as my mentors—the classic book *The Elijah Task* by the faithful pioneers John and Paula Sandford and the excellent training manual *Interpreting Symbols and Types* from the brilliant teaching ministry of Kevin Conner. There were no classes to attend, no schools of the Spirit that I knew of, no national prophetic conferences. But step by step new materials have been released, and a new generation of fathers and mothers in the prophetic has emerged. We will continue to trust the Lord to release additional tools for equipping and training in this vital area of ministry. He is not leaving us as orphans in this progressive, restorational move of His presence, thank the Lord!

In other words, training opportunities today abound. Take advantage of them! Put your training wheels on, align yourself with a body of believers or specialized ministry, and practice doing the stuff. Learn to drive the proper way, for Jesus' sake.

How Are Spiritual Gifts Received?

If this is God's revolutionary army, we must start in boot camp and investigate how gifts are received. You may have heard the statement "gifts are given and fruit is grown." How *are* gifts given? How does increase come? A father in the prophetic, Paul Cain, points us in the right direction with this insight: "We can only teach you what to do with the words. Nobody can teach you how to receive words from God. Those things are the activity of the Holy Spirit in our human experience. We can only teach you how to cooperate with the activity of the Spirit, not how to produce the activity of the Spirit."[3]

Larry Randolph, an author and powerful prophetic minister from California, states, "God, who is divinely unique, has also made us unique. Therefore, it is difficult to teach others how to hear from God who is diverse in expression. Depending on the circumstances, God speaks in many different forms, ranging from an audible voice to an inner voice, from dreams and visions and mental pictures to inner impressions. Yet, in spite of how we hear from God, we can become more receptive to His voice and attentive to His ways through prayer, fasting, meditation, worship and intense scrutiny of the Scripture."[4]

In other words, although each of us is unique, some basic principles apply to all of us. Thus, just as we can learn to hear God's voice more effectively, so can we learn to be more open to His gifting. Here are five principles to help us understand how gifts are received and to open our hearts to receiving them.

1. **Gifts are given by a sovereign God.** He gives grace, ministries and offices entirely as He pleases. These gifts may have little or nothing to do with the condition of the person. Acts 2:1–4 and 10:44–46, for instance, tell about vast numbers coming to faith and receiving the gift of tongues at Pentecost, and the results of Peter's preaching to the Gentiles at Cornelius' house.

2. **Gifts are often conveyed by the laying on of hands.** An early example is the gift of wisdom given to Joshua when Moses laid his hands on him (Deuteronomy 34:9). Another is the impartation to Saul of the gift of the Holy Spirit and the return of his sight when Ananias laid hands on him (Acts 9:17–18). People are often equipped for ministry by the laying on of hands, like the seven men chosen to oversee the daily serving of food in the early Church (Acts 6:3–6) and Barnabas and Saul before being sent out by the church at Antioch (Acts 13:1–3). This practice is to be used advisedly, however. Paul warns Timothy not to be hasty about laying hands on others for gifting lest he "share responsibility for the sins of others" (1 Timothy 5:22).

3. **Gifts can be enhanced through mentoring relationships.** The most noted example is that of Jesus and His disciples. The Lord called the Twelve and passed on His authority (Luke 10:1–11, 19). Another prominent example is Elijah's anointing of Elisha, who followed his master through years of training and service. Recall that when Elijah was taken into heaven, Elisha took up the older prophet's mantle and began his own ministry (1 Kings 19:15–21; 2 Kings 2:1–15).

4. **Gifts we have already received can be developed further.** We should mature in and grow more sensitive to the gifts we receive from God. Hebrews 5:14 tells us to practice and train our senses in order to mature. Ways to do this include prayer, fasting, self-restraint, increasing in faith, growing in character and holding to orthodox doctrine.

5. **Gifts come from God only by grace.** Self-righteousness is a serious hindrance to the development of gifts. Gifts are gifts! They do not prove how much God loves or wants to favor the prophet or teacher or evangelist; rather, they show how much God loves and wants to bless the people!

A Grace That Had Evaded Me

Years ago I just plain could not teach. I could share from my heart, but I did not have a natural propensity toward teaching. At that time my primary mentors and peers were all gifted teachers. I felt like a fish out of water most of the time. I had the heart of a shepherd with a budding call of a prophet, but a teacher I was not.

Then, at a small group meeting one night, Geoff Buck, a co-leader with me in the Jesus People movement, approached me. "I feel the Lord is saying that you are to ask for any gift that you want," he said, "and God will give it to you."

It seemed a bit unusual, yet I knew this was the voice of my Master speaking. I pondered for a bit, then responded to Geoff by expressing the desire for the grace to teach God's people.

My friend proceeded to lay his hands on me and quietly pray for me.

Something happened—two things, to be exact.

First, as I wondered why I had not asked for the gift of miracles or evangelism or something more dramatic, faith rose up in my heart and I knew I had asked for the very thing God wanted me to receive. Second, after Geoff prayed I was different. I was not sure how, but I knew I had received a grace that had previously evaded me.

Today Geoff Buck is in charge of the Outreach to America video conferences of Derek Prince Ministries, and I . . . well, I bring forth some interesting revelatory teaching. It is by grace—always has been, always will.

The Elevator or the Staircase?

Do you prefer to ride an elevator, or at least an escalator, or do you always seem to take the stairs? What does this have to do with prophetic development? Hang on.

Some profoundly gifted people, it seems, just get onto an elevator and the operator says, "What floor?" These people respond, "Well, the top, of course!" And the next thing they know, they are on the rooftop with a panoramic view of the whole city. Talk about dreams and visions—they are there! They are not exactly sure how they got there, but what does it matter? The overnight delivery package has arrived and they have taken a quantum leap into the Spirit realm.

Other people are staircasers. In their gift development they take one step at a time—step by step by hard step. They hear the stories of the others whom the Commander has called up hither, and they begin to wither! By the time they have climbed the first few flights of stairs, with much perspiration, they are beginning to wonder, *Where was I when the mail list was called? Did I miss my calling?*

God has His reasoning, and His ways are not our ways. There is the sovereignty of God and then there is man's cooperation with His calling. Both factors always come into play. I have observed the following simple points in this mix of elevator-riders versus staircase-climbers that have helped me in my pilgrimage.

THE ELEVATOR-RIDERS

- A sovereign gift; like Jeremiah, they are born with it
- Early operation, even though they may not be walking closely with God
- Anointing often greater than their training; great experiences but sometimes a lack of wisdom in their operation of it
- Sensitive in their emotional makeup
- Can suffer from an increased amount of rejection and isolation
- Can be tempted to think too highly of themselves, that they are special
- Not typically good teachers, as they do not know how they got what they have
- Should cultivate humility and gratitude

THE STAIRCASE-CLIMBERS

- Develop slowly and progressively; gift does not appear overnight; they can even be late bloomers
- Proceed one step at a time, like climbing a mountain
- Progress through faithfulness
- Can suffer from intimidation and even jealousy

- Must avoid the "if-only" thoughts
- Prone toward a works mentality and self-righteousness: "I deserve this; I earned it!"
- Should continue in faithfulness and endurance while cultivating a revelation of God's grace

Character Development: Fruit That Is Grown

We find many excruciating lessons in character development, some of which we looked at in Track 1 of this book. *God does not want us only to give a message; He wants us to become a living word.* Because the revelatory-gifted person is extra-sensitive, he or she must give the area of character development special attention. The cross of Christ will eventually become the love of any true prophetic person.

In his excellent book *Prophets, Pitfalls and Principles*, Dr. Bill Hamon shares an illustration from agriculture to drive home a spiritual point concerning character issues. A weed called Johnson grass intertwines its roots with the root system of a good crop, such as corn (to which it looks almost identical). The weed steals nutrients from the corn, but it cannot be pulled up by the roots without destroying the corn. The result: a scrawny, inferior crop, unsuited to be used as a seed corn for the next planting. Only after the harvest can the problem be fixed, when the farmer can plow up the earth to expose and remove the roots of the weed.

> In the spiritual realm as well, God will not deal with advanced root problems during a productive ministry season. He will bring the ministry . . . into a winter season of inactivity and non-productivity. He will plow the prophet upside down, exposing the root problems, and then He will either spray them with a strong anointing to destroy them or else rake the minister's soul until all the roots are removed and thrown into the fire of God's purging purpose.
>
> For that reason we must allow God and those He has appointed as our spiritual overseers to show us our weed/seed attitudes and remove the newly sprouted character flaws before they grow intertwined with our personality and performance. The longer we wait, the more drastic the process becomes.[5]

Character Signs along the Way

Here are ten stunning points for you to meditate on in your driver's education on the way to getting your prophetic license:

1. Seldom is character seen until pressures and trials come. At such times gifts may dry up and even disappear for a season, as the pruning of the Lord takes place in the character of the gifted vessel.
2. As character matures, it greatly enhances the individual and his or her gift.
3. Because of its invisible nature, character can be harder to gauge, in terms of progress and growth, than a grace gift from God.
4. Motives are the hardest to recognize. A true word can be given with an impure motive of self-promotion that is not detected by the one giving the word. Let's be kind and not judgmental with each other!
5. In time you come to understand not to sacrifice long-term goals in order to achieve short-term success.
6. Learn to value "team life." Realize you need others to help watch out for you, your family and your priorities. Become accountable in motives, finances, morality and other major areas of natural and spiritual life.
7. In character development you learn to honor others and not envy their positions, titles, functions, prestige or gifting. You learn that before honor comes humility.
8. You learn to overcome jealousy and wait on His timing in your life. For example, the Lord spoke to Jeremiah about 627 B.C. (the thirteenth year of Josiah), yet it was not until 612 B.C. that he began to prophesy. He waited fifteen years. The next year, in 611 B.C., sixteen years after Jeremiah's visitation by the Lord, certain tablets of the Law were found. Yet King Josiah did not consult Jeremiah about their meaning, but the prophetess Huldah (2 Kings 22:8–14; 2 Chronicles 34:14–15, 19–22).

9. Learn to give mercy and grace to others as they, too, are Christians under construction. This, in turn, sows a crop of mercy and understanding from others to you.

10. Give all glory, honor and praise to the Lord. Your weaknesses will glare in front of you, driving you into greater intimacies with the Lord. Embrace the cross, refuse the temporal adulation of others and revel in His unconditional love!

The Prophet and the Word

In surrendering to our Commander-in-Chief and enlisting in His revolutionary army, you must turn to the codebook given to all new recruits. This awesome resource is the only book on the planet that, when you read it, it reads you. It is your instruction manual for warfare, wisdom and the ways of God. Devour it. You will be given many pop quizzes along the way, and if you study it, you will pass the tests. In fact, if you read this driver's manual, you will not only pass the test, but end up driving on the right side of the road!

Let me share a word of wisdom with you: *Be more impressed with the word going into you than the word coming out of you.* This is particularly true for us prophetic types. Here are seven more pungent words to help you fulfill your commission:

1. **Be addicted to both the written Word (Scripture) and the living Word (Jesus).** The error of some revelatory-gifted people is that they tend to use the Scriptures as their source of validating their latest "revelation." "Study to show thyself approved," urged Paul (2 Timothy 2:15, KJV), but not by improperly stretching the Scriptures to fit your latest dream or vision. Don't make a taffy pull out of the Word of God.

2. **Always maintain your devotional place of reading and meditating on the Scriptures for your own life.** Feed yourself first. Don't misplace ministry for devotion. Be with Him.

3. **Stick with the "main and plain" things of Scripture.** Be of sound doctrine in the basics, such as the virgin birth, the cross, the resurrection of the dead, the Second Coming, being born again, the inspiration of the Scriptures and so on. Don't accept just any new twist to the age-old foundational beliefs of the historic Church.

4. **Maintain proper biblical doctrine.** Without it your interpretation of revelation might be tainted. Seek out proper historical, contextual understanding of the Scriptures, then let the Holy Spirit bring you into current-day application.

5. **Learn the symbols and types of the Old Testament,** as used in the New Testament, in order to precisely interpret contemporary revelatory experiences. Use the written to judge the spoken.

6. **Get connected with leaders.** For balance, protection and enhancement, all revelatory-gifted people should link themselves with apostles, teachers and other leaders who might be trained more systematically in Scripture and theology.

7. **Walk in mental and spiritual preparedness** through the regular exercise of the spiritual disciplines.

3. Commissioning—Getting Your Driver's License

For some of you this is a scary time. Under orders from the top, you must take those training wheels off your bike and see if you can keep your balance. You might wobble for a while, or you might take right off, but whatever the case, always remember to keep looking and moving forward. You received your driver's license! You have passed your first set of tests.

It might be helpful to warn you, in a phrase coined by Francis Frangipane, "New levels, new devils!" So don't clutch and worry if some little voice of intimidation tries to tell you to stick your hands back into your pockets, shut your mouth and just sit this one out. One of the devil's main goals is to make you into a successful observer. But don't let him succeed. Stare down those fears, be a bit adventurous and pump on down the street.

Signs of a Prophetic Commissioning

As in the military, your life and ministry can see many progressive commissionings and appointments. We are called and we continue to be called. We are trained and we continue to be trained. We are sent out and we are brought back again to be retrained, retooled and given a new vision, so that we can be recommissioned with fresh purpose and power. 1 Samuel 3:19–21: "Thus Samuel grew and the LORD was with him and let none of his words fail. All Israel from Dan even to Beersheba knew that Samuel was confirmed as a prophet of the LORD. And the LORD appeared again at Shiloh, because the LORD revealed Himself to Samuel at Shiloh by the word of the LORD."

What are some of the signs that a commissioning has been or is being granted by God (who alone can do it)?

1. God backs up the words; they do not fail.
2. People recognize the power, accuracy and consistency.
3. The Lord appears to the individual through various means.
4. The word of the Lord comes to the prophetic person more consistently.

There is another sign of a commissioning, too; it is called the sign of "da boot!" If you wait around too long expecting perfection of character before any commissioning comes, then you might be in for a rude awakening. You might be given the sign of "da boot!"

Yes, you might just get a kick in the seat of your pants, and God might have to say, "Well, do something with what you've got, and then I'll give you more!" Or He might say, "Have you obeyed My last orders?" You respond, a bit puzzled, "What orders, exactly, have I been waiting for?" And He responds with His Word, reminding us, "I have already said, 'Go, therefore!'"

So my thoughts to you are, Get to gettin'! Don't be that old religious observer just looking on and keeping all those scorecards. Get into the car and start the ignition.

Wisdom Ways for the Road

To help you stay on course, here are a few simple guidelines to help you avoid a speeding ticket or ending up in some ditch along the way:

1. When at all possible, go out in teams. Remember, Jesus sent His disciples two by two.
2. Relate to a team for correction, adjustment, encouragement, confirmation and friendship.
3. Don't alienate yourself (a prophetic tendency).
4. Go forth with assurance that God is with you. Rejoice and "do the stuff."
5. Call for intercessory covering on your many ventures. Develop a prayer shield. "Five of you will chase a hundred, and a hundred of you will chase ten thousand. . ." (Leviticus 26:8).
6. Realize that you will wear different hats or shoes for different cities, nations, time periods or events. Learn your sphere of grace and rule. Be flexible, but stay in your strength.
7. Report back home. Remember that you are a natural person. Value and take time for everyday living.

Reporting for Service

There is a cave of preparation for every prophet. There is a Commander-in-Chief who really does gives out the orders. He is God and thinks He is in charge. Sometimes it seems that the Holy Spirit is whispering, "Come out, come out, wherever you are!" If ever there was a time to report for duty, it is today! Stand up and be counted. Leonard Ravenhill stated it this way: "God's men are in hiding until the day of their showing forth. They will come. The prophet is violated during his ministry, but he is vindicated by history."[6]

So whatever your part in this time of sudden shift and change in history, take the place that is meant just for you. And remember, when you are called, you must get trained and retrained before many different levels of appointments and commissionings appear.

Listen to sage words of balance from Dr. Bill Hamon, a veteran of many prophetic wars: "The gifts and callings of God are based on His sovereignty, not on human worthiness or persistence in requesting a position. The principle Paul revealed when he said, 'Behold then the goodness and the severity of God' (Romans 11:22) applies to God's choice for ministry. The goodness of God is manifested in His gifts and callings. His severity is revealed in the process of His training to make a person ready to be commissioned to that calling."[7]

Are you ready to report for service? If so, then your heart will beat a little more loudly as you read these closing penetrating statements:

Let him be as plain as John the Baptist.

Let him for a season be a voice crying in the wilderness of modern theology and stagnant churchianity.

Let him be as selfless as Paul the apostle.

Let him, too, say and live, "This *one* thing I do."

Let him say nothing that will draw others to himself, but only what will move them to God.

Let him come daily from the throne room of a holy God, the place where he has received the order of the day.

Let him, under God, unstop the ears of the millions who are deaf or mesmerized by the clatter of shekels.

God have mercy! Send us *prophets!*[8]

OUR INTERCESSORY CRY

Holy God, we report to You, as Joshua did, and prostrate ourselves before You in worship. We might even take our shoes off at this very moment. We sense that the Commander-in-Chief of the Lord's army has just appeared and said, "I am in charge! I am the General. Now who is on My side?"

In the fear of Christ, we salute our Master and report for service. We say, with Isaiah, "Here am I, Lord. Send me." Use us, Lord. Train us, Lord. Be our Teacher. Send us forth for your holy name's sake. Amen and Amen!

POP QUIZ—KEEPING YOU ON YOUR TOES!

1. Explain the three-stage process of being called, trained and commissioned.
2. What are the areas of training that are important for the prophetic person to engage in?

3. What does it mean to you to keep the pursuit of the person ahead of the purpose?

FOR MORE, LORD!

Graham Cooke, *Developing Your Prophetic Gifting* (Kent, Sussex, U.K.: Sovereign World, 1994)

Rick Joyner, *The Prophetic Ministry* (Charlotte, N.C.: MorningStar, 1997)

John and Paula Sandford, *The Elijah Task: A Call to Today's Prophets* (Tulsa: Victory House, 1977)

5

OUR REVELATORY ARSENAL

If we are to enlist to serve in a revolutionary, prophetic, all-volunteer army, we had better have the right ammunition to load into our guns: love for the Church, mercy to sinners, no tolerance toward the powers of darkness. First Corinthians 14:1 clarifies this a bit for us: "Pursue love, yet desire earnestly spiritual gifts, but especially that you may prophesy." Remember, we must make sure our aim is straight and our target clear.

With love as the motivational aim of our hearts, we stock our arsenal with "revelation" from God. We do not shoot blanks. We get to pull the trigger with lively, powerful rounds of ammunition consisting of spiritual gifts and revelatory gracelets—the weaponry He gives out to His conscripts.

Yes, sir, we're in the army now, and it is worth getting excited about! The Holy Spirit has a revelatory arsenal ready to distribute. He wants to give us gifts to build up His people and tear down the kingdom of darkness.

Let's take a closer look at the goal of receiving and releasing the gift of prophecy. After all, if we are joining an army of passionate, prophetic, revolutionary warriors, we need to make sure we know how to load and use our weapons before we can pass on to graduate-level courses.

Earnestly desire and zealously cultivate the greatest and best—the higher [gifts] and the choicest [graces]. And yet I will show you a still more excellent way—one that is better by far and the highest of them all, [love].

1 Corinthians 12:31, AMP

This foundational Scripture holds three keys to receiving and releasing the gift of prophecy.

The first key: *We must remind ourselves that revelation from God is a gift.* You and I cannot earn that gift; it is given freely to any who are hungry.

A few years ago, as I was sitting at my desk, doing nothing in particular, not even earnestly seeking God, the voice of the Lord resounded within me. He said simply, *You are now hearing Me through a gift.*

We are not qualified to receive, but we are able to receive because of the unmerited riches of His grace that have been freely bestowed on us through the sacrifice of Christ, through the power of the Spirit. Prophetic revelation is a present from the heart of the Father. We can situate ourselves in such a manner as to cooperate with His grace, but we cannot earn it. When a word from God comes to us as we minister to others, we are hearing Him through a gift—God's grace. This puts us all on level ground.

God wants us to hear His voice even more than we want to hear it. And the way we hear Him is through a relationship. This is the second key to receiving the gift of prophecy: *We must cultivate a love relationship with the Father God.* We hear Him when we pray. We hear Him by reading His written Word. We hear Him because we are sons and daughters in relationship with our awesome Father. No gifting can ever take the place of a relationship. A love relationship with our Father God through Jesus Christ is the foundation of all true communion. Remember the words from the old hymn, "And He walks with me and He talks with me . . ."?

Paul's admonition to the church at Corinth to "pursue love, yet earnestly desire the spiritual gifts, but especially that you may prophesy" (1 Corinthians 14:1) was written not to a select group of people or only to those holding the office of prophet, but to the everyday believer at Corinth—and to you and me. The target: the character of Christ. Paul wanted their guns loaded with love (1 Corinthians 13), yet he still urged them to *earnestly desire!* This is the third key.

The word *desire* means to have a deep-seated yearning for something. It is not wrong to want, desire and crave the operation of the gifts of the Spirit in your life. In fact, the Church is exhorted by the Lord through Paul to passionately pursue these. Our Father wants us filled with His love and the gifts of His Spirit so His people are not without vision and encouragement.

With ravenous hunger, then, pursue the transforming grace packages of God so that His love will leave an unforgettable mark on the heart of another. Fan into flame your craving, your longing, your desire for the gifts and graces of God. Use this third key of passionate desire to receive and release the gifts of revelation, so that you may build up, exhort and bring comfort to many needy souls as you aim for the character of Christ. Ready. Aim. Now fire!

What Is the Gift of Prophecy?

Holding these three important keys, we can go on to define the gift of prophecy. We will look at definitions from noted teachers who have emerged from different moves of the Spirit of God—the healing revival, the latter rain movement, the charismatic renewal, the Pentecostal tradition, the liturgical Church and the perspective of the third wave. As we look at the definitions, we find that each has a particular slant. When we combine the definitions, we come up with an excellent composite picture of the gift of prophecy.

Let's lay the pieces out on the table in order to see the greater whole.

Kenneth Hagin, Father of the Faith Movement

Prophecy is supernatural utterance in a known tongue. The Hebrew word for *prophesy* means "to flow forth." It also carries with it the thought "to bubble forth like a fountain, to let drop, to lift up, to tumble forth, and to spring forth." The Greek word translated "to prophesy" means "to speak for another." *It means to speak for God or to be His spokesman.*[1]

Dick Iverson, Apostolic Leader of Ministries Fellowship International

The gift of prophecy is speaking under the direct supernatural influence of the Holy Spirit. It is becoming God's mouthpiece, verbalizing His words as the Spirit directs. The Greek word *propheteia* means "speaking forth the mind and counsel of God." It is inseparable in its New Testament usage from the concept of the direct inspiration of the Spirit. *Prophecy is the very voice of Christ speaking in the Church.*[2]

Derek Prince, International Teacher, Author

The gift of prophecy is the supernaturally imparted ability to hear the voice of the Holy Spirit and to speak God's mind or counsel. Prophecy ministers not only to the assembled group of believers but to individuals. Its three main purposes:

1. *To edify:* build up, strengthen, make more effective
2. *To exhort:* stimulate, encourage, admonish
3. *To comfort:* cheer up

Thus prophecy overcomes two of Satan's most common attacks: condemnation and discouragement.[3]

Ernest Gentile, Author, Preacher, Prophet

New Testament prophecy occurs when a Spirit-filled Christian receives a "revelation" *(apokaupsis)* from God and then declares that revelation to the gathered Church under the impetus of the Holy Spirit. Such revelation enables the Church to know something from the perspective of the Kingdom of God. The essential makeup of a prophecy is fivefold:

- God gives a revelation (communication, divine truth, message, insight)
- to a Spirit-filled Christian (one of God's people, a spiritual intermediary)

- who speaks it forth (an oral declaration)
- to the gathered Church (the public assembly of believers)
- under the impetus (inspiration, stimulation, prompting, encouragement, empowerment) of the Holy Spirit[4]

Bill Hamon, Founder of Christian International, Apostolic Prophet, Author

The Greek *propheteia*, according to Vine's *Expository Dictionary of New Testament Words*, is a noun that "signifies the speaking forth the mind and counsel of God. It is the declaration of that which cannot be known by natural means. It is the forth-telling of the will of God, whether with reference to the past, the present, or the future." New Testament prophecy functions in three realms:

1. Jesus giving inspired testimony and praise through one of His saints by prophetic utterance or song of the Lord (Hebrews 2:12; Revelation 19:10)
2. One of the manifestations of the Holy Spirit called the gift of prophecy that brings edification, exhortation and comfort to the Body of Christ (Romans 12:6; 1 Corinthians 12:10)
3. The prophet speaking by divine utterance the mind and counsel of God and giving a *rhema* word for edification, direction, correction, confirmation and instruction in righteousness (1 Corinthians 14:29; 2 Timothy 3:16–17)

A divinely inspired prophecy is the Holy Spirit expressing the thoughts and desires of Christ through a human voice.[5]

C. Peter Wagner, Author, Chancellor of Wagner Leadership Institute

The gift of prophecy is the special ability God gives to a certain member of the Body of Christ to receive and communicate an immediate message of God to His people through a divinely anointed utterance (Luke 7:26; Acts 15:32; 21:9–11; Romans 12:6; 1 Corinthians 12:10, 28; Ephesians 4:11–14).[6]

The Gift of Prophecy versus the Office of a Prophet

What, then, is prophecy? We could say that prophecy is the expressed thoughts of God spoken in a language that no person in his or her natural gift of speech could ever articulate. The substance and nature of prophecy exceed the limits of what the natural mind can conceive. God's thoughts are not man's thoughts (Isaiah 55:8). The gift of prophecy may come through human mouths or actions, but it originates in the mind of God—spiritual thoughts in spiritual words and demonstrations (1 Corinthians 2:9–16).

In this hour we must learn to distinguish among the gifts and offices of the Spirit. While they are from the same Lord and Spirit, and their functions overlap, we must yet acknowledge the distinctions so as not to act presumptuously in their outworking. Not all who prophesy are prophets. Not all authentic prophets speak and address the same spheres of life and ministry. We need clarification in this foundational area to help maintain our proper spiritual equilibrium.

Following is a brief comparison that I adapted from some of the early teachings of John Paul Jackson, author and director of Streams Ministries:

Gifts of the Holy Spirit	Ministry or Office Gifts
Given by the Spirit (1 Cor. 12 and 14)	Given by Jesus (Eph. 4)
If prophecy, given to all (1 Cor. 14:24, 31)	If prophecy, given to some (Eph. 4:11; 1 Cor. 12:29)
Given for edification, exhortation, comfort (1 Cor. 14:3)	Same, plus correction and direction
Given to the Body for the common good (1 Cor. 12:7)	Given to lay the foundation of the Church and lead and equip the people (Eph. 2:20; 4:12)
Given to the members of the Body (1 Cor. 12:12)	Act as joints, holding the Body members together (Eph. 4:16)
Involve revelations of the past and present (1 Cor. 12:8–10)	Involve revelations of the past, present and future (Acts 11:28; 21:10–11)
Speak primarily to the Body (1 Cor. 12:14–26)	Speak to the Body and also to the nations (Acts 21:10; Jer. 1:5, 10)
Deliver the Word (1 Cor. 14:12)	Become the Word (Agabus, Isaiah, Hosea)

(continued)

Gifts of the Holy Spirit	Ministry or Office Gifts (cont.)
Speak to the Church (1 Cor. 14:2–4)	Speak to the past, present and future Church, and to social, political, economic and geological arenas (Nahum, Hosea, Obadiah, Elijah, Daniel, Agabus)
Involve intercession to make the desires of the people known to God	Involve prophecy to make the desires of God known to the people
Speak of God's grace	Speak of God's grace and judgment

This is but an overview in the vast arena of the study of prophecy. Stay with me.

What Are the Present Purposes of Prophecy?

The gift of prophecy is like Jesus standing up inside a person, waving His hand and saying, "I have something encouraging I want to bring to you, My people. I have a word of comfort. I have a word of edification. I have a word of learning." The gift of prophecy is the testimony of Jesus that will motivate us to persevere and to pray. In other words, Jesus has something to say.

Jesus promised that the Holy Spirit would speak to us about the things that are to come (John 16:13). Why? To prepare us for those events ahead of time. The gift of prophecy brings hope and the restoration of faith for the days ahead. It sheds light on our sometimes dark path.

Following is a scriptural list of some of the present-day purposes of this wonderful present.

1. **Edification.** "Pursue love, yet desire earnestly spiritual gifts, but especially that you may prophesy" (1 Corinthians 14:1). God has provided this gift to edify or build up the Church (1 Corinthians 3:10–15; 14:2–4).

2. **Exhortation.** God wants us to incite, encourage, advise and warn earnestly (Hosea 6:1–3; 1 Corinthians 14:3; 1 Timothy 4). Prod others on to love and good deeds by exhorting them.

3. **Comfort.** When this occurs, it is Christ speaking in great personal concern, tenderness and care to release the comfort of His presence in times of need (1 Corinthians 14:3). Ever need comfort? You will reap what you sow!

4. **Conviction and convincing.** "If all prophesy, and an unbeliever or an ungifted man enters, he is convicted by all, he is called to account by all; the secrets of his heart are disclosed; and so he will fall on his face and worship God, declaring that God is certainly among you" (1 Corinthians 14:24–25). This relates to believers who are unlearned and uninitiated in the present-day operation of the gifts of the Holy Spirit, as well as unbelievers who have yet to come to the saving knowledge of our Lord. Here the prophetic is also used to convict us, to prick our consciences concerning sin, but with a heart to bring about repentance and reconciliation.

5. **Instruction and learning.** "You can all prophesy one by one, so that all may learn and all may be exhorted" (1 Corinthians 14:31). As the revelatory gifts open the Scriptures to us, great truth is seen and new understanding opened up. More, Lord!

6. **Gift impartation.** "Do not neglect the spiritual gift within you, which was bestowed on you through prophetic utterance with the laying on of hands by the presbytery. Take pains with these things; be absorbed in them, so that your progress will be evident to all" (1 Timothy 4:14–15). We are not to disregard the gifts that reside within us, especially prophecy. As mentioned in these verses, giftings and callings may be discerned, confirmed or even imparted. Put jumper cables onto the battery of someone's heart and charge him or her up, for Jesus' sake! Give that person a boost to go on to the next level.

7. **Testimony of and from Jesus.** "Then I fell at his feet to worship him. But he said to me, 'Do not do that; I am a fellow servant of yours and your brethren who hold the testimony of Jesus; worship God. For the testimony of Jesus is the spirit of prophecy'" (Revelation 19:10). Jesus stands in the midst of His people to tell of His works. One of the ways He does this is through the present-day operation of the gift of prophecy. When His heart is shared, people realize the Lord is near and not far off, and the hearer is drawn closer to Him.

Examples of the Gift of Prophecy

In the Scriptures prophetic gifting was not reserved for the elite, but was given by the Spirit to those in need of encouragement, instruction, impartation and the testimony of Jesus. Nor was respect given to the maturity of the recipient. Seasoned disciples as well as new converts were used in the gift of prophecy. The common denominator: All were seekers and followers of Christ. The gift was given freely to reveal a loving God who enjoys sharing His heart with His people and who wants to make them increasingly aware of His attentive presence in their lives.

The following Scriptures give us examples of the gift of prophecy operating in and through believers in the New Testament:

Luke 1:66–67: "All who heard them kept them in mind, saying, 'What then will this child turn out to be?' For the hand of the Lord was certainly with him. And his father Zacharias was filled with the Holy Spirit, and prophesied. . . ." Zacharias began prophesying concerning the birth of his son, John. A measure of the purposes of God was revealed through this prophetic utterance. This was the experience Michal Ann and I had concerning the births of our four children. By grace the Holy Spirit signified through dreams and visions and revelatory utterances the names and callings of each of them.

Acts 13:2: "While they were ministering to the Lord and fasting, the Holy Spirit said, 'Set apart for Me Barnabas and Saul for the work to which I have called them.'" A directive word of wisdom was given to Barnabas and Saul and the others, apparently through prophecy, while they ministered to the Lord with prayer and fasting.

Acts 19:6: "When Paul had laid his hands upon them, the Holy Spirit came on them, and they began speaking with tongues and prophesying." At times prophesy is one of the signs of the Spirit's overflowing presence in the life of a new believer, as it was for these Ephesians. This is the way it worked with me, too. Before I was ever released into the gift of tongues, I first bubbled up and started speaking God's plan of a great end-time revival covering the earth!

Acts 20:23; 21:4, 11: "'. . . The Holy Spirit solemnly testifies to me in every city, saying that bonds and afflictions await me.' . . . And they kept telling Paul through the Spirit not to set foot in Jerusalem. . . . 'The Holy Spirit says: "In this way the Jews at Jerusalem will bind the man who owns this belt and deliver him into the hands of the Gentiles.""" Prophecy and other ministries apparently combined to give Paul warnings and direction. The apostle was made aware of the cost that confronted him as a result of his interaction with the prophetic. May true, nonjudgmental warnings be released to us as well, to prepare us for life's journey.

1 Timothy 1:18: "This command I entrust to you, Timothy, my son, in accordance with the prophecies previously made concerning you, that by them you fight the good fight. . . ." Prophecies were used to reveal Timothy's appointed ministry calling, and later to strengthen him in fulfilling that ministry. In Timothy's experience, prophecy was used by the presbytery with laying on of hands for a commissioning of a gift or ministry. This model was restored through the latter rain movement of the late 1940s and early 1950s.

Releasing the Gift of Prophecy

Now that we have romped through the pasture of receiving the gift of prophecy, let's lay some elementary, practical principles for releasing this (and other) gifts of the Holy Spirit.

Faith must be active in order for a person to receive and express the gift of prophecy. We have to step out on the limb in order to get the fruit that hangs at the end of it. To respond to God's word in faithful obedience, we must sustain a belief that the Lord does speak and is speaking. The following Scriptures are examples of the ways prophecy comes to us, the ways it can be expressed through us and the ways it can be administered in the church body.

Prophecies may come:

1. As spontaneous utterances, unpremeditated impressions or thoughts (1 Corinthians 2:12–13; 14:30).
2. Through visions or trances (Numbers 24:2–9; Isaiah 6; Acts 9:10–16; Revelation 1:11).
3. Through dreams and night visions (Genesis 37:5–9; Numbers 12:6; Daniel 7:1–28; Joel 2:28).
4. Through the avenue of an angel (Acts 10:22; 27:23–26; Revelation 1:1).

Prophecies may be expressed or delivered:

1. By simply speaking them (1 Corinthians 14:4, 6, 19).
2. Through demonstrative actions (1 Samuel 15:26–28; Acts 21:10–11).
3. Through writing them down (Jeremiah 36:4–8, 15–18; Revelation 1:11).
4. Through song or musical instrumentation (2 Kings 3:15; 1 Chronicles 25:1, 3; Ephesians 5:19; Colossians 3:16).
5. Through anointed intercession, privately or publicly (e.g., Daniel), or by praying a prophetic blessing releasing God's grace.
6. As a *rhema* word in the midst of preaching or sharing.
7. In the context of "the spirit of counsel" (Isaiah 11:2) without the endorsement of "thus saith the Lord."
8. By an individual and then submitted to the local pastoral eldership team for judgment, appraisal, prayer and application. It is then their responsibility; the prophet's responsibility has been fulfilled.
9. Not right away. You do not have to release everything you receive. Wait for a confirmation of two or three witnesses. Put it into your spiritual filing cabinet (called "pending") and wait for the other pieces of the puzzle to appear before you speak.
10. Not at all! Some things are not to be shared. They are God's revelatory treasures just for you, as one friend speaking to another.

Each local eldership or apostolic/pastoral team is given the responsibility to determine the wisdom administration of the revelatory gifts. The following are some options concerning the congregational release of these revelatory graces.

1. *Small groups.* This is the starting block, the entrance gate.
2. *Prayer line ministry teams.* These are often utilized at the close of a meeting. Volunteer for practical help!
3. *Congregation.* An assigned captain (point person) to judge, then release the prophetic flow at the appropriate time so as to cooperate with the overall flow.

An approved word gift section of approved, trusted men or women assigned weekly or monthly to seek the Lord ahead of time and during the celebration services. This approach has often been used for large conference settings.

Prophetic singers releasing the song of the Lord. Practice does make perfect. Practice His presence at home, and it will deliver you from the performance spirit.

Open microphone (popcorn style) under leadership oversight.

4. *Written submissions.* These can be submitted to leadership before or during services for them to judge and discern. I have done and continue to do this. Just don't write a book and expect them to read it. Be concise.

5. *Prophetic fellowship groups.* In these peer groups, under the oversight of local pastoral/eldership team, insights are shared and confirmation or consensus determined.

When Prophecy Does Not Flow

You might be saying, "I feel all blocked up. Something just is not right! Do you have any help for me?" Well, let's take a stab at it. There is no one solution that fits all, but here are some principles to follow.

Scripture says that if you are faithful in a little, you will be given much. Don't despise small beginnings in operating in the gift of prophecy. If you are faithful to give the small word the Spirit gives, your capacity to receive more will increase and the gift will begin to flow richly and freely.

If you or your church body seems to be stuck or has stopped flowing altogether, there may be some sin or error that has not been recognized and corrected. The Lord is quick to forgive and cleanse once repentance has been expressed, and you can ask Him to restore the gift and then believe for a renewal to occur and increase to come. Remember that you will mess up from time to time, but your Father desires to express His love to you through His kind discipline and correction. His mercies are new every morning! So be quick to forgive yourself, too, and move on in the flow of the Spirit. Dust yourself off and get going again.

The following is a list of some major reasons why the prophetic does not flow. Read it prayerfully and ask the Lord to highlight anything that might apply to your experiences. The light of God's truth brings healing and freedom.

1. **Ignorance.** "My people are destroyed for lack of knowledge" (Hosea 4:6). Due to insufficient teaching, areas of ministry may appear weak or undernourished. Instruction needs to be given; then faith and hunger will result.

2. **Fear.** "God has not given us a spirit of timidity, but of power and love and discipline" (2 Timothy 1:7).

   Fear of people, even leadership (rejection, being misunderstood).

   Fear of missing God and saying something wrong, or of saying something out of one's own mind.

   Fear that one's faith will fail in the middle of the delivery.

   Fear of embarrassment, failure.

3. **Pushing prophesying out of reach.** By taking the attitude that prophecy is out of the reach of the ordinary believer, or by making the detailed word of knowledge of the prophetic the standard, we can intimidate others from sharing their "less impressive" gifting. Share the thoughts of God.

4. **Closed environment.** By not staying exposed to an environment in which the prophetic is flowing, you miss out on associational training. If you drink from a river long enough, you, too, will be involved. Association and environment must be created and maintained for the revelatory presence to be sustained.

5. **Not living in the Word.** If the Word of Christ is not dwelling in a person richly, then the Spirit has little to draw from. The breath of God blows upon the written word of God. Again, be more impressed with the Word going into you than the Word coming out of you.

6. **Inconsistent prayer.** It is by being in God's presence that we receive His word. We must be consistent in prayer. No prayer life, no revelatory life. Active prayer life, active revelatory life.

7. **Pride.** By wanting to start at the top, we circumvent the natural progression of growth. With a desire to be deep and profound rather than stick with the simple, we stop up the prophetic flow. Motivation is the central issue. The Lord honors humility. Be a servant and increase will come.

8. **Grieving the Holy Spirit.** Due to errors of the past (by an individual, a fellowship, even a denomination or region), the Holy Spirit may have been grieved. We must confess our ways and seek His restored prophetic life flow again. This may take months or even years, but eventually we will see new growth in burned fields. I have seen this pattern in many cities. As repentance is cultivated, old wells can and are often redug. Like Isaac, redig the ancient wells of His presence!

Practical Points of Wisdom

"The king's favor is toward a servant who acts wisely" (Proverbs 14:35). As we step out zealously in the gift of prophecy, let's pursue a heart of wisdom so we find favor with our King. After all, we are Jesus' servants as we share His testimony with the Body of Christ and with the world.

Michael Sullivant in *Prophetic Etiquette* has some masterful thoughts for us on the issue of "Gifts, Fruit and Wisdom." Let's ponder the words of one who has both moved in the prophetic and pastored prophetic people:

> There is a "prophetic etiquette" that needs to be taught and learned in the Lord's house so that the gift of prophecy can be utilized to its fullest intent and extent. Four governing values—love, integrity, humility and passionate pursuit. I have identified four basic values that will make prophecy more helpful if embraced. I am certain there are others that could be added to the list. Actually, these values do not apply only to prophecy, but also to any ministry in the body of Christ.[7]

With this in view, I have listed some valuable bullets of wisdom for your revelatory arsenal. They can help keep you from grieving the Holy Spirit and the hearts of those to whom you serve the word of the Lord.

- **Avoid prophesying your pet doctrine.** For a pure stream to come forth, you must yield your favorite opinions and prejudices.
- **Refrain from scolding.** Don't lecture people through prophecy. Condemnation does not come from the Spirit of Christ (Romans 8:1).
- **Avoid publicly correcting leadership through prophecy.** Honor those in authority. We are not called to criticize but to pray for them (Romans 13:1–5; 1 Peter 2:17; Jude 8–9). Do not release words that create pressure for people to perform.
- **Be careful with your words.** Take care when speaking about courtship, marriages, births and deaths. Rare exceptions occur, but stick to the main and the plain. Do not put a heavy word on people, pressuring them into personal directions that violate their individual consciences.
- **Don't focus on problems.** Speaking only from known problems and current circumstances creates unnecessary stress. Prophesy life! See the problem but search out the solution. (See the last chapter of this book for more on this.)
- **Avoid preaching.** Don't preach for extended periods under the guise of prophesying. Know when to stop. Don't use a gifting as a soapbox to display your latest revelation, but serve with humility in order to exalt Christ, not your own ego.
- **Refrain from redundant and repetitive prophecies.** When the mind of God has been clearly communicated by others, there is no need for another to jump in and say it over. Be encouraged knowing that you heard the Lord.
- **Stay in tune.** If prophesying during a meeting, stay in tune with the tenor of the meeting. Do not go cross-current and frustrate the overall message of the Lord. A word wrongly spoken is like a clanging symbol.
- **Speak inspirationally.** The ideal is to speak encouragingly and avoid yelling, whining or harshness. This is part of edifying and doing all things decently and in order.
- **Avoid confusion.** Refrain from speaking if you have an unclear or obscure message. If the trumpet makes an uncertain

sound, it produces confusion (1 Corinthians 14:33). Simply push the pause button and continue to seek the Lord.

- **Stick to the Word.** This is especially true for beginners. Don't swim out too far from shore until you are sure your vessel is seaworthy. Be addicted to the Scriptures.
- **Refrain from injecting self.** Avoid inserting self and personal problems into your words. This includes moods, pressures, frustration, bitterness, haste, opinions, legalism or times when you are sick or on major medication. Be a clean vessel for the Lord to use.
- **Purge negative emotions.** It is important to let the Holy Spirit purge any negative elements from your spirit. Avoid speaking on issues on which you know you have negative emotional involvement. Be an intercessor in these situations, not a mouthpiece.
- **Stay within your measure of faith.** Step out, yet stay within your boundaries (2 Corinthians 10:15). "Since we have gifts that differ according to the grace given to us, each of us is to exercise them accordingly: if prophecy, according to the proportion of his faith" (Romans 12:6).
- **Be governed by love.** Let the love of Christ be your aim (1 Corinthians 13:1–3; 14:1; 2 Corinthians 5:14).
- **Don't subject yourself to the fear of man.** Shoot for the mark of the overall unity of the Body of Christ. Avoid the snare of the people-pleasing spirit and the fear of rejection. Strive for the goal of pleasing the Lord.
- **The major principle is edification.** Does this prophecy sound like Jesus? Will it build up this person, ministry or church? Like weight-lifters let us learn to be Body-builders.

Lessons for the Beginner, Guidance for the Mature

Many mark 1988 as a year when the prophetic movement was reintroduced to the Body of Christ. This was one generation (or forty years) after the beginning of the latter rain movement and the birth of Israel as a nation. During the late '80s and early '90s I was privileged to be part of the company of prophetic voices emerging nationally. Here is some practical advice I wrote for getting started—lessons for beginners and a stake in the ground to which the mature can always return.[8]

1. **Earnestly desire the gifts of the Holy Spirit,** especially that you may prophesy (1 Corinthians 14:1). God wants to speak to you and through you.

2. **Trust the peace of God.** Beware of speaking when your spirit is uneasy, in turmoil or feels forced to speak. Look for the peace of God in every word you hear (Psalm 85:8; Philippians 4:7–9).

3. **Obey the urging of the Spirit.** Remember that the prophetic spirit is under your control. It will not impel you to speak against your better judgment. You can turn it off or turn it on by an act of your will.

4. **Don't rely on physical sensations.** When you begin to move in prophecy, the Lord frequently gives you physical sensations—knots in the stomach, fluttering heartbeats, intense heat, a feeling of euphoria, impressions, visions and so on. The Lord does this to prepare you to receive or deliver His word. As time goes on, however, the Lord often withholds these promptings so you can grow in the ability to hear Him apart from physical sensations.

5. **Speak clearly and naturally.** You don't have to speak in King James English to get your point across. Nor do you always have to say, "Thus saith the Lord." If your word is truly from God, the Spirit will confirm it in the hearts of the listeners (John 10:4–5, 16). Also, speak loudly and clearly enough to be heard by everyone.

6. **Timing is everything.** A prophecy that comes at the wrong time during a meeting sounds like a noisy gong or clanging symbol. It will draw attention to you, not to Jesus.

7. **Leave corrective and directional words to experienced and mature brothers and sisters.** The simple gift of prophecy is for exhortation, edification and comfort (1 Corinthians 14:3). If you do receive a directional word, write it down and submit it prayerfully to your leadership for evaluation.

8. **How do you receive a message?** You don't have to be struck by a lightning bolt to prophesy! A message can come in a variety of ways: literal words; dreams; senses or inklings; pictures of words

like print in your mind; and so on. More often than not, a seasoned individual receives the sense of what God wants to say. Your duty is to then express that sense clearly and appropriately (Psalm 12:6).

9. **What do you do with a word after you have received it?** That depends. Not all words are for the purpose of proclamation; many are for intercession. Some words should be put on file, waiting for confirmation. Others should be written down and submitted for evaluation by more mature Christians with a prophetic ministry. Some prophecies should be spoken only to an individual, others to a group. Some prophetic words are delivered as songs.

10. **What if you mess up?** No one is perfect. Maturity comes from taking risks and occasionally failing. Proverbs 24:16 says, "A righteous man falls seven times, and rises again." Learn from your mistakes, ask the Lord to forgive and cleanse you, and get back up and humbly receive His grace (1 Peter 5:5).

Nine Scriptural Tests

The following nine Scripture tests on judging prophecy are inspired by a teaching tape of Derek Prince.[9]

1. **1 Corinthians 14:3:** "One who prophesies speaks to men for edification and exhortation and consolation." The end purpose of all true prophetic revelation is to build up, admonish and encourage the people of God. Anything not directed to this end is not true prophecy. Jeremiah's commission was negative at first, then given with a promise (Jeremiah 1:5, 10). 1 Corinthians 14:12 sums it up best: "Seek to abound for the edification of the church."

2. **2 Timothy 3:16:** "All Scripture is inspired by God. . . ." All true revelation agrees with the letter and spirit of Scripture. Read 2 Corinthians 1:17–20, where the Holy Spirit says *yea* and *amen* in Scripture. He also says *yea* and *amen* in revelation. He does not contradict Himself.

3. **John 16:14:** "He will glorify Me, for He will take of Mine and will disclose it to you." All true revelation centers in Jesus Christ, and exalts and glorifies Him (Revelation 19:10).

4. **Matthew 7:15–16:** "Beware of the false prophets, who come to you in sheep's clothing, but inwardly are ravenous wolves. You will know them by their fruits." True revelation produces fruit in character and conduct that resembles the fruit of the Holy Spirit (Galatians 5:22–23; Ephesians 5:9).

Among aspects of character or conduct produced that are clearly not the fruit of the Holy Spirit, we may mention the following: pride, arrogance, boastfulness, exaggeration, dishonesty, covetousness, financial irresponsibility, licentiousness, immorality, addictive appetites, broken marriage vows, broken homes. Any revelation responsible for results such as these is from a channel other than the Holy Spirit.

5. **Deuteronomy 18:20–22.** If a revelation contains a prediction concerning the future that is not fulfilled, then (with a few exceptions) the revelation is not from God. Exceptions:

   a. When the will of the person is involved
   b. When it involves national repentance (e.g., Nineveh)
   c. When it concerns a messianic prediction (hundreds of years until fulfilled)

6. **Deuteronomy 13:1–5.** The fact that a person makes a prediction concerning the future that is fulfilled does not necessarily prove he or she is moving by Holy Spirit–inspired revelation. If such a person, by his own ministry, turns others away from obedience to the one true God, then that person is false, even if he makes correct predictions concerning the future.

7. **Romans 8:15:** "You have not received a spirit of slavery leading to fear again, but you have received a spirit of adoption as sons by which we cry out, 'Abba! Father!'" True revelation given by the Holy Spirit produces liberty, not bondage (1 Corinthians 14:33; 2 Timothy 1:7). The Holy Spirit never brings God's people into a condition in which they act like slaves, motivated by fear or legal compulsion.

8. **2 Corinthians 3:6:** "[God] made us adequate as servants of a new covenant, not of the letter but of the Spirit; for the letter kills, but the Spirit gives life." True revelation given by the Holy Spirit produces life, not death.

9. **1 John 2:27:** "As for you, the anointing which you received from Him abides in you, and you have no need for anyone to teach you; but as His anointing teaches you about all things, and is true

and is not a lie, and just as it has taught you, you abide in Him." True revelation given by the Holy Spirit is confirmed by the Spirit within the believer. The Holy Spirit is "the Spirit of Truth" (John 16:13). He bears witness to what is true and rejects what is false. This ninth test is the most subjective of them all, and must be used in conjunction with the previous eight objective standards.

Taking the Prophetic to the Streets

So far we have dealt with the operation of our revelatory arsenal only from the setting of a typical congregational meeting. But, oh, there is so much more! Yes, the Church is to be built up. But aren't we supposed to do something once we have been equipped?

We need to adopt a new mindset of what "church" is and where it takes place. We need a paradigm shift into the "church without walls." The Holy Spirit wants to incite a revolution!

Do you recall my thesis statement? *If there is to be a revolution in the prophetic, there must be revolution in the Church. If there is an authentic revolution in the Church, there will be the greatest spiritual awakening society has ever seen.* For this to happen, we must aim our prophetic arsenal at the streets and marketplaces of real life.

Recall the lesson of Numbers 11. While the seventy elders prophesied around the tent of meeting, Eldad and Medad, also moved by the Holy Spirit, "prophesied in the camp" (verse 26). Moses refused to forbid them, and there is no indication that they stopped. But after the seventy elders prophesied, "they did not do it again" (verse 25). They just used their gift at "church," went home and never did it again. How horrible! Maybe someday we will become so frustrated with "practice sessions" with believers that we explode for Jesus' sake and do some real damage to the kingdom of darkness outside the four walls of the church!

Consider these concepts and targets as ways of coloring outside the lines:

- Pursue a revelatory conversation with a waiter or waitress at a restaurant under the leadership of the Holy Spirit. (Sounds like Jesus counseling with the woman at the well to me!)

- Go to a New Age festival and wisely share the truth of God's Word. (Sounds like Paul going to Mars Hill, don't you agree?)
- Help an acquaintance with AIDS receive the word of the Lord and get healed. (How about Elisha and his interaction with the leprous man in 2 Kings 5? Naaman's friends persuaded him to obey the word, and he got healed.)
- Go to a public park or bridge underpass to the homeless. Give them a meal and ask if you can pray for them. (Sounds like Jesus feeding the five thousand with a couple of buns and five fish. More, Lord!)

My point? You are beginning to catch on, I think. Most accounts in Scripture in which the gifts flowed took place when believers sought out nonbelievers—not just inviting them into their nice, cultured church world, but visiting them where they lived. In addition to congregational settings, let's take the prophetic to the marketplace, the judicial system, the public school environment, the poor. Let's color outside the lines!

As you meditate and pray over the principles in this chapter, remember that the Holy Spirit is with you to teach and train you in the gift of prophecy. You will make some mistakes, but He will redeem every one of them if you humble yourself and receive His loving correction. Becoming God's faithful servant in the gift of prophecy will involve you in His intimate thoughts and plans for His children and for the lost souls of the world. Be encouraged as you step out in faith and dare to grow up in the testimony of the Lord Jesus Christ!

Our Intercessory Cry

Father, we present ourselves to You right now and ask that You equip us with the gracelets of Your Holy Spirit as our revelatory arsenal so that we can be effective warriors for Your Kingdom's sake. Fill us with Your Holy Spirit right now. Stir up the dormant callings within us so we can be empowered revolutionaries. Grant us wisdom beyond our years to keep us charted on the right course. Give us opportunity to impact the lives of others by allowing us to speak, pray and act out Your thoughts, O God, to edify, exhort and comfort others. Let love be our aim, but help us to passionately pursue, with a deep-seated hunger, the spiritual gifts, especially that we might prophesy. Help us to serve revelation with wisdom to further Your Kingdom purposes. In Christ's name. Amen.

POP QUIZ—KEEPING YOU ON YOUR TOES!

1. What are the scriptural purposes of the gift of prophecy?
2. What are some different models or approaches of releasing the revelatory gifts in a congregational setting?
3. What are some of the guidelines or tests for judging prophecy?

FOR MORE, LORD!

Cindy Jacobs, *Hearing the Voice of God* (Ventura, Calif.: Regal, 1995)

David Pytches, *Prophecy in the Local Church: A Practical Handbook and Historical Overview* (London: Hodder & Stoughton, 1993)

Steve Thompson, *You May All Prophesy!* (Charlotte, N.C.: MorningStar, 2000)

6

THE ANATOMY OF
A PROPHETIC WORD

Counsel in the heart of man is like water in a deep well, but a man
of understanding will draw it out.

Proverbs 20:5, AMP

If we are going to have a revolution on our hands,
we had better get not only the right ammunition, but some good
old-fashioned common sense and understanding to ground us, lest
we shoot ourselves in the foot before we even get started! Too often
that is what we have done with our revelatory arsenal—hurt ourselves instead of the kingdom of darkness.

In order to release the revelatory counsel of God correctly, we
need *His understanding.* There are at least nine principles concerning revelatory gifts that we must understand so that we will
not dismiss a genuine word of God or diminish the impact He wants
that word to produce. As we look at these factors, we will gain a
better understanding of the anatomy of a prophetic word and how
it works to bring about the results God desires. Let's get the most
out of each word that we can!

The ditches are littered with too many prophetic sideswipes and
bumper car junkies who bounce from one meeting to another, one
word to the next. It is time for a revolution to take place in the

prophetic stream. As David Ravenhill says, "For God's sake, grow up!" That is an in-your-face way of saying it, but it is true nonetheless. Let's clean up our act, learn from the mistakes of the past and call forth a purer and clearer stream.

I have had the privilege of walking and conversing with many of God's choice servants. Much of what follows is what I have gleaned over many years from these divergent voices. I have held onto these precious truths and added my own insights along the way. I trust these nine points will help you avoid being another prophetic casualty and instead see fulfillment with understanding.

1. The Starting Block of Revelation

Hup, two, three, four . . . you gotta start somewhere to get ready for war! We will start by examining the three possible sources of revelation.

Source #1: God

"Beloved, do not believe every spirit, but test the spirits to see whether they are from God, because many false prophets have gone out into the world" (1 John 4:1). There can be mixture in a revelatory word—not because the word is mixed when it comes from God but because it is filtered through the tainted soul of a man or woman. It can be flavored with our unsanctified opinions, prejudices and emotions. This is particularly true in the area of our learning to interpret and apply the prophetic word.

Source #2: Self

"'I did not send these prophets, but they ran. I did not speak to them, but they prophesied'" (Jeremiah 23:21; see also Ezekiel 13:1–2). These prophets spoke out of the inspiration of their own souls or hearts. They were prophesying what they wanted instead of what God was really saying at the time. This is why we must emphasize the centrality of the cross of Jesus—because we must die to our own desires.

Source #3: Satan

"[Jesus] turned and said to Peter, 'Get behind Me, Satan! You are a stumbling block to Me; for you are not setting your mind on God's interests, but man's'" (Matthew 16:23). Peter had just spoken by the gift of prophecy when he declared, "You are the Christ, the Son of the living God" (verse 16). Then, as Jesus referred prophetically to His own crucifixion, Peter protested and elicited this strong rebuke. One minute Peter was speaking by inspiration of the prophetic, and the next he was disagreeing with Jesus, whose words did not line up with his own strong-willed opinion. Peter thus became an instrument of Satan to speak in opposition to the purposes of God.

Our own preconceived, prejudicial mindsets can hinder us from rightly interpreting or responding to revelation. The enemy uses these mindsets to twist and diminish true revelation from God, as well as to fabricate his own supposed revelations that ultimately oppose the purposes of God.

Looking to God

We must recognize that revelation comes from one of these three major sources. Yet as believers in Christ we must also accept that if we ask our Father, in Jesus' name, He will give us good gifts. Let's trust the Holy Spirit.

2. Modes of Revelation

"He said, 'Hear now My words: If there is a prophet among you, I, the LORD, shall make Myself known to him in a vision. I shall speak with him in a dream'" (Numbers 12:6). God has limitless ways to communicate with His followers. I have had angelic visitations, dreams in which I prophesied, open-eyed visions, visions in my mind, feelings, "knowings," audible voices and many other leadings. I have experienced doorbells ringing, phone calls coming, fire alarms occurring spontaneously and lightning bolts shooting forth. The greatest mode of revelation, however, comes from two sources: the written Word and the living Word.

The following scriptural examples portray the diversity of tools the Holy Spirit uses to release the voice of God to man:

The powerful, majestic voice of the Lord in water, in thunder, in breaking cedar trees and flames of fire, shaking the wilderness and stripping the forest bare (Psalm 29)

God speaking once, twice, through a dream, vision (Job 33:14–18)

A voice in a trance (Acts 10:9–16)

The voice of many angels (Revelation 5:11)

The voice of the archangel (1 Thessalonians 4:16)

The sound of many waters (Revelation 1:15)

The sound of the Lord walking in the Garden (Genesis 3:8)

The sound of the army of God marching in the tops of the trees (2 Samuel 5:23–25)

The audible voice of God (Exodus 3:4)

God speaking peace to His people (Psalm 85:8)

God's written Word as our primary source of His voice (Psalm 119:105)

Wonders in the sky and on the earth (Joel 2:30–31)

Visions and parables to the prophets (Hosea 12:10)

Words and physical metaphors to the prophets (Jeremiah 18:1–6)

The Holy Spirit speaking to a group (Acts 13:2)

Men moved by the Holy Spirit declaring God's voice (2 Peter 1:21)

Heavenly visitation in which one is brought up before the Lord (2 Corinthians 12:1–4)

The Holy Spirit bearing witness to our spirits (Romans 8:16)

A dumb donkey speaking with the voice of a man (2 Peter 2:16)

One person speaking the revelatory counsel of the Lord to another (James 5:19–20)

In these last days, God's own Son (Hebrews 1:2)

Numerous genuine words have been judged false because of wrong interpretation. The opposite can be true as well. False words can be deemed appropriate due to a lack of discernment and inadequate interpretation skills. We must seek the Lord, therefore, for wise counsel and wise counselors.

Special examples in Scripture show us the need for wedding prophetic revelation with accurate interpretation. Through the process of seeking God for understanding, we build faith in God's desire to communicate with us, and confidence in our own ability to hear His voice. Like Joseph, we can also declare, "Do not interpretations belong to God?" (Genesis 40:8).

What Does It Mean?

Recall the account of Peter's vision (revelation) when the Lord declared all animals clean in His sight. This sat crosswise with Peter's good Jewish upbringing, dictating that certain animals were unclean and should not be eaten. When Peter awoke and pondered the Lord's declaration, he "wondered within himself what this vision which he had seen meant" (Acts 10:17, NKJV). Peter needed understanding to benefit from the vision.

In Acts 11 Peter had gained the proper interpretation of the vision, as he was now speaking with brothers astonished that he had eaten with "uncircumcised men" (verse 3). This was a turnaround that affected all of Church history.

Steve Thompson, vice president of MorningStar Publications, has some wise words on the subject of correctly interpreting revelation:

> While uninterpreted revelation is often useless, misinterpreted revelation is even more disconcerting. When misinterpreted, prophetic revelation will become a stumbling stone instead of a building block. As such, we must grow in our understanding of symbolism and have our hearts purified as we grow closer to the Lord.
>
> Knowing God is the single most important element in interpreting dreams, visions, and revelation. Not just knowing about God or about prophetic symbolism, but knowing Him personally. The testimony of Jesus is the spirit of prophecy, so knowing Him is a key to knowing His testimony. In other words, knowing God is foundational to knowing what He is saying to us.[1]

Seek to Know

"As to this salvation, the prophets who prophesied of the grace that would come to you made careful searches and inquiries, seeking to know what person or time [here is the interpretation] the Spirit of Christ within them was indicating [here is the revelation] as He predicted the sufferings of Christ and the glories to follow" (1 Peter 1:10–11).

The Key Is Humility

"I saw at night [the revelation]. . . . Then I said, 'My Lord, what are these?' [This is his inquiry for the interpretation] . . . And the angel who was speaking with me said to me, 'I will show you what these are'" (Zechariah 1:8–9). Notice that when Zechariah asked, the Lord answered. The key here is humility, which admits weakness and need and compels you to seek divine strength.

Seek to Understand

"When I, Daniel, had seen the vision [the revelation], I sought to understand it [the interpretation]; and behold, standing before me was one who looked like a man" (Daniel 8:15). The Lord answered Daniel's seeking by granting living understanding. Should we not do the same?

Discern God's Call

"When he had seen the vision [the revelation], immediately we sought to go into Macedonia, concluding [the interpretation] that God had called us to preach the gospel to them" (Acts 16:10). Again, proper interpretation of the vision resulted in the altering of Church history. Macedonia received the Gospel!

Listen and Hear

Genesis 40 recounts when the Pharaoh's butler and baker had dreams they shared in prison with Joseph, hoping to get some understanding. The dreams were the revelation. After listening to them, Joseph provided the interpretations (verses 12, 18). The skills of listening intently and hearing God's voice helped him receive the correct interpretations from the Lord.

Confirm!

"Joseph said to Pharaoh, 'Pharaoh's dreams are one and the same; God has told to Pharaoh what He is about to do'" (Genesis 41:25). In this case Pharaoh told Joseph his dream (revelation), and Joseph told Pharaoh the meaning (interpretation). Then Joseph gave a detailed interpretation of the symbolic figures in the dream and how it applied to Egypt. The key here was understanding the tool of confirmation.

The principle of Scripture is that God will always confirm His word by more than one witness, experience or testimony (Deuteronomy 19:15; Matthew 18:16; 2 Corinthians 13:1). Pharaoh's dreams interpreted one another; they conveyed the same meaning in different symbols. God will do this for us as well.

3. Determining the Best Application

You might hit the target on the first couple of shots, but let's keep our aim steady so our application of properly interpreted revelations will keep hitting the bull's eye. I feel like posting a warning sign: *Needed: Correct Application!*

The apostle Paul provides us with a fascinating, poignant example. He had been hearing in every city, through the Holy Spirit, that "bonds and afflictions await me" in Jerusalem (Acts 20:23). The prophet Agabus actually "took Paul's belt and bound his own feet and hands, and said, 'This is what the Holy Spirit says: "In this way the Jews at Jerusalem will bind the man who owns this belt and deliver him into the hands of the Gentiles"'" (Acts 21:11). Paul's friends "began begging him not to go up to Jerusalem" (verse 12).

Wouldn't the apostle be better off avoiding certain death and prolonging his ministry to the churches? But Paul knew the Lord was leading him to Jerusalem and giving him opportunity to count the cost. He was ready, he said, "not only to be bound, but even to die at Jerusalem for the name of the Lord Jesus" (verse 13).

Paul did not let the affection or emotional display of those who loved him persuade him to stop. What an incredible example of the discernment and tenacity of a totally committed soul! *Lord, build in us this wisdom and surround us with people who will accept Your will for our lives and support us as we step out in faith.* We must not only interpret God's revelation correctly, but count the cost, pick up our crosses and follow Him. This is the only acceptable application for a consecrated warrior.

4. Appropriation: Calling It Forth

"This command I entrust to you, Timothy, my son, in accordance with the prophecies previously made concerning you, that by them you fight the good fight" (1 Timothy 1:18).

When a prophetic word comes to us, what do we do with it? We have been taught to hold it with an open hand before God and trust Him to bring it to pass. This is, I believe, a true teaching. But we must also respond to the word with faith and obedience. Below are some simple keys that will help us appropriate true prophetic words so they may be fulfilled in our lives. We must declare those things that are not as though they are (Romans 4:17).

Faith: The Tool of Appropriation

"The word they heard did not profit them, because it was not united by [or *with*] faith in those who heard" (Hebrews 4:2). The word of God given through prophecy is like a seed with a hard covering around it. Faith unlocks the seed so it can grow into fullness. Our primary faith must be in God Himself. We "must believe that He is and that He is a rewarder of those who seek Him" (Hebrews 11:6). Our trust is in God alone to fulfill the word.

But we must also believe that the word itself is true and that it came from God. He may speak a word many times, but if we do not unite it with our faith, it will be unproductive. Unite your faith to genuine words of prophecy, and faith will unlock the promise.

In the book *Developing the Prophetic Ministry*, Frank Damazio offers a sobering warning:

Whenever the prophetic word comes to us, we must adhere to that word with faith. Hebrews 4:2 says, "For unto us was the Gospel preached, as well as unto them, but the word preached did not profit them, not being mixed with faith in them that heard it." When we receive a word from God, that word must be united with faith in order for that word to profit us and come to pass in our lives. There have been many instances of people receiving a prophetic word from the Lord, but who stumbled in disbelief or through their narrowness of mind and smallness of heart. They have canceled the great promises of God.[2]

A Tender Heart: Ground That Grows a Crop

"Other seed fell into the good soil, and grew up, and produced a crop a hundred times as great" (Luke 8:8). The parable of the sower emphasizes the importance of the right kind of heart soil. The same seed was sown all over, but only the good soil produced fruit. Shallowness, worry, anxiety, deceitful riches and desire for the pleasures of worldly life made the other soils unproductive.

A prayerful look at this parable can reveal trouble spots in the ground of our own hearts. Are there rocks in your heart? Ask the Holy Spirit to reveal any hard places, then call for His tenderizing agent to be released.

Diligence: Seek God's Meaning

"I, Daniel, observed in the books the number of the years which was revealed as the word of the LORD to Jeremiah the prophet for the completion of the desolations of Jerusalem, namely, seventy years. So I gave my attention to the Lord God to seek Him by prayer and supplications, with fasting, sackcloth and ashes" (Daniel 9:2–3). We see the process Daniel used to receive the word of the Lord through the writings of the prophet Jeremiah, to mix that word with faith and finally to respond to it by diligently seeking the Lord with supplication, prayer and fasting.

It is important to take prophetic revelations to the Lord diligently so we can appropriate them in our lives. We can gain greater understanding of God's purpose in granting us a particular revelation and apply it in a way that will bring forth rich fruit for the glory of God.

Be tenacious like a bulldog—get hold of the pant leg of God and don't let go! There is a time for holy, diligent stubbornness.

5. Searching for the Conditional Clauses

Often there are conditions behind words of prophecy that must be met in order for the word to be fulfilled. *Sometimes these conditions are present in the heart of God but not spoken to the mind of man.* This is a principle we do not like, because all we really want to do is get a word from God and then go on our merry way. Our flesh does not want to press into the heart of the Father to find out if some requirement or qualification might be involved.

But God's words are designed to draw us to Him in relationship. He desires to communicate with us intimately about His plans for our lives, so He makes it necessary for us to seek Him for more understanding about His words. If *we* will, *He* will! Most words are not like flying a plane on autopilot. They do not automatically come into being. We must seek the Lord for the conditional clauses that must be met.

Here are some conditions set forth in scriptural words from God.

Turning from Evil

"If that nation against which I have spoken turns from its evil, I will relent concerning the calamity I planned to bring on it" (Jeremiah 18:8). This statement was the condition for the Lord's relenting from destroying the nation over which He had declared destruction.

Humility, Prayer and Repentance

"[If] My people who are called by My name humble themselves and pray and seek My face and turn from their wicked ways, then I will hear from heaven, will forgive their sin and will heal their land" (2 Chronicles 7:14). Four conditions are mentioned in this prophetic word that any nation must meet in order to receive the three promises that are declared. A full hand of repentance has to be dealt before we can win the whole promise!

Looking to God for Mercy

"'Yet forty days and Nineveh will be overthrown.' . . . When God saw their deeds, that they turned from their wicked way, then God relented concerning the calamity which He had declared He would bring upon them. And He did not do it" (Jonah 3:4, 10).

Wow! Watch this one more closely. Nineveh was in Assyria, a country to the north of Israel and one of northern Israel's worst enemies. Jonah was given a prophetic invitation from God to deliver to an enemy of Israel so that He could have compassion on her. Jonah was angry because he knew that if she would repent, God would spare her. Notice that, as given by Jonah, God's word included no condition. Still, Jonah knew God was compassionate and would relent from destroying Nineveh if the people repented.

And they did—from the greatest to the least, even the livestock! They all went without food or drink for three days, God relented and Israel's chief enemy was spared for 110 years. Even though the condition was unstated, the recipients of the word met the conditions in God's heart through their genuine repentance. Although no promise was given that God would relent, they believed the word as true and responded to it, hoping for mercy.

Cry to the Lord; He will be merciful to you as well.

Another Sincere Appeal for Mercy

"In those days Hezekiah became mortally ill. And Isaiah the prophet the son of Amoz came to him and said to him, 'Thus says the LORD, "Set your house in order, for you shall die and not live""" (2 Kings 20:1). But in verses 5–6 we see that the Lord healed Hezekiah and gave him fifteen more years. Was Isaiah a false prophet? Why didn't this word come to pass?

What happened in verses 2–4 holds the answer: "Then [Hezekiah] turned his face to the wall and prayed to the LORD, saying, 'Remember now, O LORD, I beseech You, how I have walked before You in truth and with a whole heart and have done what is good in Your sight.' And Hezekiah wept bitterly."

The Lord heard the sincere prayer of this man and, in a matter of moments, changed His word. As Isaiah was still on his way out of the palace, "the word of the Lord came to him" that God had heard Hezekiah's prayer, seen his tears and would heal him (verses 4–5).

The original word given by Isaiah was indeed a true word of prophecy. No condition was stated, but again, behind the word of judgment was a God of mercy. Hezekiah appealed to His mercy and God responded with another word that he would be healed. Sincere prayer was a key to God's heart, who desires merciful relationship, not judgment.

Gaining this understanding would stir a revolution among many of our prophetic brothers and sisters!

6. The Kairos Moment: The Timing of a Matter

Being able to discern the timing of a word of prophecy is sometimes crucial to the proper impact of the revelation. It takes practice, patience and wisdom to discern timing accurately, but the Lord gives us great grace and is very patient with us as we learn. The Greek word *kairos* refers to an appointed and strategic time for a matter to come into being. The Lord may give us revelation far in advance of the actual manifestation in the natural realm, and He may require us to hold it in our hearts until a strategic time, when the word can be received with grace by those who are to receive it.

This has been the case in my ministry experience. In 1979 I had a brief encounter with a young Korean man. A snapshot picture went off inside me, and I knew he had a calling of apostolic proportions with a power gift to release in the nations. But I prayed and wept over that word for fifteen years before I had the release and *kairos* divine appointment to do anything with it. Today this man, Dr. Che Ahn, heads up a wonderful, fast-growing network of churches called Harvest International Ministries across the world.

Timing is everything! Learning to discern the timing of the Lord becomes a great test of character in our lives. As we wait on Him for direction and fulfillment of revelation, God is patiently weaving His character into the tapestry of our lives.

The following Scripture passages help us see the importance of *kairos* timing.

To Tell or Not to Tell?

"Joseph had a dream, and when he told it to his brothers, they hated him even more. . . . Then his brothers said to him, 'Are you actually going to reign over us?' . . . So they hated him even more for his dreams and for his words" (Genesis 37:5, 8). Joseph definitely had a revelation from God, and he also had the right interpretation. But it appears that his timing was disastrous. (Have you ever gotten out of timing?) We also have to consider the sovereignty of God, however, whose mercy and faithfulness came into play even if Joseph's timing was off. Praise God! And, as Joseph said later, what his brothers meant for evil, God turned for good (Genesis 50:20), even the good of a whole nation!

A Time to Tarry

"The LORD answered me and said, 'Record the vision and inscribe it on tablets, that the one who reads it may run. For the vision is yet for the appointed time; it hastens toward the goal and it will not fail. Though it tarries, wait for it; for it will certainly come, it will not delay'" (Habakkuk 2:2–3). This is also a lesson in the importance of journaling, because timing is vitally important. There is a time for tarrying and waiting (while holding onto the word and remembering it), but there will also come a time to run with it.

The Fullness of Time

"When the fullness of the time came, God sent forth His Son, born of a woman, born under the Law" (Galatians 4:4). God waited until the fullness of time to send His Son to redeem the world. Certain elements had to be in place before Jesus' entrance into the natural would affect mankind in the way God planned.

Letting God Bring It About

"The soil produces crops by itself; first the blade, then the head, then the mature grain in the head" (Mark 4:28). Many times we may get a prophetic word that we know in our hearts is a genuine word from the Lord, but it looks overwhelmingly unlikely, like an Abraham and Sarah situation. That is a very real and common place to be in when the Lord has spoken about our future. But He wants us to look away from ourselves and our present circumstances and look up to Him in faith. Then, as we gaze on Him and His faithfulness, first comes the blade, then the head, then the mature grain. We have to realize we are not going to bring a particular word to pass in our own strength, but the Lord, in His perfect timing, will bring forth the manifestation of the revelation as we trust and obey.

Waiting for the Impossible

"A child will be born to us, a son will be given to us" (Isaiah 9:6). No one could comprehend how that was going to be fulfilled, let alone the timing of that incredible word. A virgin would conceive? Who had heard of such a thing? Yet in the fullness of time God brought forth His Word.

7. Proper Heart Motivation

God looks deeply into the heart of a man or woman to find the inner motivation. Do we want glory for the Lord or promotion before man? He is a loving but jealous God, and out of His mercy He searches the hearts of His people for idols that would take His place. Paul writes, "The love of Christ constrains us, because we judge thus: that if One died for all, then all died; and He died for all, that those who live should live no longer for themselves, but for Him who died for them and rose again."(2 Corinthians 5:14–15, NKJV). Love for God, and not the love of recognition or of approval from man, should be our motivation.

Let's look at two Scriptures to get a deeper understanding.

Worship the Giver

"Therefore speak to them and tell them, 'Thus says the Lord GOD, "Any man of the house of Israel who sets up his idols in his heart, puts right before his face the stumbling block of his iniquity, and then comes to the prophet, I the LORD will be brought to give him an answer in the matter in view of the multitude of his idols, in order to lay hold of the hearts of the house of Israel who are estranged from Me through all their idols"'" (Ezekiel 14:4–5). The issue on God's heart is relationship. He was jealous after Israel and wanted to seize her for Himself. Her idols had taken His place in her heart. He also desires a motivation of pure love to energize the revelatory gifts and cause them to pierce the hearts of those who receive them. We are to worship the Giver, not the gifts or the glory they carry.

Keep Your Heart Clean

"They soon forgot His works; they did not wait for His counsel, but lusted exceedingly in the wilderness, and tested God in the desert. And He gave them their request, but sent leanness into their soul" (Psalm 106:13–15, NKJV). God answered the children of Israel according to their lust, for the purpose of revealing to them what was in their hearts, so that they might deal with it. He sent leanness into their souls, which caused them great distress. But what seemed harsh was a merciful move on the part of their God to draw them back to His love and protection.

Let's turn again to Steve Thompson in *You May All Prophesy:*

> In addition to understanding interpretive principles, we must also have "clean hearts" to accurately interpret prophetic revelation. Interpretations are often derived through an interplay between our understanding of interpretative principles, our sensitivity to the Holy Spirit, and our heart attitude. To accurately interpret God's mind, we must also possess His heart.
>
> There are two basic "heart problems" that can cause misinterpretation even when we understand prophetic symbolism. The first is when our heart is not right with God. Heart issues such as pride and "unteachableness" often cause wrong interpretations. The second problem is when our hearts are not right toward the people to whom we are ministering. These heart problems come in the form of offenses, bitterness, or prejudices. We must have our heart right towards God and people in order to accurately interpret prophetic revelation.[3]

8. Surface-Level Contradictions

On some occasions the Holy Spirit speaks very clearly, but when the promise is being birthed, it can appear quite different than what we expected it to look like. We have to cry out to the Lord so we will not miss the day of our visitation, due to misunderstanding the manner in which the promise first appears.

In coming to understand the issue of surface-level contradictions, let's lean on the years of experience of Dr. Bill Hamon:

> Keep in mind . . . that life has its own seasons, each one unique. One prophecy may refer to one season in a person's life, and another prophecy to another season. So if one word, for example, talks about financial abundance, while another predicts lean times, they probably do not contradict, but rather describe different periods in the future.
>
> Also be careful of reading too much into words. Sometimes the contradictions are actually in our assumptions about what prophetic utterances say, not in what they truly say.[4]

Here are some scriptural examples.

Acknowledging Deeper Principles

"Unto us a Child is born, unto us a Son is given" (Isaiah 9:6, NKJV). Israel was looking for the birth of a king. She expected a child of royal birth; instead she got a little boy born in a stable to poor parents. This was beyond her comprehension. God was employing principles of pride and humility that she could not understand. The circumstances of Jesus' birth seemed to contradict the promise the Lord had given.

Trusting God with the Contradictions

"When His mother Mary had been betrothed to Joseph, before they came together she was found to be with child by the Holy Spirit. And Joseph her husband, being a righteous man and not wanting to disgrace her, planned to send her away secretly" (Matthew 1:18–19). Joseph's first response to his fiancée's pregnancy seems like a noble thing to do. He was trying to protect Mary from shame and ridicule. He decided to put her away secretly because, to his mind, it seemed like the righteous thing to do. It came out of his own heart of compassion and his principled thinking. He could have been saying to himself, *Let's just ignore this prophetic revelation about a virgin being pregnant (who happens to be my betrothed!) and just hide it away!*

But something happened to Joseph as he was contemplating these things. He had a second revelation that changed him. "An angel of the Lord appeared to him in a dream, saying, 'Joseph, son of David, do not be afraid to take Mary as your wife; for the Child who has been conceived in her is of the Holy Spirit. She will bear a Son; and you shall call His name Jesus, for He will save His people from their sins'" (verses 20–21). The man of principle was also a man of fear. God visited him with revelation to dispel the fear and bring him faith to believe in the prophetic word already spoken. "And Joseph awoke from his sleep and did as the angel of the Lord commanded him, and took Mary as his wife" (verse 24).

Revelation came to Joseph and he was changed from a man of principle and fear to a man of faith and obedience. This is what God desires to do in each of our lives through the revelations He brings to us. But when things appear contradictory, we must learn to trust Him.

This is ultimately what the Lord did with Michal Ann. Through a series of dramatic supernatural visitations—including angels appearing and the fire of God manifesting Himself—my wife was delivered from fear and made into a bold powerhouse for God. If He did it for Joseph, He can do it for you, too.

Discerning the Paradox

"Elijah said to Ahab, 'Go up, eat and drink; for there is the sound of the roar of a heavy shower'" (1 Kings 18:41). In this passage Elijah was proclaiming something that was not happening. It had not rained for three and a half years; it was dry as dust. Yet this guy was proclaiming, "I hear rain, and it's a deluge."

Definitely sounds like a contradiction to me! Then Elijah sent out his servant to look. He came back and said nothing was happening. Seven times he did this, until finally that little cloud that was only the size of a man's hand appeared. Even that report seems like a contradiction, because Elijah heard a roar, and this little cloud could not produce such a downpour. But eventually the sky grew black and the deluge came.

We must learn to discern things that appear paradoxical and not despise the day of small beginnings.

9. Properly Discerning the Ways of God and Man

I saved one of the best points for last. I think I will hear a sigh of relief from the prophetic company and a shout of *Amen!* from the recipients of their words. This one point will help clear up a lot of the mud in the revelatory stream.

One of the greatest potential problems for the prophetic person is that others assume they are in the gift mode whenever they speak. This not only shows a lack of wisdom on the part of the listener; it also dishonors the prophetic person. We must prayerfully, with godly, trusted counsel, seek proper discernment. Consider the following examples:

Speaking from One's Natural Mind

"The king said to Nathan the prophet, 'See now, I dwell in a house of cedar, but the ark of God dwells within tent curtains.' Nathan said to the king, 'Go, do all that is in your mind, for the LORD is with you.' But in the same night the word of the LORD came to Nathan, saying, 'Go and say to My servant David, "Thus says the LORD, 'Are you the one who should build Me a house to dwell in?'"'" (2 Samuel 7:2–5). Until God corrected him, Nathan spoke to David out of his natural mind, not having received a word from the Lord. David could have taken that as a word to proceed with his plans, and it would not have been the revelation of God. (As God planned it, David did not end up building the Temple, but rather his son Solomon.)

Prophets Are Just People!

"When they entered, he looked at Eliab and thought, 'Surely the LORD's anointed is before Him.' But the LORD said to Samuel, 'Do not look at his appearance or at the height of his stature, because I have rejected him; for God sees not as man sees, for man looks at the outward appearance, but the LORD looks at the heart'" (1 Samuel 16:6–7).

When Samuel was sent to the house of Jesse to anoint one of his sons as king, the prophet had no idea which one he would anoint. God's word of instruction contained no information as to which son it would be. As Samuel looked at the firstborn son of Jesse, he thought (in part out of his good Jewish tradition) that Eliab would be the one, because he looked good and the firstborn usually got the birthright. But no. As the divine checkmark of God went across his heart, he had to stop, listen and get discernment quickly!

This example contains important principles about proper discernment. Just because someone has a mature gifting does not mean all his thoughts and statements are genuine words from the Lord. Don't make the mistake of assuming that every word that comes out of his or her mouth in natural conversation is some sort of high-level word. We need to allow people with prophetic graces to function as normally as anyone else. They are just people!

We must not take ourselves too seriously, either, if the revelatory gifting flows from time to time in our own lives. We all have room to grow, and we need to make allowances for others.

Sound Practical Wisdom

There are times that people come up to my wife and me when we have our four children with us; it might be in a mall or at church. I know they are hungry for God. But my kids are hungry to have a dad! I just have to say, "Sorry, I'm being a dad right now, not a prophet." I'm afraid people turn away at times disgusted. But I have other priorities in life; I am not a jukebox on which someone can push the buttons anytime to play a tune. We must learn when to "step into the gift" and when to "step out."

Aren't you glad God does not look on the outward appearance to deem men and women worthy of His anointing? Samuel had to wait patiently through the passing of seven sons, only to be told by God that none of them was the right one. Did Jesse even *have* another son? Then Samuel had to wait again until David could come in from the sheepfold before the prophet finally got the O.K. from the Lord to anoint this last son to be king. Apparently David would not have been Samuel's natural choice. But God knew which heart He could trust with the authority of being made king of Israel. We, too, must learn to wait patiently and listen, as Samuel did, for the wisdom and direction of the Spirit, and stay out of presumption!

We must also give grace to the one who offers a prophetic word but who may not have the interpretation for that revelation. For example, the Lord may say through someone, "I see a move ahead of you." The one hearing that word could interpret it to mean a physical move when, in fact, the Lord means there is a move of His Spirit coming. The person speaking can be accurate in delivering the word but not understand what kind of move it means. And the person receiving the word may misinterpret it based on his own inward desires or expectations.

We must remain in constant dependence on God, whether we are delivering revelation or receiving it. David was the eighth son; number eight is symbolic of a new beginning. There may be an eighth "son" in your life that *you* cannot see, but at the right time God will clearly declare, "This is the one I have spoken of."

When all these wisdom parameters are in place, they will create a safe atmosphere where we can walk into fruitful prophetic maturation and faith can move freely. Let's not err either on the side of license or on the side of stifling the Spirit's presence and power. With this understanding of the anatomy of a prophetic word, we can line up as enlisted soldiers in God's revolutionary army, prepared and ready for war.

OUR INTERCESSORY CRY

Father, we stand in awe of Your desire to include Your children in the work of Your Spirit. We ask that You give us grace to wait on You with patience as You weave Your own character and wisdom into our lives. Help us eliminate the idols and fears from our hearts so that we may fully enter into the ministry of reconciliation with You, as You seek to encourage and direct others through us. May love for You be our one ambition, and may love for others flow out from our spirits into those around us. Grant us grace to load, with understanding, the revelatory ammunition we need in order to march forward in Your progressive purposes. Thank You for teaching us Your ways. In Jesus' great name. Amen.

POP QUIZ—KEEPING YOU ON YOUR TOES!

1. At times what seems to be a contradiction can be an accurate fulfillment of the revelation. Give an account of this from Scripture.
2. Give an account from your own life when you misinterpreted a prophetic word. What was the result?
3. What are some of the wisdom ways of God that you can gain from this chapter?

FOR MORE, LORD!

Kevin Conner, *Interpreting Symbols and Types* (Portland: BT Publications, 1980)

Larry Randolph, *User-Friendly Prophecy* (Shippensburg, Pa.: Destiny Image, 1998)

Michael Sullivant, *Prophetic Etiquette* (Lake Mary, Fla.: Creation House, 2000)

THREE

A REVOLUTION
OF WISDOM

The Broken Vessel

When His disciples James and John saw this, they said, "Lord, do You want us to command fire to come down from heaven and consume them?" But He turned and rebuked them.

Luke 9:54–55

Have you ever been scorched by the hot words of Jesus? Has He ever spoken something so deep into your heart that you were cut to the very core of your being? I think this is exactly what happened to John, the zealot, in the above example. I believe he was pierced by God in his fleshly strength, never to recover.

John started out like most of the rest of us—zealous, jealous and on hot fire. But along the way he became a broken vessel in the Lord's hands. Remember, disciples are made, not born. This John had made a radical surrender to his new Commander-in-Chief. Imagine having to learn new ways, a new vocation, hanging out with a bunch of men day and night, and following some itinerant around the country. Yeah, it would be exciting for a while. But when you get a prophetic word like, "You don't know what spirit you are speaking from!" that might set you back for a spell.

Realize that most of these new followers were probably just in their early twenties or so. John and James were even named *Boanerges* by the Lord, which means "Sons of Thunder" (Mark 3:17). After they had followed Jesus for almost three years, they were still jostling for position, and their mother, Salome, was even stirring them up to do it. They were contending to see which one could sit on Jesus' right hand and which on His left (Mark 10:35-41). Sounds as if John and his brother had more zeal than wisdom. Does that sound familiar?

But every "son of thunder" needs the wisdom of a father to help nurture and love him into all God has created him to be. Did you ever have more zeal than knowledge of God's ways? Ever get in His way instead of out of it? Ever have the wrong concept of what prophetic ministry looks like, and you just wanted to call down fire on everyone? After all, you are called to be a prophet of judgment, and you know God has chosen you to call it down. (And in your high and mighty opinion, sooner would be better than later!)

Maybe mercy needs to triumph in your life, as it did in John's. We need prophets who love mercy and who want to call *that* kind of fire down on people, cities and nations. Judgmental, prophetic lone rangers do not last long; team ministry is the higher pathway. Are you in this for the long haul or just the short range? Determine your destiny. Aim the right way. Seek the wisdom of the Holy Spirit. And cultivate the character necessary to carry the amazing anointing of God.

Yes, there are pits to avoid and wisdom to be gained. There are valuable lessons to grasp that selfish ambition is not the Kingdom way. Promotion does come from the Lord, but normally after you have been in the game and endured a few rounds. John became a broken vessel, and it was pleasing to the Lord. See him yielded, merciful and leaning on the Master's chest. I wonder how He got that way?

Maybe it will be the same for you and me. Lessons from the journey of becoming—that is what this track is about. Material here might just save your life, or that of a friend. So take a deep breath and continue on. Destination? "A Revolution of Wisdom" is the antidote for the day.

7

THE PITS AND PINNACLES OF PROPHETIC MINISTRY

Before we examine the pits and pinnacles of moving in the prophetic, we must identify the two foundational purposes for the existence of prophetic ministry. If a true revolution is to bring forth a more excellent display of the Gospel to the world, we must stay focused on the plan of our Commander-in-Chief. And without a clear understanding of these two foundational purposes, we will misuse revelation and miss the main objectives of the prophetic revolution.

Purpose #1: Testifying About Jesus

We are to carry within our bosoms the fire of the testimony of Christ, an aching longing to know Him and to make Him known. Glimpsing details of the future or making grand and glorious statements cannot be our primary motivation. *The enflaming passion for knowing this glorious Man, Christ Jesus, and for making Him known, is the empowering force within that will cause us to exude the fragrance of His wonderful presence.* Without this solid foundation in place, we will expend our energy for no eternal purpose and fail to reveal the testimony of Jesus through our lives.

He was asking His disciples, "Who do people say that the Son of Man is?" And they said, "Some say John the Baptist; and others, Elijah; but still others, Jeremiah, or one of the prophets." He said to them, "But who do you say that I am?" Simon Peter answered, "You are the Christ, the Son of the living God." And Jesus said to him, "Blessed are you, Simon Barjona, because flesh and blood did not reveal this to you, but My Father who is in heaven."

Matthew 16:13–17

There was much debate over who Jesus really was and what He was about. Many looked at His marvelous works and mannerisms and compared Him to prophets who had come before Him. These observers used their natural understanding to explain who He was. But Peter received his understanding from the Father, God Himself.

True prophetic revelation comes from no other source but the living God. We cannot figure Him out by natural perception or educated guesses. Peter received a personal testimony of Jesus from the Spirit of God, then spoke it out by the power of the spirit of prophecy. Once Peter (along with the other disciples) had received the testimony of Jesus, then the Father revealed to Peter who Jesus was.

"I also say to you that you are Peter, and upon this rock I will build My church; and the gates of Hades will not overpower it."

verse 18

Jesus was saying to Peter (*petra*—a little stone) that the Church would be built on the large Rock, Jesus, and that hell itself could not prevail against it. That solid foundation is the revelation of Jesus Christ, and no storm can blow you off that Rock.

It takes the Holy Spirit to know who God is, to show us who Jesus is. The Holy Spirit is the first Person of the Godhead we meet. He takes Jesus from being some religious icon and illuminates Him as the Christ, the Son of God. He makes Jesus real to us.

The Holy Spirit also releases the spirit of conviction of sin, righteousness and judgment to come on our lives, and thereby reveals the centrality, the glories and the wonders of this glorious Man, Christ Jesus. *It takes God to know God!* This is the foundation of the prophetic. If prophetic revelation does not make us fall more in love with Jesus, then we have missed its main purpose.

The true purpose of the prophetic is to not only reveal the Man Jesus but to reveal the Lordship of Jesus. "No one can say, 'Jesus is Lord,' except by the Holy Spirit" (1 Corinthians 12:3). We cannot understand Jesus' Lordship and His right to authority over our lives without the revelation of the Holy Spirit operating in our behalf.

The revelation of Christ Jesus and His Lordship is the foundational purpose and focus of all prophetic revelation. If we are not fully grounded here, we will have no prophetic revolution.

Purpose #2: To Pierce Defenses

The Holy Spirit is the master at detecting and piercing the defenses of the enemy, and He uses prophetic gracelets as antitank missiles. Jesus demonstrated this second purpose of prophetic ministry in His interaction with Nathanael in John 1:45–51 and with the woman at the well in John 4:7–26. Jesus' execution of prophetic revelation pierced their defenses of skepticism and prejudice and cut through to the hidden places in their hearts. The Holy Spirit anointed Jesus to reveal these hidden things in order to bring these individuals to an understanding that He was the Messiah.

Piercing the Defense of Skepticism

Nathanael had just been approached by Philip, who had told him that they had found the One "of whom Moses in the Law and also the Prophets wrote—Jesus of Nazareth, the son of Joseph" (John 1:45).

> Nathanael said to him, "Can any good thing come out of Nazareth?" Philip said to him, "Come and see." Jesus saw Nathanael coming to Him, and said of him, "Behold, an Israelite indeed, in whom there is no deceit!" Nathanael said to Him, "How do You know me?" Jesus answered and said to him, "Before Philip called you, when you were under the fig tree, I saw you." Nathanael answered Him, "Rabbi, You are the Son of God; You are the King of Israel."
>
> verses 46–49

Even though Nathanael appeared skeptical in his response to Philip about Jesus as the promised Messiah, the Lord saw by the spirit of revelation that he was being true to his understanding. Nathanael was speaking honestly and transparently, calling a spade a spade. But Nathanael was shocked that Jesus professed to know him even though they had never laid eyes on one another. Jesus' word of knowledge about the fig tree served only to confirm to Nathanael that this was no ordinary man. Jesus' revelation of God's pure view of Nathanael's heart pierced his defense of skepticism.

Piercing the Defense of Sin

In a second prophetic account we see a stark contrast between Jesus and the woman at the well. Because He was a Jew, there was an immediate barrier between Him and this woman. Hebrews had nothing to do with the half-breed Samaritans. A good Jew considered them less than nothing. Not only that, but she was an adulterous woman who worshiped false gods, and He was a pure single man. They could not have been any more separate if a brick wall had stood between them.

Yet Jesus, by the power of the spirit of prophecy, dared to break through the wall of tradition and prejudice and reach out to a lost soul. She was touched not only by His daring to speak with her, but by the fact that He knew what her personal life was like.

> He said to her, "Go, call your husband and come here." The woman answered and said, "I have no husband." Jesus said to her, "You have correctly said, 'I have no husband'; for you have had five husbands, and the one whom you now have is not your husband; this you have said truly."
>
> John 4:16–18

Jesus' penetrating revelation had the power to break down her defenses and convince her that He was a prophet—better yet, the Messiah! Soon she ran out and told the whole town about the man who must be the Christ, "a man who told me all the things that I have done" (verse 29). God had exposed the deceitfulness of her life, and she knew that God knew her. Awesome! Not only did she experience a swift change in her personal history, but she turned her city upside-down. Personal revolution can lead to a city revolution, if you let it!

An Airport Encounter

About ten years ago I was coming back from a crusade on the island nation of Haiti with my dear friend Mahesh Chavda, and we had a layover in Atlanta. The meetings had been wonderful and we had seen many miracles, such as a 77-year-old woman, blind from birth, being given her sight on the last night we were there. As some of us from the team, including my sister, Barbara, were sitting in the airport in the afterglow of success, an unkempt man appeared. His hair was a mess, his clothes were ragged and he reeked of nicotine from his chain-smoking. On top of all that, he was wearing one of those sandwich board signs with something like *Prophets Are of No Profit* written on it.

As he approached, I became agitated, feeling protective of my sister and wary of his coming too close. Then he flopped down in the same row of chairs we were occupying, just a few seats away.

As we were contemplating moving, suddenly my spiritual antennae went up and I began to ask the Lord if He had something to say about this man. As I prayed quietly in the Spirit, the Lord began to speak to me about the man. Then, in question form, I began to address him.

"Sir, you've been really wounded by the Body of Christ, haven't you?"

The guy turned his head and looked at me.

"In fact," I continued, "you've been kicked out of the church you'd been part of. Is that right?"

He continued to stare.

"And you don't have a place to live. You've been living out of a garage. Is that right?"

Tears began coming down his face.

"And your wife left you about three years ago, and you've been rejected by the Body of Christ, and you carry great pain in your life."

As soon as I started speaking out of the place of compassion, the lens of judgment came off and I knew the Lord was speaking to the man's heart. By then a lot of tears were dripping onto the floor, as the people with me on the team were weeping, too, and repenting for their own judgmental attitudes.

The man responded by saying all of this was true. Then we stood to our feet and embraced one another. I prayed for the Lord's cleansing to come into his life and for healing to come into his heart.

I tell you the truth, the spirit of prophecy breaks down barriers and defenses. Even more than that, the Holy Spirit—the prophetic presence of God—can build bridges with people we are totally unlike.

Revelatory gifting is part of God's defense system that releases missiles and destroys the defenses and barriers erected by the enemy to cut off the plan of God. What power we wield through the prophetic! If we want to use these powerful missiles with greater accuracy and effectiveness, we must deploy them with love and the testimony of our Lord Jesus Christ resounding in our hearts.

Now, remembering these two foundational purposes, let's take an honest look at six pitfalls we face in the prophetic arena. Then we will look at seven pinnacles, and finally three simple guidelines that will help us avoid the pits and prepare us for the pinnacles.

The Pits!

Have you ever said, "Now that's the pits!" It is *bad*—you know, God knows and He alone knows who else knows! But through the grace of God and a greater understanding of the tactics of our enemy, we can advance and learn for God's Kingdom and glory. But beware. There are numerous pits that must be avoided as we advance. Snares and hostility await us as we venture forward. We are going to look at six of these pitfalls.

Pit #1: Hostility

The risk is not so much in wrongly promoting the prophetic as it is in putting prophets to death with the sword of the tongue. All throughout biblical and Church history and into the present time, there have been many misconceptions about prophets and prophecy that lead to hostility toward prophetic people. "The prophet is a fool, the inspired man is demented" (Hosea 9:7). What are some of the reasons for such hostility? Here are four.

Human sin. The original sin of humankind is rebellion against God's word. The heart of man harbors hostility toward the entrance of God's word. The Holy Spirit does an intrusive work that brings the cutting edge of conviction, making us feel discomfort or outright pain. It is natural to resist these feelings. Prophetic revelation is a sharp knife! But remember, the revelatory word does not compete with the Word of God (Scripture); it complements it. And because of the sin in the human heart, hostility often arises not only toward God's Word but toward prophetic revelation.

The "offensive" way gifts are packaged. "God has chosen the foolish things of the world to shame the wise" (1 Corinthians 1:27). He often packages His gifts in an offensive manner. Moses is an excellent example of offensive packaging. He grew up with a silver spoon in his mouth, as an Egyptian prince in Pharaoh's house. He offended the Israelites ethnically, racially and socially. But God chose him as their deliverer. That does not compute in the religiously correct mind!

Paul is another example of offensive packaging. "On the contrary, seeing that I had been entrusted with the gospel to the uncircumcised. . ." (Galatians 2:7). Paul was a blueblood Pharisee sent to bring the message of salvation to the Gentiles, who despised the Jews because of their attitude of separation and religious superiority. Go figure! As some say today, "God offends the mind to reveal the heart."

The veiled way God chooses to reveal Himself. God's methodology also arouses hostility and creates snares. Numbers 12:6 addresses His methodology: "[The LORD] said, 'Hear now My words: If there is a prophet among you, I, the LORD, shall make Myself known to him in a vision. I shall speak with him in a dream. Not so, with My servant Moses, he is faithful in all My household; with him I speak mouth to mouth, even openly, and not in dark sayings. . . .'"

God has chosen to speak prophetically in various veiled ways. How did Jesus do most of His teaching? Through parables. Why would God purposefully choose to create obscure messages? To create in us seeking hearts and the grace of humility, and because He is more than an answer box. He provokes questions within us to whet our appetites and stir up divine curiosity so we will seek the answer—God Himself! His desire is to draw us into closer communion and relationship through our seeking.

Lack of appreciation for the prophetic process. Most people do not appreciate what many teach as a three-stage process: revelation, interpretation, application. After *revelation* comes, we must get proper *interpretation;* but proper *application* of the interpretation is also vitally important. Many receive the revelation initially but forget to finish the process by interpreting and applying it. Then they become hostile toward the messenger because they view it all as soooo complicated. Our tendency is to want revelation, interpretation and application dropped into our laps without our having to consult personally with the Source of revelation, the Holy Spirit. Remember that prophecy is designed to promote relationship. Hence, hostility arises out of a lack of true appreciation for the process of receiving God's word through relationship.

Pit #2: The Effects of Hostility on the Prophet

Gifted creatures often react in unhealthy ways to the hostility directed at them. After all, if you are getting stoned, it is natural to want to run and hide, or to build up a wall to avoid the wounding of those stones! But such natural reactions ensnare and paralyze prophetic people. As a result, they become:

Adversarial. Prophetic people may begin to look at the people who have reacted with hostility toward their revelations as the enemy, instead of recognizing that our real enemy, the devil, is the one stirring up reactions. Sin is our enemy, not sinners.

Judgmental. The pain of experiencing hostility can cause prophetic people to begin to judge the motivations of everyone who disagrees with them. Then, in turn, they become overly critical of others.

Isolated. As the pain continues to fester, the prophetic person may isolate himself and refuse to submit to any counsel, correction or authority within the local church. They are now lone rangers taking potshots at their brothers and sisters for whom Jesus died.

Dropouts. Finally prophetic people under attack may choose to drop out of the ranks of the local church and give up on the Body of Christ. Isolation leads to alienation. Alienation creates quitters.

THE ELIJAH SYNDROME

Elijah experienced hostility toward the prophetic ministry as he dealt with King Ahab and his wife, Jezebel. In 1 Kings 18 the man of God experienced a powerful pinnacle of the prophetic when he confronted Ahab's wickedness, killed the 850 false prophets and prayed for the end of the long drought that had caused severe famine in the land. "The hand of the LORD was on Elijah" (verse 46). What a fantastic series of events to have experienced!

But something happened to Elijah. He suffered a blow from Ahab's evil wife, Jezebel, who sent a messenger of death to him. "So may the gods do to me and even more," she said, referring to her slain prophets, "if I do not make your life as the life of one of them by tomorrow about this time" (1 Kings 19:2). She was really sore about those prophets and the fact that Elijah was making her husband look foolish and weak.

Even after all God had done, the blow hit Elijah so hard that his first reaction was to *run*. Then the Lord came to Elijah where he was hiding in a cave and asked him, "What are you doing here, Elijah?" (1 Kings 19:9).

Remember in chapter 1 when we reflected on why God asks us questions when He already knows the answers? Could it be that He just wants us to be aware that we have fallen into a pit?

Elijah's pitiful response: "I have been very zealous for the LORD, the God of hosts; for the sons of Israel have forsaken Your covenant, torn down Your altars and killed Your prophets with the sword. And I alone am left; and they seek my life, to take it away" (verse 10).

Boy, was he depressed! He was hiding out in that cave, feeling all alone and thinking he was the only righteous guy left. I think you could call this a messiah complex. Ever been there? I have, and it felt really lousy.

THE INCUBATION BED OF REVELATION

The enemy, through various demonic forces (for example, the spirits of Jezebel, Antichrist, discouragement, depression and heaviness), attempts to alienate prophetic vessels from participation in the Body of Christ. Darkness hates the light of revelation, and if it cannot put the light out, it will at least attempt to push the "fire-starter" so out of the loop that its impact is limited.

Yet prophetic warriors also need space, quiet and a measure of seclusion to function well. Aloneness is a vital part of the prophetic lifestyle. *Quietness and aloneness is the incubation bed of revelation.* Being quiet and alone with God helps relationship and revelation to flourish. Turning to some words from my book *Kneeling on the Promises* may give us some additional insight:

> Yes, just pause for a while. . . . We must learn to quiet our souls before God in order to commune with Him. Remember, prayer is not just talking our heads off to God and telling Him all the things we think He has not done! Prayer is not so much something we do as Someone we are with. This requires a rare commodity—actually pushing the pause button!
>
> True prayer involves *selah.* We must pause long enough to quiet ourselves and bend our ears in His direction in order to listen. You cannot hear what another is saying if you are talking all the time. It is impossible! So pause. Wait. Rest. Slow down. You will be amazed how this alone will revolutionize your life.[1]

Seclusion is a discipline, but it is absolutely necessary in order for God to teach us and fill us with His life-changing words. Our gas tanks run dry after much ministry, and we need to fuel up again so we can move out in strength and deploy those antitank missiles in the love of God. It helps us maintain our mental health. It gives the Holy Spirit opportunity to heal our wounds from previous battles and to ready us for the next offensive.

Jesus Himself knew this place of aloneness and went there often. Why should we think we can survive on the battlefield with anything less than what the incarnate Son of God required Himself? We must learn to maintain the quiet aloneness that fosters an intimate relationship with our God and restores our arsenal of revelation against the enemy.

BACK TO ELIJAH

The Lord came to the prophet again with the same question—"What are you doing here, Elijah?" (verse 13)—and his response was the same the second time. But the Lord did not leave him in that place. He declared the truth to Elijah: "I will leave 7,000 in Israel, all the knees that have not bowed to Baal and every mouth that has not kissed him" (verse 18).

Elijah was not really the only good guy left, was he? He just thought he was! But then the Lord called him out to anoint others: "Go, return on your way to the wilderness of Damascus, and when you have arrived, you shall anoint Hazael . . . Jehu . . . and Elisha. . . ."

Our Father God has a special plan for the protection and nurturing of His people as they step out in faith to be His ministers of grace. His design is to bring us together as a team of friends and peers to give one another the mutual support of caring, challenging and blessing one another. We are the family of God! But it takes humility and time to develop this kind of a team atmosphere and relationship. The safety net of a caring community and team ministry is vital to the growth and development of the revelatory gifts (as well as other ministry gifts).

Pit #3: Confusion Over Personal Identity

Prophetic people often seem to be extra-sensitive. That is partially the means by which we get revelation. We are receptive to the gentle nudgings of the Spirit. This sensitivity can enable us to perceive things quickly in the spirit realm. God created us this way. But if our personal identity and security rest on the wrong things, that sensitivity can cause us to overreact to certain words, innuendoes, judgments or criticisms from others.

Gaining a deep understanding of the following points can help us avoid those personal identity pitfalls.

Your identity is who you are, not what you do. Your primary identity is found in who you are in Christ, not what you do in obedience to Him. You are a child of God and your identity is found in your relationship with Him. I love prophetic ministry. It is exhilarating and exciting. But I am first a child of God, not a prophetic minister. I have many roles in the earth—husband, father, teacher, minister, intercessor—but none of these roles makes me who I am. They only tell you what I do in response to being a child of God created in His image. Don't build your foundation of identity on what you do, either in the ministry or in earthly responsibilities, or you will be blown away with the changing of the winds.

Your function is what you do. The same is true for gifts ministry. The ministry gifts with which God graces us are not who we are. These gifts enable us to function as dispensers of the love and mercy of our Creator. But our function will go through many changes. Who we are in Christ remains constant. Thank God!

You are not what you do. We are to be identified as true and authentic Christians who bear the resemblance of our Father God and carry the family name. Paul, an apostle, never identified himself as such, but called himself "a bondslave of the Lord Jesus Christ." Also, if we label ourselves "Apostle Jones" or "Prophet Smith" and it is not true, we diminish the identity and function of that position in the Body of Christ. If I am to be called anything, it will not be because I put it on some business card or fancy website. It will be because fruit has been borne and others have eaten of it. Again, functions change. We are Christians first. Others are to declare who we are by the fruit borne. May a revolution occur even in this simple arena!

You are loved because of God's grace, not because of your performance. We love Him because He first loved us. God extended grace and mercy to us before we ever knew He existed. Your performance does not qualify you to be His child, called by His name. You receive His grace and love through faith, and that never changes. Your performance does not change His love for you, and His grace and mercy are held out to you continually as you toddle through the growth process.

What are the results of personal identity pits into which we fall?

Stubbornness and dogmatism. This happens not because the prophetic person is rebellious or wicked, but because he is trying to survive! Our aim is not survival, however, but death to self.

Extravagant deliveries. When you are trying to survive, the claim of "thus saith the Lord" gets louder and more emotional with every delivery. Simplicity is thrown out the window and self-promotion becomes the norm.

An unteachable spirit. "I hear from God, and I learn from no man!" Have you ever heard that one? We are members of a local body because God knew we needed each other to fulfill our destiny in Him. We will always need the Body of Christ.

While we are on the subject of personal identity, I want to identify three possible misconceptions concerning our prophetic ministry.

Public ministry is the goal. This is a wrong goal and focus in life. We are called first to function at home, at work, at school and then elsewhere according to His will. Let the platform people inspire and equip a company of passionate, consecrated warriors to invade the earth!

The highest release of the prophetic is the spontaneous and ecstatic spoken word. This is also a misconception. One of the highest forms of prophetic release is to pray back to God a word we have received from Him. Intercession is praying God's burdens back to Him and fellowshiping with Him concerning His revelation to us.

Our goal is to be known as the best, or at least to be right. No, our goal is the testimony of Jesus. The prophetic presence will make Him known *to* us and make Him known *through* us. What is the prophetic presence and gifting for, then? First of all, to reveal God to us; and then for us to emanate His presence wherever we go.

Pit #4: Guilt by Association

Have you ever fallen into the pit of guilt by association? You think you are doing O.K., when suddenly a list of bad comments about some group you are associated with pops up out of nowhere. As far as you know, you have not done any of those things. Then someone points a finger at you and says, "You are one of *those people*, aren't you?" What is your reaction? Don't you just want to hide and say, "Who, me?"

We can learn a lot from the life of Peter concerning guilt by association. After he claimed boldly that he would never forsake the Lord, Jesus was arrested. Peter followed Him at a distance into the courtyard of the high priest's home where Jesus had been taken for questioning. Peter tried hard to stay loyal to the Lord, but when people began to associate him openly with Jesus, embarrassment, shame and fear suddenly raised their ugly heads, and Peter stumbled headlong into the pit of guilt by association.

First, people made statements (quoted in Luke 22) about Peter's identity:

"This man was with Him too." (verse 56)

"You are one of them too!" (verse 58)

"Certainly this man also was with Him, for he is a Galilean too." (verse 59)

Peter denied not only his Lord but also his own identity:

"Woman, I do not know Him." (verse 57)

"Man, I am not!" (verse 58)

"Man, I do not know what you are talking about." (verse 60)

"The Lord turned and looked at Peter. And Peter remembered the word of the Lord, how He had told him, 'Before a rooster crows today, you will deny Me three times.' And he went out and wept bitterly" (verses 61–62). Can you imagine the pain Peter must have felt when Jesus, his Lord and Friend, turned and looked deeply into his soul? That glance must have cut through to the very core of his being and divided spirit and soul. Peter was at the very bottom of the pit, in the throes of death to self.

God wants to heal that pain, but He also wants to us to die. The devil and God have one thing in common: They are both out to kill us!

Have you ever experienced the fame and glory that come with the name of Christ? I hope so, because it is a sign that you are authentic. When people see evidence that you are associated with Jesus, it means there is something real about your message or lifestyle. But the pointing finger of accusation and the reactions you may feel can cause real pain. It is a time to die to self and be identified with the sufferings of Christ.

The pain of denial is much worse than the pain of being associated with Jesus and those who follow Him. You may have done nothing wrong, but persecution is a very real part of following Christ.

In the realm of prophetic revelation, your image of being a "wonder boy" can quickly change into "blunder boy," especially when people do not like the message (and particularly if it calls for a revolution of change). We can learn from Peter's experience—that denying our true identity with Christ and our associations in Him is more painful than dying to our own self-image.

Pit #5: Revelation Without Compassion

The pit of anger is another common trap that awaits prophetic people. The story of Jonah, which we looked at earlier, gives us an excellent picture of an angry prophet.

THE JONAH SYNDROME

Jonah had a great dilemma. The word of the Lord had come to him to go and prophesy to Nineveh. But because Ninevites were notorious for their atrocities against the Hebrew people, Jonah probably hated them. Not only was God asking him to speak to them concerning their sin, but if they truly repented, Jonah knew God would listen and turn away His anger from them.

Can you imagine what it might feel like if God gave you a word that He was going to pour out His mercy on someone who had given you a lot of grief? He might tell you to prophesy to the church down the road that dragged your name through the mud, to tell them He was going to pour down His fresh fire of the Spirit on them and bless their socks off! That would be a hard word to give. You would have to swallow your hurt and put away your pain to give your persecutors a word of mercy.

That is what Jonah was called to do. The prophet fled from the presence of the Lord and jumped right into the pit of anger. God may have been gracious, compassionate and slow to anger toward Nineveh, but Jonah was despondent, bitter and very angry! He did not have the heart of God and did not really want it. Even after his obedience to give the word of the Lord to Nineveh, and after its repentance, he held onto his anger: "'Therefore now, O LORD, please take my life from me, for death is better to me than life.' The LORD said, 'Do you have good reason to be angry?'" (Jonah 4:3–4).

Years ago I was part of a fellowship in Kansas City that came under some persecution and criticism from another ministry that had blessed me personally. I grew angry over the situation. I felt caught between these two groups, since I had been nurtured by both. It was the pits! I have never tasted anger such as I did then. I was hurt and confused by the reactions on both sides.

During the midst of that turbulent time, Mike Bickle, the senior leader of the team I was part of, talked openly about his own anger and the wisdom God had given him. The Lord revealed to him that the degree of his own anger was the degree of his own ambition. What a measuring stick! And did I ever have to check my heart on that one!

God gives us revelation, and then we face situations, like this one with Jonah, in which He instantly plumbs the depths of our sin-sick souls. His words and acts of mercy toward others can expose the amount of unforgiveness and lack of mercy in our own souls.

Jonah continued to wallow in the pit of anger and took a spot above the city to watch and see what God would do. God had mercy on him by providing a shade plant, keeping him from the discomfort of the heat of the sun. Jonah was happy with the plant. But then the Lord sent a worm to eat it up, and Jonah was exposed to the elements.

> When the sun came up God appointed a scorching east wind, and the sun beat down on Jonah's head so that he became faint and begged with all his soul to die, saying, "Death is better to me than life." Then God said to Jonah, "Do you have good reason to be angry about the plant?" And he said, "I have good reason to be angry, even to death." Then the LORD said, "You had compassion on the plant for which you did not work and which you did not cause to grow, which came up overnight and perished overnight. Should I not have compassion on Nineveh, the great city in which there are more than 120,000 persons who do not know the difference between their right and left hand, as well as many animals?"
>
> Jonah 4:8–11

God's compassion extended even to the dumb animals of that city. He wanted to reveal to Jonah the depth of compassion and mercy lacking in his own life. Jonah's heart was hard and God's mercy exposed it, but in the process God saved a whole city from destruction for another 110 years.

God will use all the circumstances in our lives to reveal Himself and expose our hearts so that we can be changed "from glory to glory" (2 Corinthians 3:18). If you will permit me for a moment, I want to take some liberty with this phrase. I believe God takes us from "gory to glory." He exposes the "gory" places of our hearts and, through repentance and forgiveness, changes them to "glory" places where He can bring His mercy and compassion. So we go from gory to glory and from glory to glory!

Mercy Points

We must move away from the Old Testament prophetic stereotype with the loud voice, pointy finger and hard, judgmental attitude.

God restored a fallen spiritual leader in the 1940s named Rex Andrews. The Lord gave this man the following thoughts that altered his course:

> Mercy is God's supply system for every need everywhere. Mercy is that kindness, compassion and tenderness that is a passion to suffer with, or participate in, another's ills or evils in order to relieve, heal, or restore. It accepts another freely and gladly as he is and supplies the needed good of life to build up and to bring to peace and keep in peace. It is to take another into one's heart *just as he is* and cherish and nourish him there. Mercy takes another's sins and evils and faults as its own, and frees the other by bearing them to God. This is the glow of love. This is the anointing.[2]

One of the necessary ingredients in prophetic maturation is cultivating such a heart of compassion. Author Ken Blue writes, "The kind of compassion Jesus was said to have for people was not merely an expression of His will but rather an eruption from deep within His being. Out of this compassion of Jesus sprang His mighty works of rescue, healing and deliverance."[3] We must see the heart of God behind a matter and become problem-solvers, not problem-pointers.

Mercy Scriptures

Mercy Scriptures to pray over your life:

Hebrews 4:16: Let us draw near with confidence to the throne of grace, so that we may receive mercy and find grace to help in time of need.

Matthew 9:13: "Go and learn what this means: 'I DESIRE COM-
PASSION, AND NOT SACRIFICE,' for I did not come to call the righteous, but sinners."

Micah 7:18: Who is a God like You, who pardons iniquity and
passes over the rebellious act of the remnant of His posses-
sion? He does not retain His anger forever, because He delights
in unchanging love.

James 2:13: Judgment will be merciless to one who has shown
no mercy; mercy triumphs over judgment.

Mark 1:41: Moved with compassion, Jesus stretched out His
hand and touched him, and said to him, "I am willing; be
cleansed."

Psalm 78:38–39 (NKJV): But He, being full of compassion, for-
gave their iniquity, and did not destroy them. Yes, many a time
He turned His anger away, and did not stir up all His wrath;
for He remembered that they were but flesh, a breath that
passes away and does not come again.

Pit #6: Ditches on Both Sides to Avoid

Here are some attitudes and reactions to avoid on both sides of
the street as they, too, will send you into the pits:

- People treat you special.
- People quit treating you special.
- People want to wind you up like a toy and get you to proph-
  esy on demand.
- You're not prepared but are called "up front" to prophesy.
- You are ready but nothing comes.
- You are ready but you are not called on.
- You are ready but nobody wants it, likes it or responds to it.
- You make messes for yourself and others to clean up.
- There are so many parameters in place that you are afraid to
  do anything.
- You are afraid to risk your reputation.
- You have exaggerated a word and everyone knows it.

- You have exaggerated a word and no one knows it except you and God.
- Your gift exceeds your character. Woe!

These might sound a bit humorous, but most people don't laugh much when it happens to them. Pastors might want to add a line here also. To pastors, at times, the P.I.T.'s are "prophets-in-training." (Ouch, that hurt!)

Remember, our loving Father offers a way out of all the pits we have mentioned. It is His great *grace and mercy!* "Let us draw near with confidence to the throne of grace, so that we may receive mercy and find grace to help in time of need" (Hebrews 4:16).

The Pinnacles

Finally we get to the joyous pinnacles of prophetic ministry. The highest pinnacle of prophetic lifestyle is this: *Jesus Christ magnified, Jesus Christ glorified, Jesus Christ lifted up, and the life of God being released to other people.* This happens when a man or woman follows the two foundational purposes of prophetic ministry—knowing Christ and making Him known; and using prophetic words as missiles to pierce the defenses of the enemy.

Pinnacle #1: When It Really Works!

I got ruined in January 1994 on a trip to Albania, in a city on the northern coast of the Adriatic Sea.

Albania is an Islamic nation that came under the control of Communism, and was opened in 1990 and 1991. In 1967 all church buildings were destroyed. Most of the people were also closed to the Gospel. In the Albanian language the name of the city we were visiting, Sein Gein, means St. John. Residents claim it is a city where the apostle John ministered. The evangelistic team I was with knew of only five or six Christians in the whole town.

Before we were scheduled to begin the evangelistic meeting—one of the first this town had seen maybe even in centuries—I was standing on a cliff overlooking the Adriatic Sea. I began asking the Lord, "What do You have for the people of Sein Gein?" Although we were there for only one night, I could sense their destiny with God, knowing that possibly John, the apostle, had walked that very spot.

Suddenly the name *Sarah* floated through my mind.

Again I said, "But Lord, what do You have for these people of Albania?"

Again the name *Sarah* ran through my mind.

Then it was time for the meeting. "Oh, well," I said, and made my way back down the bluff.

Only a few in the small gathering of eighty to a hundred people were Christians. A friend of mine shared his testimony. Then it was time for me to preach.

About halfway through my talk on Jesus Christ—the same yesterday, today and forever—that name *Sarah* floated through my mind again. So I turned to my interpreter and asked how to say *Sarah* in Albanian.

"Sabrina," he said.

So through the interpreter I asked if someone was present named Sabrina. Almost at the back of the building, a young woman raised her hand. I called her to come up front.

As Sabrina stood in front of the interpreter, the thought came to me to tell her how old she was. (Strange thought to tell a woman!) Then I asked the interpreter to tell her the following things: "Your name is Sabrina. You have never been to a Christian meeting before in your life. You are 32 years old. You have a tumor in your left breast. And Jesus wants to heal you."

As the Holy Spirit moved on Sabrina, a Muslim, it looked as though the rest of the people present had their eyeballs popping out! Sabrina got saved right on the spot.

After that wonderful meeting, it was raining. The other team members and I grabbed the first available car and driver. As this gentleman was driving us to the next town to spend the night, I suddenly got the feeling I was like Philip, who climbed into the chariot with the Ethiopian eunuch in Acts 8.

"Jesus knows your name," I said to this driver through my interpreter. "He knows how many hairs are on your head. In fact, a woman at the meeting tonight, Sabrina, is 32 years old and had a tumor in her left breast. She's a Muslim, has never been to a Christian meeting before. But tonight she met the Lord Jesus Christ!"

As we headed down this bumpy old road, the driver started shaking. Guess what? Sabrina was his wife! I led him to the Lord as he drove the car that rainy night.

That kind of pinnacle in the prophetic ministry ruins you for sure! I want to see hundreds of thousands more of these demonstrations of God's revelatory power and love. It's the real thing!

Pinnacle #2: When Character Matches Prophetic Giftedness

When our character and fruit match the gifting God graces us with, it seems as though He drops an extra portion of anointing on us called "the authority of God." We do not have to say or do anything different than before, but God puts a little extra seal of His life on us. When He puts His authority on our words, it is as though we are E. F. Hutton and people stop to listen. What a pinnacle!— and a new test as well.

Pinnacle #3: Learning from Past Mistakes

Don't stop! Learn all you can. Keep going. Be like Paul, the apostle, who said, "Brethren, I do not regard myself as having laid hold of it yet; but one thing I do: forgetting what lies behind and reaching forward to what lies ahead, I press on toward the goal for the prize of the upward call of God in Christ Jesus" (Philippians 3:13–14).

Pinnacle #4: Denial Turned into Correct Identity

When we say, "Yes, I am one of them, and I am willing to bear the cost," we can turn a pit into a pinnacle. You might just graduate like Joseph from a pit to a palace!

Pinnacle #5: When the Prophetic Spirit Is Imparted to Others

It is a pinnacle to impart God's presence to others. One of my chief joys is giving the measure of prophetic presence that I have to others. What a joy to equip others and teach them how to drink in the prophetic presence of Jesus in their lives. But this revolution will not come about until we each load our guns with His presence.

Pinnacle #6: When We Embrace the Cross and Are Changed

The pit feels horrible emotionally. It can cause torment and bruising. But I can truthfully say that I would not trade those times of learning for anything. Embracing the cross has been good and needful, and it, too, is a pinnacle. Don't let the devil keep you in the pits; go to the cross and be transformed.

Pinnacle #7: When We Step Aside and Jesus Is Glorified

This is the pinnacle of all pinnacles. Once we get past the cross, resurrection life awaits us on the other side. It is then that we have stepped out of the way, and only Jesus can be seen. When He alone is magnified, we have reached the real pinnacle of success. Then the revolution has truly begun.

How to Handle Genuine Prophetic Ministry

Following are three simple guidelines that will help us avoid some of the pits and prepare us for the pinnacles of prophetic ministry.

Guideline #1: Test the Spirits

"Test the spirits to see whether they are from God" (1 John 4:1). What idea, concept, teaching or information is coming forth? What is the heart of the issue? Is Jesus presented as the Source of life? Is His cross lifted up?

Graham Cooke, author and prophetic minister from England, states, "Allowing prophecy without testing it . . . leads to abuse within the ministry, a discrediting of the gift in general, a poor model for local believers to follow, and frustration of the purpose for which true prophecy is given."[4]

International Bible teacher Derek Prince adds, "To permit the exercise of prophecy without requiring it to be subjected to scriptural judgment is against the teaching of the New Testament, and commonly leads to abuses which discredit prophecy as a whole and frustrate the purposes for which true prophecy is given."[5]

Guideline #2: Don't Be a Prophecy Junkie!

The revelatory word complements and does not compete with the written Word of God. Be a Wordaholic first. Let the revelatory gifting be the dessert, not the main course. Store the Word of God in your heart and meditate on the written Word, giving the breath of God something to blow on to quicken as a spoken word in your life.

Guideline #3: Understand the Nature of the Prophetic

Knowledge is not our primary goal; prophetic revelations are signposts pointing the way to the One who is the answer. We want more than information; we want intimacy with God! Here are some related guidelines.

- Few words are declarations that something will automatically come into being. Most words are invitations to respond to God with conditions that must first be met. (See chapter 6 for more on this subject.)
- Few prophetic words are immediate, "now" words. Most help us in the process of becoming.
- Few prophetic words get us out of a dilemma. They are used to shed light, comfort and encourage us to continue on. There are no shortcuts with God!
- Focus not on the promise but on the God who promised. Direct your faith onto the God of the Word. When our faith is misplaced, it produces fantasy and unreal expectations.
- Realize the clarity and cost equation. What God counts as significant will often arouse great opposition by the enemy. Paul was warned repeatedly of how much he would suffer for Christ's sake. Every promise contains a cost.

- Give room for "time lapse." As most words are invitations toward an end, there is a duration of time in between while the person is being prepared for the promise that is on the way.

Don't Throw It Out!

When learning to discern prophetic revelations and trying to process them effectively, we may experience some frustration and confusion. At some point we may be tempted to throw the whole package of this gifting out the window. Don't do it! It takes time and patience to develop your spiritual antennae, and that is what this relationship with Jesus is all about—communicating. We must be committed to learning God's methods of communication.

Here are some helpful tactics to employ while you are in training for the coming prophetic revolution.

Don't Put Out the Spirit's Fire

"Do not put out [despise, quench] the Spirit's fire [passion, zeal]; do not treat prophecies with contempt" (1 Thessalonians 5:19–20, NIV). Due to errors, failures and abuses, we may be tempted to despise the whole mess. But don't put out the Holy Spirit's fire by overreacting.

Don't Be Quickly Shaken

"[Don't] be quickly shaken from your composure or be disturbed either by a spirit or a message or a letter as if from us, to the effect that the day of the Lord has come" (2 Thessalonians 2:2). Don't become easily unsettled or alarmed by some prophecy. And avoid two ditches: discarding and rejecting prophecy altogether; and being enamored of and captivated by it.

Hold Fast to What Is Good

Moving in the prophetic is well worth the journey, even though there are pitfalls along the way. Great benefit will come as we cultivate the character we need to carry the revelatory gifts. "I, the prisoner of the Lord, implore you to walk in a manner worthy of the calling with which you have been called" (Ephesians 4:1). First Thessalonians 5:21 urges us to "examine everything carefully; hold fast to that which is good."

Hope for the Wounded

"Come, let us return to the LORD. For He has torn us, but He will heal us; He has wounded us, but He will bandage us. He will revive us after two days; He will raise us up on the third day, that we may live before Him. So let us know, let us press on to know the LORD. His going forth is as certain as the dawn; and He will come to us like the rain, like the spring rain watering the earth" (Hosea 6:1–3).

This is a prophetic word about the Messiah—His death, burial and resurrection. But it is also a message for the people of the Messiah, the Body of Christ. It is a comforting word of God's grace and mercy toward us as we experience the pits and pinnacles of a prophetic revolution.

There will be times of wounding and dying to selfish ambition, but our Father promises hope and help for the weary soldier. He has not left us alone in the battle to perish. The Holy Spirit will come and bind us up and resurrect the prophetic graces He has imparted, so we can continue to fight the good fight with the strength and power of His grace, and with His merciful hand leading us on to victory. Be encouraged in your journey, and give away the valuable lessons you learn to those who are coming along behind you. Impart His presence to all those He gives you.

OUR INTERCESSORY CRY

Lord, we stand in great fear and trembling at the awesome power You have manifested in all creation. But we also bow and worship You for the tender grace and mercy You display through the testimony of Your Son, Jesus Christ. Lord, our desire is to be carriers of the glorious presence of the Man Christ Jesus. We ask that You come by the power of Your Holy Spirit and heal all the broken places in our hearts that keep us from holding onto Your merciful graces.

Bind us up and teach us to listen to Your loving words and freely give them away to those in need of a revelation of Jesus. Our desire is to glorify You, magnify You on this earth and loyally serve You in the fields of harvest. Dear Father, lead us out of the pits and take us to the pinnacles by the power of Your Holy Spirit. May we learn from the past and move on in response to the upward call in Christ Jesus. For the glory of the Son of Your love. Amen.

Pop Quiz—Keeping You on Your Toes!

1. What are some of the pits of prophetic ministry?
2. What are some of the pinnacles?
3. From observing the experiences of others, what are some wisdom lessons that have given you insight?

FOR MORE, LORD!

Mike Bickle with Michael Sullivant, *Growing in the Prophetic* (Lake Mary, Fla.: Creation House, 1996)

Jim and Michal Ann Goll, *Encounters with a Supernatural God* (Shippensburg, Pa.: Destiny Image, 1998)

Dr. Bill Hamon, *Prophets, Pitfalls and Principles* (Shippensburg, Pa.: Destiny Image, 1991)

8

TOO HOT
TO HANDLE?

We need to put on the mittens of wisdom so we can carry the large, hot pan of His great anointing that simmers on God's stove—otherwise we might end up mishandling it, spilling it and getting burned. We need to pursue the presence and face of God, and we must nurture a deep-seated craving for the spiritual gifts, especially that we might prophesy (1 Corinthians 14:1). God's recipe calls for an equal proportion of each of the ingredients—gifts and fruit—to be blended together. But the stew is too hot to handle with bare hands—human strength, ego and soulish promotion. So let's find the lost mittens of the wisdom ways of God so we can serve up the anointing to a hungry world without getting burned and burning others in the process!

Church history is full of reports of anointed leaders who rose quickly to prominence only to become shooting stars, falling from their places of influence in front of the eyes of many who painfully observed their downward spiral. The world has mocked the Church as we have become ensnared by political and religious spirits. We have slept with the enemy. Unperceived ambition and the need to be needed have been the motivating forces propelling many of us into the limelight. Many ministers, like many business and government leaders, have more of a "driving spirit" than the Holy Spirit pushing them forward. God, have mercy on us. Lord, drive the "driving spirit" out of us!

We are called to "be shrewd as serpents and innocent as doves" (Matthew 10:16), but when we persistently, knowingly allow mixture in our lives, we open ourselves eventually to deception.

I could be a little less shocking and term the next section "Misconceptions about the Anointing." But our lack of understanding of the ways of God leads to many misapplications of revelation affecting our presentation of God. Eventually it causes some to end up on the trash heap of being deceived and also deceiving. So I am sticking with *deception*—"the act of deceiving or misleading; the habit of deceiving; the state of being deceived or misled."[1]

Samson: The Deception of the Anointing

Samson is a classic example of a person anointed by God who fell into the trap of deception. In just four chapters in the book of Judges, we find some peculiar and significant keys to understanding the anointing and the ways of God with man. Samson, one of the judges, was misled into a pattern of immorality while yet able to minister under the anointing, resulting in a swirl of chaos that only God can redeem (which He does, thank the Lord!).

First let's read a few verses concerning the calling of this man mightily used of God:

> There was a certain man of Zorah, of the family of the Danites, whose name was Manoah; and his wife was barren and had borne no children. Then the angel of the LORD appeared to the woman and said to her, "Behold now, you are barren and have borne no children, but you shall conceive and give birth to a son. Now therefore, be careful not to drink wine or strong drink, nor eat any unclean thing. For behold, you shall conceive and give birth to a son, and no razor shall come upon his head, for the boy shall be a Nazirite to God from the womb; and he shall begin to deliver Israel from the hands of the Philistines."
>
> ... Then the woman gave birth to a son and named him Samson; and the child grew up and the LORD blessed him. And the Spirit of the LORD began to stir him. ...
>
> Judges 13:2–5, 24–25

Supernatural intervention was required in order for Samson to be born. We read on in Judges that the Spirit of God would move on him suddenly, and an unusual anointing of strength would come on him to subdue the Philistines, the enemies of God's people. There was a mysterious secret to Samson's anointing: the length of his hair. Not cutting it was an outward prophetic representation of his inward vow of being a consecrated warrior to the Lord, a Nazirite.

Supernatural strength would come on Samson and he would perform an act of violence, sending terror into the enemy's camp. You can imagine how the Philistines felt about this strong man of God! But Satan devised a nasty game plan to pull him down. The devil has strategies and tricks up his sleeve that are always loaded with corruption. In this case the usurper, moving forward in a stealthy attempt to discover the key to Samson's anointing, hit below the belt. Samson's wife was given to his best friend (Judges 14:20). Samson avenged his loss by setting the Philistines' fields of grain and olive orchards on fire (Judges 15:4–5).

The battle of jealousy, anger and competition escalated. The outraged Philistines had had enough of this man; they devised a plot to capture Samson and bind him with ropes. Once again the gift of God came into operation. The ropes burst off his arms and Samson, in a mixture of anointing and rage, took the jawbone of a donkey and killed a thousand men (Judges 15:14–17). God's anointing continued to prevail over Israel's enemies.

Samson's Tumble into the Gutter

Judges 16:1 graphically depicts the scene: "Samson went to Gaza and saw a harlot there, and went in to her." What was going on here? (Have you ever asked that question when one of God's anointed has fallen?) More than likely the enemy had been doing a study on Samson's manly weakness. He was apparently turning away from his inward vow of consecration and now wanted the best of both worlds—the realm of the Spirit and the realm of the flesh.

As Samson started to play around with the precious things of God, the "deception of the anointing" began to settle in and have its effect. ("I must be special; I can do anything I want.") But notice that God did not remove His gift from Samson. This is one of the bizarre things, and where the principle as found in Romans 11:29 comes into play: "The gifts and the calling of God are irrevocable."

Word circulated quickly concerning what and where the man of God was, and the Gazites waited at the gate of the city, hoping to capture and kill him when he came out of his fling of fleeting pleasure (Judges 16:2). Instead the strength of God came on Samson once again (verse 3). He ripped off the city gates and carried them triumphantly to the top of the mountain outside Gaza.

Seemingly Samson got away with playing around. But the issue here is not the immediate outcome; rather, it is the long-term consequences of his actions. Ask yourself, *Where will the results of my action lead me a year from now? Five years from now?* Samson's Achilles' heel—a small but potentially mortal vulnerability— was now openly exposed, and the enemy was going to get him there if he could.

Samson's Enemies Set a Trap

Seemingly out of nowhere Delilah appeared on the scene. Samson loved her (Judges 16:4). So the Philistines wove a conspiracy of sexual intrigue, employing the forces of the bloodthirsty god of mammon to coax out the secret to Samson's great strength.

"Delilah said to Samson, 'Please tell me where your great strength is and how you may be bound to afflict you'" (Judges 16:6).

Excuse me, but can't you see the scene? The enemy's camp was following the plot. The woman seduced her way right into his face, wearing who knows what, just to destroy the man of God. Do you think she really cared about Samson? She was in it for what she could get—eleven hundred pieces of silver from each of the lords of the Philistines (verse 5). The Philistines were in it to smear the name and reputation of the one true God. It was a spiritual war, and demonic hosts were being called on to wear Samson down.

Probably Samson was thinking, *The last time they bound me, I snapped the cords, and then took a jawbone and killed a thousand men. I'll just play along with her little game. After all, I'm indestructible. I'm God's anointed.*

So as Delilah persisted in her question, Samson, playing a little closer to the edge of the cliff, wove a tale of where his secret lay:

If he was bound with "seven fresh cords" (verse 7), he would lose his strength. She tied him up with these and set the Philistines on him. Again the strength of God was released, and Samson triumphed over what seemed a trivial escapade. But the lady would not give up.

So it is in our day. Give the devil an inch and he'll take a mile. So don't give the seducer the time of day.

Without realizing it, Samson was beginning to get worn down. As he weakened, Delilah got a little closer to knowing the truth of his strength. He concocted tales starting with seven fresh cords, then "new ropes" (verse 11), and then—slipping a bit—said, "If you weave the seven locks of my hair" into the web of the loom, "then I will become weak and be like any other man" (verse 13). At this point, speaking about his hair, he was flirting around with his secret.

The Philistines failed once again to capture him, so the seductress really turned on the charm: "How can you say, 'I love you,' when your heart is not with me?" (verse 15). The demonic power encounter was now turned up to level ten. "It came about when she pressed him daily with her words and urged him, that his soul was annoyed to death" (verse 16). Beaten down, Samson finally spilled the beans. What difference did it make? He was still God's anointed. "He told her all that was in his heart" (verse 17), the secret to his strength.

Delilah lured him into her lap, lulled him to sleep and had a man shave off his seven locks of hair. Sure enough, they got their payoff: "His strength left him" (verse 19). When the Philistines came in to get him, Samson assumed he would shake them off as before. But he had played one time too many with the devil's fire. Listen to these ominous words of Scripture: "He did not know that the LORD had departed from him" (verse 20).

Captured by the enemy, Samson was tortured and his eyes were put out. Now he was just another backslidden, natural, tormented man. God's destiny had evaded him as he became a grinder in a Philistine prison. What a tragic state of affairs!

The Results of Losing Your Strength

The sad thing is, whole denominations, ministries, movements, congregations and individuals find themselves in the same state of affairs. All that remains is a mere skeleton and shadow of the authentic creation God called them to be. When wisdom is not the guardian of the anointing, drastic results may occur, as they did with Samson.

- He lost his hair, his strength, his joy—the loss of covering and protection.
- He lost his sight—the absence of prophetic revelation and vision.
- He lost his function, left to grind at the prison mill—the torment of lost destiny and purpose.

I have long since seen too much—everything from senior pastors running off with their secretaries; to flaming evangelists becoming beguiled by the "I-am-special" syndrome; to cultish exclusivity due to the pride of a supposed prophet's revelation. (You can add to the list.) Such lapses are expected in the world. The problem is, the worldly system is in the Church! Delilah and Jezebel run rampant, and we act as if we do not know what hit us.

Enough is enough! It is time for an authentic prophetic revolution. It is time to tell Delilah and her demonic hosts to pack their bags. It is time to learn wisdom from the past, to avoid the pointing of the judgmental finger, to cry out to God for a shift in society and history. It is time for a revolution that will restore the radical roots of the Church. It is time to wake up from sleeping in Delilah's lap and escape while we can. Oh, may a holy deliverance come forth to cleanse the bride of Christ!

The Mercy of God at Work

In the midst of it all, mercy was at work in Samson's life. "The hair of his head began to grow again after it was shaved off" (verse 22). Praise the Lord! Yes, I said, Praise the Lord! Thank the Lord for the recovery and restoration of any individual or ministry. Do whatever you can to help restore a fallen brother or sister (Galatians 6:1–3). Your attitude and response to his or her condition might just determine your own next level of grace, promotion or demotion. Together let's learn the lesson of crying out for wisdom, and for Jesus' sake let's fall out of agreement with the accuser of the brethren.

It isn't over till it's over. The Philistines, celebrating in the temple of Dagon, called for their prime-time prisoner to entertain them (Judges 16:25). Little did they know, he was no longer weak and bald. I think he had learned some lessons in his prison cell concerning the fear of the Lord, and about correctly handling the gifts of God.

"Samson called to the LORD and said, 'O Lord GOD, please remember me and please strengthen me just this time, O God, that I may at once be avenged of the Philistines for my two eyes'" (verse 28). His final act of power and ministry was fulfilled as he pulled on the two middle pillars, and the whole building came crashing down, crushing three thousand Philistine men and women—and Samson himself.

Yes, he was restored to his calling. But what a high price to pay, and what a poor way to end up—sacrificing his own life. Thank the Lord for His merciful heart, as Samson's strength returned, and along with it a measure of his purpose and calling. The Lord did triumph over His enemies.

Every individual, like Samson, has a special gift from God (1 Peter 4:10–11), a special way the supernatural presence of God works with and through him or her. But, like Samson, each gifted person also has an Achilles' heel or distinct place of vulnerability. Samson had Delilah; you have your weaknesses as well (1 Corinthians 10:13–14). But those places of weakness, when surrendered to the Lord, can become the very mechanisms that keep you in humility and connectedness with our Messiah. Your weakness will either become the place where the enemy beguiles you, or else the place where God's power is perfected in you. The choice is yours.

When Deception Settles In

I have seen it happen many times. So have you. A setup occurs in which individuals or groups begin to see themselves in an elitist category, an "I'm the exception to God's standards" line of thinking, what I call the Superman syndrome: "I am invincible!" You begin to think you can get away with things because you are right, better, holier or smarter than other people, even other spiritual leaders.

Deception trickles in when people draw up false equations of *why* they are anointed. "It's because we have the right doctrine" is a real killer. "God is vindicating the truth of our teaching!" There are elements of reality here; the Holy Spirit does bear witness to truth and does set a dramatic seal on a person's life. But when you think you deserve the anointing, that you earned this special grace, that special treatment is owed you as the man or woman of God, then self-justification has captured you, and deception is close at hand.

A veteran of 53 years of national prophetic and local church ministry, Ernest Gentile, adds some additional insight here: "When people are enthralled with prophetic ministry, it is easy to assume that a minister's odd traits (and doctrines!) are part of the anointing and revelation that God is restoring to the Church. This, of course, is not so. Also, a simple word from God can be embellished with additional supplemental, grandiose words that only serve to promote the messenger and not the Sender. These factors all dilute the simplicity that is in Christ and His gifts."[2]

Sexual Issues and the Anointing

Looking at this new subhead, you might be getting nervous and thinking I am treading on thin ice, that I should not be skating in this arena. Well, if we want a revolution to take place, somebody had better spell it out. So here we go. The following truths pertain to young and old, male and female, married and single.

Ministering in the anointing of the Holy Spirit is a real rush. You can become so caught up in the Spirit that everything natural temporarily fades into the background. Even natural, physiological desires and appetites seem to be put on pause. You are engaged with God. It is heavenly! The power is flowing. The divine intelligence of the Holy Spirit seems to be flying around the room, available for everyone to capture. His awesome presence is among us!

But when the ministry engagement is over, the anointing gradually wears off and you are left a hunk of flesh, just like the next person. It seemed as if you were changed into another person in the anointing, a very spiritual person, but now you are a physical creature altogether! Ouch! Fatigue, tiredness and appetites all come to visit. Sometimes loneliness hits people who are anointed by God, and times of greater vulnerability and spiritual warfare hit them after direct ministry engagement. Instead of those sexual appetites lessening, now they are building up. Apparently they were only put on hold.

You are in a hotel room, you flick on the TV and Ms. or Mr. Temptation happens to appear. You are tired. As a result of real-life issues and the deception finding a place, the enemy plants the thoughts in your mind of illicit activity as a "service" to the man or woman of God. A phone call comes . . . and thus the story goes, time and time again.

Wake up, brothers and sisters. This is a real, live war. No wonder Jesus sent His disciples out by twos!

The enemy has a set a trap for you, just as he did for Samson. Or maybe he is getting hooks into you through the Internet. Jezebel has weaseled her way onto the worldwide web, which today is one of the major nesting grounds of the enemy to ensnare teenagers, let alone adults. Help us, Jesus! A Trojan horse has been rolled into the Church and is releasing hordes from hell.

The Eye Gate

In his book *The Prophetic Ministry* Rick Joyner gives some good old-fashioned fatherly advice: "We can let either light or darkness into our soul through our eyes. If we are going to function as eyes for the Lord's body, we must give our eyes to Him, to be used only for His holy purposes. We must not let darkness into our soul through what we allow ourselves to look at. Lust is one of the primary destroyers of prophetic vision. Lust is selfishness in its basest form—the exact opposite of the nature of the Lord, whom we are seeking to emulate."[3]

The battle of passions is being waged on a different level than ever before. Catalog and newspaper ads from today's retail chains and department stores would have been considered pornographic in years past. We have lost our way in this glitzy society. We need an awakening to occur. If we in prophetic ministry are to be considered the eyes of the Body (Isaiah 29:10), then we must lead the way by calling for a cleansing of the eyes and a guarding of the eye gate. We need to make a covenant with our eyes so that our vision will be clear (Job 31:1; Luke 11:34).

When the Hand of God Is Lifted

A few years ago I was given a vivid, wisdom-filled dream in which I was shown three things that can occur when the hand of God is lifted off a man or woman. God's hand brings protection, covering, blessing and giftedness. But due to persistent sin, disobedience or other issues, God might lift His hand off a person for a season. This seems to be what happened with Samson, through sin: God's hand lifted and Samson was not aware of it. These are times of great testing. Run to God; He will help you.

In this dream I saw three things that will try to come and camp out at your doorstep if you do not run to Him:

1. The issue you have struggled with in private becomes more difficult, and it is sometimes revealed or exposed in public.
2. The thing you have feared in the past becomes drawn to you like a magnet.
3. The desire for former sinful habits (weaknesses, compulsions or obsessions) escalates.

Triumphs are now about to become tragedies.

After I woke up from this dream, the fear of the Lord came on me (may it also come on you!), and I cried out to the Lord, "O God, I am dependent on Your hand of protection. May Your hand never lift off me. May I never give You a reason that Your hand would have to lift off my life—for my family's sake and for Your holy name's sake. Help, Lord!"

I encourage you to lift a gut-level prayer and commit the conduct of your life to Him.

Exaltation and Worship of Human Vessels

I was given another stunning dream depicting plausible reasons for the failures of three major spiritual leaders from the heartland of America. Each of these charismatic leaders had had major followings regionally and nationally. Their real-life falls produced reverberations that are still being felt today. Each leader had a successful ministry. Each situation was distinctly different. But the enemy struck them in the place of their Achilles' heel. The problems, as depicted in my dream, centered around:

1. **Exaltation of position.** This resulted in the soulish manipulating, pushing and pressuring of others. The heart of a bully was more at work than the character of the Lamb! In contrast, we are to function for the purpose of servanthood. We wage war with a sword in the heavenlies but with a towel on earth.
2. **Exaltation of revelation.** This resulted from the profuse display of giftedness as people became addicted to getting "words," and the gifted one became addicted to the attention of giving words. No gift, as I have said, is to overshadow the main and plain devotion to the Scriptures. The revelatory is to complement, not compete with, the Word of God.
3. **Exaltation of interpretation.** This resulted in the elevation of one's personal interpretation as higher than that of others. Elitism crept in. Pride set in. Then new doctrines were formed out of the concept that these leaders were special—the elect ones! There is no private interpretation of Scripture. We must walk with others and avoid elitism and isolationism from the larger Body of Christ.

The Perils and Blessings of Weakness

Consider the following points as we continue down the path of learning some of the wisdom ways of God. A revelation of weakness can be used redemptively to save you from many perils.

- The anointing on a person can develop more rapidly than the character of that individual. But keep going. Gifts are given; fruit is grown.
- No one builds a tower unless he counts the cost (Luke 14:28).
- We say zealously at first, "Lord, I'm ready!" He will use us in that condition, but eventually to show us that we are *not* ready.
- Then we often say, "Lord, send someone else." *Now* we are ready, because we know we cannot do it in our own strength. Now the problem becomes getting us off our seats!

- We are typically ready first in our ability; then we become ready in *His* ability, out of the revelation of our weakness.
- "When I am weak, then I am strong" (2 Corinthians 12:10)
- "Most gladly, therefore, I will rather boast about my weaknesses, so that the power of Christ may dwell in me" (2 Corinthians 12:9)
- You start at *a*, *b* and *c* before you get to *x*, *y* and *z*. The foundational steps are the most important ones.
- Just as the process of childhood development and formation must not be speeded up, so discipleship and maturation take time—but they are worth the price.
- There are two kinds of ministries. Shooting stars are here today, burn out and are gone tomorrow. The north star is a fixed light that inspires over a lifetime. Joining *giftedness*, *character* and *wisdom*, all woven together, creates a three-cord strand that cannot be broken.

Let me close this portion of this pivotal chapter by quoting the awesome passage found in Joel 3:10: "Let the weak say, 'I am a mighty man.'" When our weaknesses are identified and brought to Him, He turns the power of weakness into a confounding and powerful weapon. His power is perfected in our weakness. We do not have to repeat the mistakes of previous moves of God. We can learn from the past and walk together as passionate, consecrated warriors called to a prophetic revolution. Yes, I am weak, but He is strong. Deception does not have to grip us. When we keep hold of God, and let Him keep a tight hold on us, the devil won't be able to get in edgewise!

Guidelines for Discernment

At certain times caution lights should be going off inside of you. The following paragraphs describe some such situations. Put these guidelines in place and they will help you in your discerning process.

- **Understand "second heaven revelation."** Different terms are used for this by different groups and individuals, but not everything you receive is a declaration of what is supposed to come to pass. It is possible that the Holy Spirit might give you insight into one of Satan's schemes or plans. (Paul said in 2 Corinthians 2:11 we are not to be ignorant of his schemes.) Regarding the term itself: Since Paul was transported into paradise, "the third heaven" (2 Corinthians 12:2), and since we may assume that the first heaven is the universe and sky over our heads, therefore "the second heaven" is considered by many to be Satan's likely place of residence. The term *second heaven revelation* refers to information that derives from the enemy's camp and is used to enlighten us, so as to prepare us or to cut off the event from taking place.

- **Be careful with your curiosity.** Is it the Holy Spirit leading you into this experience, or passion for Jesus, or could an enticing spirit be pulling on your curiosity? The fruit is distinctly different. With an enticing spirit you are left beaten up. By God's invitation you are left enlightened and empowered.

- **Give your revelation with gentleness.** Try brokenness. Hard confrontation is the exception, not the norm. Go through the standard procedures of first speaking, then exhorting, and only then reproving with all authority. This is according to the pattern of Titus 2:15 (see Galatians 6:1; 2 Timothy 2:23–26).

- **Realize that some words are conditional.** Some prophetic words are given without articulating the conditions. Remember Jonah's message to Nineveh, which was not destroyed in forty days. Behind every word of judgment stands a merciful God ready to forgive. And consider the example of Amos. He was given five visions of judgment, which were true revelatory experiences. Yet Amos' intercession blocked two of the five words from coming to pass—forty percent! Again, an example of a merciful God.

- **Wisdom shouts the fear of the Lord.** "The fear of the LORD is the beginning of wisdom" (Proverbs 9:10). Do not use revelation as a tool of punishment. The Holy Spirit said to me once, "Be careful not to stretch the rod of your mouth out against the house that the Lord builds."

- **Don't borrow and snatch!** Avoid using others' revelation as your own, as a means of gaining credibility. If necessary, ask another if you have permission to restate his or her word. When asked by others about another's word, stand secure and simply say, "I'm sorry, I don't know. You'll have to consult that person."
- **You can be tainted by an evil report.** You can become polluted by an evil report given to you by a person about another person under the guise of revelation. Numbers 13–14 are important chapters for us to read and learn today. Get washed in the blood of Jesus from the defilement of gossip and evil reports.
- **Be alert to the activity of the accuser of the brethren.** He tries to spew his filthy inspiration on believers (Revelation 12:10; see also Proverbs 10:18). "Be on the alert. Your adversary, the devil, prowls around like a roaring lion, seeking someone to devour" (1 Peter 5:8).
- **Don't cast aside your own relationship with God.** Even in the midst of high-level prophetic activity through others, you must hear God for yourself. Look to the lessons of 1 Kings 13. Don't let someone else hear for you; you must hear God for yourself first.

Five Big "No's"

A few issues are gray—shades of in-between, but some things are clearly black or white. Here are five big no-no's when it comes to issues that are hot to handle.

1. **Never replace hearing through others as a substitute for hearing for yourself.** You must hear the voice of the Holy Spirit yourself. Never let your hearing through others override your devotion to the Scriptures, to spiritual disciplines and to cultivating your own relationship with your heavenly Father (Exodus 20:5; 1 Kings 13). God is a jealous God. He wants you to spend time with Him. Keep to the basics.

2. **Never lift up the vessel who brings the word.** Lift up Jesus! Remember, the testimony of Jesus is the spirit of prophecy (Revelation 19:10). Let Jesus be the chief Prophet in our midst.

3. **Don't be naïve** (Proverbs 14:15). "Do not believe every spirit, but test the spirits to see whether they are from God" (1 John 4:1). Ask for the gift of discerning of spirits and test the source of the activity.

4. **Don't twist the meaning of a word.** Don't twist a prophetic word to comply with your desires, wishes, hidden agenda, mixed motives, timing or aspirations. Hold onto words with open expectancy, watching a supernatural God fulfill His words in an unexpected manner. Ask for His wisdom ways (Psalm 25:4; James 1:5).

5. **Don't quench the Holy Spirit.** 1 Thessalonians 5:19–21 warns us not to despise prophecy. Counterfeits and mixtures do occur, but don't be disillusioned. Believe God for His full restoration of the prophetic ministry. It is worth the journey.

Five Big "Yes, Sirs!"

We need to be positive, not problematic, in our approach. Let's round out this section out by spelling out five clear ways we must *always* respond to the anointing of God and the activity of the prophetic.

1. **Earnestly desire the gifts of the Holy Spirit, "especially that you may prophesy"** (1 Corinthians 14:1). Not only does God want to speak *to* you, but He wants to speak *through* you. Desire the gift of prophecy!

2. **Believe God's prophets and you will succeed.** 2 Chronicles 20:20 gives us 20–20 vision. Rejoice at the privilege you have been given! Mix faith with God's words and receive the Lord's results. But place your faith in the "God of the Word," not in the "man of the word."

3. **Pray the promise back to God.** Follow Daniel's example and remind God through intercession of His word (Daniel 9:1–19; Jeremiah 29:10). Bathe the prophetic invitation in prayer. (For further study see my book *Kneeling on the Promises.*)

4. **Fight the good fight** by using the spoken *rhema* word of prophecy as equipment for spiritual battle (1 Timothy 1:18). Do

spiritual warfare against discouragement, doubt, unbelief and fear through declaring and reciting prophecies made concerning you.

5. **Seek confirmation at all times.** Remember, out of the mouth of two or three witnesses every fact is to be confirmed and established (Deuteronomy 19:15; Matthew 18:16; 2 Corinthians 13:1).

Cherish the Anointing

You can trust the Holy Spirit. He is the one who anoints us and comes to make Jesus into a living reality. The Spirit is the gift of the Father sent to empower us to be victorious over the kingdom of darkness.

Some use our very real need to get wisdom—the subject of this section—as an excuse for not stepping out in faith. These folks will overly caution you, "Now, brother, you know others have fallen before!" But I want to encourage your heart and motivate you on to love and to good works. The enemy wants to magnify the mistakes of the past, as well as the weaknesses of others and ourselves, and turn them into tools of fear. But "God has not given us a spirit of timidity, but of power and love and discipline" (2 Timothy 1:7). Let's learn wisdom, but let's also get up and do some damage to the darkness in Jesus' name!

South African evangelist Rodney Howard Browne offered the following prophecy: "The great men and women of God that I am using in the earth today are not being used because they are something special. I am using them for one reason and one reason alone. It is because they've touched Me and I have touched them."[4] I say a loud *Amen* to that! We are His conduit in the earth to release the brilliance of His great presence. When we walk in the laws and wisdom of the Kingdom of God, His stuff is not too hot to handle. It is our right, our privilege and our mandate! So I lift a cry now and say with the thousands around the world, "More, Lord!"

Keys to Increasing in the Anointing

I want to increase the tangible "felt" stuff of God. Don't you? I want more sick healed, more dead raised, more lost saved and more fruit to offer to God in worship. Here are some *ABC's* to help us increase in the anointing.

Hang out with those who love the anointing. Watch, observe and learn from those who know these ways of the Lord. Build mentoring relationships and friendships with those more experienced than you. Carry someone's bag!

Get in the right environment. If you want to be prophetic, get in a place where the prophetic is flowing. If you want to move in healing, go get exposed to places where authentic healing is occurring. Some things are easier caught than taught.

Cultivate force-feeding yourself. What you eat, you become! Read books and testimonies of great women and men of God. Do word studies from the Scripture on the anointing, on the gifts of the Holy Spirit, on the power of God. Study the revivals of past Church history.

Sit in God's presence for an hour and drink in His love. Hunger and thirst for His presence more than anything else in this life. Soak in His manifested presence.

Be an avid worshiper at all times. In everything give thanks. Remember, God's address is spelled *p-r-a-i-s-e*. Worship Jesus!

Give away the little bit you have and you will get more. Give and it shall be given to you. Hold the little you have with your hands in your pockets and you will have empty pockets. Give away what you have and you will find multiple quantities of revelation, presence and power.

Never give up! Be persistent. Be faithful. The only losers are quitters! Faithfulness brings increase. It is a law of the Kingdom.

When it comes to meetings, I have found three basic elementary principles:

1 Seek the Lord beforehand.
2. Be attentive to Him during.
3. *Risk.* Step out as He gives you enough to get you moving, but just enough to keep you looking to Him.

These principles apply to more than just meetings, of course. Remember to color outside the lines.

Honor, Ask and Give Him Liberty

Here are three final admonitions for carrying that large, hot pan of His great anointing that is simmering on God's stove, so we can serve it up to a hungry world.

1. **Honor the Holy Spirit and make Him comfortable.** The Holy Spirit is God. Welcome and honor Him as more than just a special guest. He possesses the house! Acknowledge Him as the third Person of the Godhead, with His own distinct personality (John 16:13). Desire His presence. He does not tend to manifest Himself where He is not wanted. Hunger for Him and ask the Father to release more of His manifested presence. The Spirit's presence makes all the difference in the world!

2. **Ask for the anointing of the Spirit and ask our Father to equip you by Him** (Luke 7:7–10). He is our gift-distributor, our fruit-bearer, our convicter of sin, our heavenly Dove. Cherish the Dove. Woo Him and keep asking our Father for more of Him.

3. **When the Spirit shows up in His manifested presence, give Him freedom and liberty.** Let the Holy Spirit change your agenda. But whatever you do, yield to Him. Where the Spirit is moving, there will be freedom for the people (2 Corinthians 3:17). Let Him be in control.

Is the Holy Spirit too hot to handle? No! We just need to get out those lost mitts of wisdom, and then take what's cooking on the Father's stove and serve it up to the people. Let's learn to honor the Dove of God, ask for the gift of the Father and give Him liberty. He is God and wants to be in charge of His own house.

Our Intercessory Cry

Father, we cry out to You in Jesus' name that You will forgive us for treating Your tools as toys in past historic moves of Your Spirit. Reveal to each of us our Achilles' heel, and deliver us from any spirit of deception. Help us not be ignorant of the devil's schemes. Teach us wisdom so we can be good stewards of Your presence and power.

Give us more of Your Holy Spirit. Anoint us with encounters of a heavenly kind. Lead us into truth and Your Kingdom ways.

Give us mentors who will help to be eyes for us. Teach us how to handle the precious gifts of God, that others will see the real Jesus. In His precious name we pray. Amen.

POP QUIZ—KEEPING YOU ON YOUR TOES!

1. As you consider the life of Samson, where do you think he went wrong?
2. What are some of the misconceptions that can deceive people concerning the issues of handling the anointing?
3. What are some of the keys to walking in the anointing over the long term?

FOR MORE, LORD!

Mahesh Chavda, *Only Love Can Make a Miracle* (Ann Arbor, Mich.: Vine, 1990)

R. T. Kendall, *The Anointing* (London: Hodder & Stoughton, 1998)

Don Nori Sr., *The Power of Brokenness* (Shippensburg, Pa.: Destiny Image, 1997)

9

COMRADES
OR COMPETITORS?

The "school of the Spirit" and the "school of the Word" have often been at war with each other. This war within the ranks of the Church throughout history has caused numerous casualties and great separation within the Body of Christ. Today a clarion call is coming from the heart of the Father for the prophets and teachers to work together. When opposites attract, a new birth occurs. Let's list our own cry for healing and reconciliation to arise.

In this chapter we will examine some of the reasons for the misunderstandings that have led to unrest and animosity within the army of God. There is room for change and correction in both schools, and the Holy Spirit is well able to facilitate this retraining for every soldier with a willing heart. The Lord of hosts will not lead a dysfunctional army into battle!

Around five years ago I was given a dream that I have chewed like a cow with its cud ever since. In fact, when I was awakened from the dream, I sighed and heard myself say, "Now that would be a dream!" It was a dream that I want to see come into being with my very own eyes.

In my dream I was pointing to a leader and prophesying to him. These words were very clear: "It's time for the A-Team. It's time for the ATM. It's time for the authentic Apostolic Team Ministry to begin. It will be apostolic—authentic, abandoned Christianity. It will be telescopic—the prophets looking through the lens of time and the evangelists telling the Good News. It will be microscopic—the pastors and administrators caring for the flock of God."

As I awoke from the dream—which appeared to emphasize genuine relationship rather than structural authority—I was catapulted into an open vision in which I took a key card and inserted it into an ATM banking device. Cash started pouring out. A supply of finances beyond my dreams was now available.

As I pondered the vision, I realized that when two or three come into agreement (Matthew 18:19), they will use the ATM card of the Kingdom of God, asking in prayer for heavenly withdrawals from God's bank account to be released, in order to have ample supply to do whatever He wants done. The Apostolic Team Ministry would have an abundant supply to freely equip the Church, so that she in turn could do the work of ministry (Ephesians 4:11–13). Now that *would* be a dream!

As we understand the differences between the roles of revelatory gifting and of governmental leadership within the local church, we will learn to appreciate each role as equally vital and necessary to the health and soundness of the Body of Christ. There is only one Head and there is only one Body (with many parts) that serves the Head. We need one another in order to function and contribute fully as part of God's great army.

Let me emphasize, too, that when I speak of "government" in this chapter, I refer to the leadership within the local church, including the pastoral and apostolic ministries. I am not addressing the function of the prophetic in relationship to secular government. There is a great need for the prophetic to function in that arena, although at the present time only a few voices are skilled and ready to speak to government leaders. But they are arising! Maybe we have to get it right within the Church world first.

Foundational Principles

Some foundational principles will help us to make needed corrections, from a variety of angles, to prepare us to take our places in God's revolutionary army and to carry out His plan for reconciliation within the Body of Christ. First, some definitions by way of reminder:

The role of the prophetic is to stand in the council of God and then be an oracle or spokesman for Him. The prophetic part of the Body points the way, like a road sign, to the plan of God or to God Himself. *The roles of governmental leadership within the Church (pastoral, apostolic and eldership) is to steward designated resources and responsibilities for God.* They bring applications into being.

These giftings and ministries diverge by definition but not purpose. They are both serving God's purposes. Sometimes the prophetic and governmental leadership of the Church have seemed to be at opposite poles. It has appeared to the world, to the Church and even to the Lord that they want nothing to do with each other. But that is a dangerous relationship for these important members of the Body as they venture out onto the battlefield as part of the same army! We need a revolution of wisdom to honor one another, to cooperate together and to show one another mutual esteem.

Honor One Another

Jesus lives in each of us as believers, yet He does not give the whole meal deal to a single individual. That is why the Church is made up of *members* of the Body.

One individual may serve in a role (or grace) more proficiently than another, but never to the exclusion of that other person. Overgeneralization or simplistic stereotyping can prevent our getting the whole counsel of God. We must learn to honor and discern the Body of Christ in order to receive the fullness of Christ.

One of the most strategic issues is honoring the spiritual fathers and mothers among us—and grandfathers and grandmothers, also. The joining of the generations occurs as this is done. The older must, in turn, bless the younger generation, becoming their coaches and best cheerleaders. Investing and honoring are keys to a movement's being continual and progressive rather than stagnant.

Cooperate

All ministries, offices and gifts, which are given to build up the Body of Christ, should function cooperatively, not in opposition to one another. "To each one is given the manifestation of the Spirit for the common good" (1 Corinthians 12:7; see also 1 Corinthians 14:12; Ephesians 4:11–16; 2 Timothy 3:16–17; 2 Peter 1:19–21). Examine these to gain a better feel for the cooperative functioning of the Body.

God has the idea that we need each other. But do prophets and apostles also need each other?

Dr. Jack Deere, prominent theologian, became swept up in the things of the Holy Spirit during the so-called "third wave" of God's Spirit in the 1980s. Dr. Deere states, "If the gifts were lost in history, the most important question is not whether they were lost, but why they were lost. . . . It is possible that God never intended that these gifts should cease, but rather it is the church that has rejected the gifts. The loss of these gifts could be due to the rise of an ungifted bureaucratic leadership who put out gifted people."[1]

A prophetic veteran from Great Britain, Bryn Jones, brings additional wisdom on the cooperation between prophets and apostles:

> The apostle is primarily an architect, concerned with the overall design of the local church. The prophet, on the other hand, is first and foremost a seer, who sees beyond the present situation and brings the purposes of God into sharp focus. He has revelation of the mind of God. . . . The prophet is primarily concerned about keeping things moving, whereas the apostle tends to concentrate more on what is being built and how it is being achieved. . . . People sense that the apostle has an anointing that embraces God's purposes on a scale far wider than the immediate issues. They can respond to a prophet's inspiration for the immediate but they find security in an ongoing relationship with an apostle.[2]

Esteem One Another

Gifted individuals must find one another and operate in a context of mutual respect and esteem. Teaming with others is not only biblical, but it might just keep you from shipwreck! In recent years I have experienced great strength by associating with local, national and international councils in which mutual respect is a hallmark.

There is a saying that opposites attract. But in the Church that does not always ring true. Often the opposites repel each other and create great havoc. Consider magnets as an example. Each magnet has a positive and negative pole. When you put the opposite poles of two magnets together, one negative with one positive, they are attracted and form a bond. It can be hard to pull them apart! On the other hand, if you put two positive poles or two negative poles together, they will repel each other, causing the magnets to flip and flop all around each other. Not only is no bond formed, but there is a pushing and opposing action going on. Unfortunately, this is too often the way prophetic and governmental leaders in the Church have functioned. They have pushed each other's sensitive buttons and repelled one another, diminishing the effectiveness of both of these vital parts of the Body.

God's wants us to learn and appreciate the sensitivities of the gifting in each person and let His grace draw us together in the bond of love. By His wisdom and patience, we can learn how to move toward each other in mutual respect and esteem, and form a strong bond.

The Prophetic in Context of Leadership Community

Sometimes prophetic people put on eye masks and ride their horses in and out of town crying, "The Lone Ranger!" God has another idea.

What is the relationship of the prophetic and the community of believers to look like? Where does the prophetic gifting fit into the everyday lives of the Church community? To get an idea, let's ponder some Scripture.

> You are no longer strangers and aliens, but you are fellow citizens with the saints, and are of God's household, having been built on the foundation of the apostles and prophets, Christ Jesus Himself being the corner stone, in whom the whole building, being fitted together, is growing into a holy temple in the Lord, in whom you also are being built together into a dwelling of God in the Spirit.
>
> Ephesians 2:19–22

The Church is one house under one Head, Jesus, with delegated responsibilities and spheres of authority. Do you believe that? Jesus does the delegating, and appoints who He wants, where He wants.

From Outside the Camp . . .

The following prophecy exemplifies how the prophetic ministry and its relationship to the community of believers gets stereotyped:

> Hear this word which the LORD has spoken against you, sons of Israel, against the entire family which He brought up from the land of Egypt. . . . Hear this word, you cows of Bashan who are on the mountain of Samaria, who oppress the poor, who crush the needy, who say to your husbands, "Bring now, that we may drink!"
>
> Amos 3:1; 4:1

Many times in the Old Testament, the prophetic operated from a position of isolation and alienation. When Israel persisted in rebellion, the Lord raised up voices from outside the camp to speak with hard words meant to prick the hearts and consciences of the leadership and community, and bring them to repentance and back to obedience. This is the case with Amos.

Because of the alienation that occurs between the prophetically gifted and the community of believers as a whole, many still view the prophetic as a hard and critical ministry.

. . . To Inside the Camp

At other times in the Old Testament, and especially in the New Testament, God appointed voices from within the camp of believers to speak words that would bring encouragement and correction.

> The LORD stretched out His hand and touched my mouth, and the LORD said to me, "Behold, I have put My words in your mouth. See, I have appointed you this day over the nations and over the kingdoms, to pluck up and to break down, to destroy and to overthrow, to build and to plant."
>
> Jeremiah 1:9–10

Jeremiah was called while he was in his mother's womb. The Lord instructed him as he grew not to be afraid, even though he was a youth, but to go wherever He told him. Jeremiah often functioned from a place outside the camp, but God required him to deal with governmental leadership just the same.

Then there was Isaiah:

> The vision of Isaiah the son of Amoz concerning Judah and Jerusalem, which he saw during the reigns of Uzziah, Jotham, Ahaz and Hezekiah, kings of Judah.
>
> Isaiah 1:1

We mostly think of Isaiah as having a great revelatory understanding about the suffering Messiah. Recall, for example, Isaiah 53. But in this passage we see that the prophet had to deal with the potentially horrendous headaches of relating to four different rulers. Isaiah could not just drop the words God gave him like bombs and leave, never to return. When he spoke the death sentence over Hezekiah (2 Kings 20), he no sooner got out the door than the Lord made him turn around and revoke the sentence and speak life to him. What fun! (Have you ever had to eat your own words as your next meal? I have!)

Even if a prophetic person speaks from outside the local community of believers, he or she may still have to deal with governmental leadership in order to clear up any misunderstandings and confusion related to the prophetic words. Doesn't that sound glorious?! The point is, a relationship must be established in order for the prophetic ministry and the general community of believers to benefit from each other.

But the stereotype of the harsh prophetic voice is not the norm through which that gifting should function. We need some new lens to look through. Prophets are not anarchists fomenting rebellious revolution, but voices crying God's heart.

The Wedding of the Prophetic and the Governmental

The prophetic must minister through responsible relationships with the leaders and the community of believers at large. This should be the normal operating mode for the prophetic in the Body of Christ. But consider the prophetic voices of David, Joseph, Daniel and Nehemiah. They all functioned as governmental leaders themselves.

We have often looked at the very different graces of prophet and apostle and considered each of them one-sided. Elders and pastors often think the prophetic person is totally right-brained, with no aptitude for logical thought, while the revelatory-gifted ones may view those with governmental giftings as hopelessly left-brained, with no creativity or vision for the future. In a way each sees the other as half-witted! Need I say that God does not create half-wits— just opposites who need to learn how to dwell together?

Yes, there is a great diversity of gifts and functions. Ephesians 4:11–12 describes what is commonly known as the fivefold ministry: apostles, prophets, evangelists, pastors and teachers. According to Dr. Bill Hamon, these are "to minister to the saints for their equipping and maturing so that they can enter into the work of their membership ministry in the living, corporate Body of Christ." Dr. Hamon urges us to keep in mind five important insights, which relate to our discussion of the relationship between prophets and governmental leaders:

1. All fivefold ministries are headship ministries—that is, they are an extension of Jesus Christ, the Head of the Church.
2. All five are called to govern, guide, gather, ground and guard God's people; but each has been given special grace and gifted ability in one of these areas more than the others.
3. It is unscriptural and unwise to place any of these into a box of limited anointings and activities.
4. It is detrimental to the function of the fivefold ministries to categorize them with details concerning personalities, performances and positions.
5. Each fivefold minister knows best his or her own calling and ministry.[3]

The Lord wants the prophetic and the governmental to be wedded in purpose. When the two come together in the unity of the

Spirit, the whole counsel of God can be revealed, with both groups making a vital contribution to that wholeness.

At times these two graces are brought together in a unique package, even in the life of one person. Here are a few scriptural examples.

Abraham: The Pilgrim of Faith

In the following passage Abraham (at that time Abram) was given a wonderful prophetic encounter:

> The LORD said to Abram, "Go forth from your country, and from your relatives and from your father's house, to the land which I will show you; and I will make you a great nation, and I will bless you, and make your name great; and so you shall be a blessing; and I will bless those who bless you, and the one who curses you I will curse. And in you all the families of the earth will be blessed."
>
> Genesis 12:1–3

Through this prophetic revelation, Abraham learned he was to become the leader of an entire people. Did you realize he was a military leader as well?

> When Abram heard that his relative had been taken captive, he led out his trained men, born in his house, three hundred and eighteen, and went in pursuit as far as Dan. He divided his forces against them by night, he and his servants, and defeated them, and pursued them as far as Hobah, which is north of Damascus. He brought back all the goods, and also brought back his relative Lot with his possessions, and also the women, and the people.
>
> Genesis 14:14–16

So Abraham was given prophetic revelation, he had a gift of leadership and he was a military leader as well. And we can see through the following incredible, powerful and visionary experience of Abraham's that he was definitely a prophetic person:

> When the sun was going down, a deep sleep fell upon Abram; and behold, terror and great darkness fell upon him. God said to Abram, "Know for certain that your descendants will be strangers in a land

that is not theirs, where they will be enslaved and oppressed four hundred years. . . . It came about when the sun had set, that it was very dark, and behold, there appeared a smoking oven and a flaming torch which passed between these pieces [of Abram's sacrifices]. On that day the LORD made a covenant with Abram, saying, "To your descendants I have given this land, from the river of Egypt as far as the great river, the river Euphrates. . . ."

Genesis 15:12–13, 17–18

As a prophet, a leader of people and a successful military leader, Abraham is a beautiful example of the wedding of the prophetic and governmental graces, resulting in the whole counsel of God.

Moses: The Law and the Prophet

"The LORD your God will raise up for you a prophet like me from among you, from your countrymen, you shall listen to him."

Deuteronomy 18:15

In this verse Moses was speaking to the people under the prophetic unction of the Spirit of God, who was calling him a prophet. But was Moses governmental? Let's see:

It came about the next day that Moses sat to judge the people, and the people stood about Moses from the morning until the evening. Now when Moses' father-in-law saw all that he was doing for the people, he said, "What is this thing that you are doing for the people? Why do you alone sit as judge and all the people stand about you from morning until evening?" Moses said to his father-in-law, "Because the people come to me to inquire of God. When they have a dispute, it comes to me, and I judge between a man and his neighbor and make known the statutes of God and His laws." Moses' father-in law said to him, "The thing that you are doing is not good."

Exodus 18:13–17

Was Moses governmental? Absolutely. He was acting as judge and interpreter of the laws of God. In order to do that, he had to have studied the Law that God had given him. But he did have a prophetic propensity to try to do his job alone. He was wearing himself out and his father-in-law came to the rescue, suggesting a plan for him to use the gifts in others to help him in the task.

God sent him help because it was not good for Moses to be a lone ranger. He needed help and more time to hear from the Lord so he could prophetically point the way for those wandering children of Israel. He had to learn how to go in and go out before God and before the people.

We can see from this story that Moses, far from being a half-witted prophet *or* pastor, was an example of the marrying of the prophetic and the government graces of God in one package.

David: The Prophet King

> The LORD says to my Lord: "Sit at My right hand until I make Your enemies a footstool for Your feet."
>
> Psalm 110:1

David was given this great revelation (and many others) of the ruling and reigning authority of the coming King. Now we know David was a king, so he was definitely governmental. He was also a bit "artsy" as he sang and wrote songs. But was he prophetic? If there is any doubt, listen to this New Testament perspective:

> Peter stood up in the midst of the brethren (a gathering of about one hundred and twenty persons was there together), and said, "Brethren, the Scripture had to be fulfilled, which *the Holy Spirit foretold by the mouth of David* concerning Judas, who became a guide to those who arrested Jesus."
>
> Acts 1:15–16, emphasis added

Can you see it? *The Holy Spirit foretold by the mouth of David.* This king had a prophetic grace, too. Peter continued:

> "For David says of [Jesus], 'I saw the LORD always in my presence; for He is at my right hand, so that I will not be shaken. Therefore my heart was glad and my tongue exulted; moreover my flesh also will live in hope; because You will not abandon my soul to Hades, nor allow Your Holy One to undergo decay. You have made known to me the ways of life; You will make me full of gladness with Your pres-

ence.' Brethren, I may confidently say to you regarding the patriarch David that he both died and was buried, and his tomb is with us to this day. And so, because he was a prophet and knew that God had sworn to him with an oath to seat one of his descendants on his throne, he looked ahead and spoke of the resurrection of the Christ, that He was neither abandoned to Hades, nor did His flesh suffer decay."

Acts 2:25–31

Wow! This whole second chapter of Acts is full of prophetic revelation. Another governmental person—a king!—was also a prophet and received prophetic revelation. Peter declared this phenomenon loudly to all of Jerusalem on the glorious Day of Pentecost by the unction and power of the Holy Spirit. This passage is a hammer smashing all our stereotypes and misconceptions concerning these two wonderful gifts that God has created.

Paul: Revelatory Teacher and Apostle

There were at Antioch, in the church that was there, prophets and teachers: Barnabas, and Simeon who was called Niger, and Lucius of Cyrene, and Manaen who had been brought up with Herod the tetrarch, and Saul. While they were ministering to the Lord and fasting, the Holy Spirit said, "Set apart for Me Barnabas and Saul for the work to which I have called them." Then, when they had fasted and prayed and laid their hands on them, they sent them away.

Acts 13:1–3

In this New Testament example of the wedding of the prophetic and governmental graces, we read about a gathering of both prophets and teachers—a bunch of righties and lefties all in the same room. They were actually fasting and praying together. I love it! Then they laid hands on Barnabas and Saul and sent them out.

We know Saul had probably been leaning toward the teacher gift because he was a student of the Law, although he hung out with prophets. After this ordination service, however, his grace package was expanded to include apostolic gifting.

So these graces can be expanded within a single person. Because Paul was associated with prophetic types, he gained an understanding of the prophetic. And, likewise, prophets can learn systematic theology from teachers with whom they are associated. That is the wonderfully efficient economy of God—bringing gifts and graces together to aid and learn from each other.

> Boasting is necessary, though it is not profitable; but I will go on to visions and revelations of the Lord. I know a man in Christ who fourteen years ago—whether in the body I do not know, or out of the body I do not know, God knows—such a man was caught up to the third heaven. And I know how such a man—whether in the body or apart from the body I do not know, God knows—was caught up into Paradise and heard inexpressible words, which a man is not permitted to speak.
>
> 2 Corinthians 12:1–4

Paul was probably speaking of himself here but, not wanting to bring attention to himself, left out his name. But he had experienced a prophetic revelation of great magnitude. A few verses later he stated:

> I have become foolish; you yourselves compelled me. Actually I should have been commended by you, for in no respect was I inferior to the most eminent apostles, even though I am a nobody. The signs of a true apostle were performed among you with all perseverance, by signs and wonders and miracles.
>
> verses 11–12

Paul was well aware of the apostolic or governmental graces resident within him, but he also experienced tremendous prophetic revelation. Again God married the prophetic with the governmental.

Peter: The Prophetic Apostle

We can see clearly Peter's apostolic, governmental gift:

> Simon Peter, a bond-servant and apostle of Jesus Christ, to those who have received a faith of the same kind as ours, by the righteousness of our God and Savior, Jesus Christ.
>
> 2 Peter 1:1

Peter identified himself clearly as an apostle, which is a governmental grace. He was a church planter and worked with leaders. But did he have a revelatory gift?

> So we have the prophetic word made more sure, to which you do well to pay attention as to a lamp shining in a dark place, until the day dawns and the morning star arises in your hearts. But know this first of all, that no prophecy of Scripture is a matter of one's own interpretation, for no prophecy was ever made by an act of human will, but men moved by the Holy Spirit spoke from God.
>
> 2 Peter 1:19–21

I would say, at the very least, that Peter had a deep understanding of the prophetic and how it functioned. In verse 21 he gives one of the best descriptions of how a prophetic gift works within a person that we have available in Scripture. So was he prophetic? Very possibly, because he had a profound appreciation for and understanding of the function of the prophetic protocol and its appropriate operation.

John: The Seer Lover

> The Revelation of Jesus Christ, which God gave Him to show to his bond-servants, the things which must soon take place; and He sent and communicated it by His angel to His bond-servant John, who testified to the word of God and to the testimony of Jesus Christ, even to all that he saw. Blessed is he who reads and those who hear the words of the prophecy, and heed the things which are written in it; for the time is near.
>
> Revelation 1:1–3

The great Revelation of Jesus was given to John the beloved, the man who leaned on Jesus' bosom and had the most intimate relationship with Him of all the disciples. John was an apostle, but boy, was he ever gifted with revelatory grace! Not only was he prophetic; he also had the gift of a prophetic seer. God gave the entire book of Revelation to him through an angel.

So John was an apostolic person granted entrance into the incredible seer realm. Not only did he hear and repeat the words that he heard, but this apostolic, governmental man was enveloped with the seer (prophetic) gift.

Through these examples from the Old and New Testaments, we can see God's great design to wed the prophetic and the governmental graces within His Church. His Word has given us a wonderful vision to work toward as we press on in this prophetic revolution.

Contrasting the Prophetic and the Governmental

Before I wear you out, let's go on now to contrasting these two gifts. Remember that the purpose of both of these grace packages, the prophetic and the governmental, is for charging up the batteries of the everyday believer. Let's look at the contrasting strengths found in each gift as tools we might use on a building site. The tools are quite different in function, but are used together to facilitate the construction of the building. Different grace tools are also used in different seasons or stages of the building process. (The contrasts here are generalized and not true in every instance.)

Prophetic	Governmental
subjective	objective
emotional	structural
more itinerant	more residential
functional	relational
intuitive	logical
idealistic	practical
spontaneous	premeditative
personal	corporate
inspirational	informative
creative	managerial

Here are some Scriptures to explore that will shed more light on these contrasts: Matthew 16:3–19; Acts 20:17–38; 21:8–11; 2 Peter 1:19–21.

Here are more contrasts:

- The prophetic role is to hear the instruction of God.
- The governmental role is to be accountable for the instruction of God.

- Without the prophetic, people become institutional without life.
- Without the governmental, everyone does "what [is] right in his own eyes" (Judges 21:25).

Revelation without application means there is no receptacle present to contain and hold the revelatory content. Without a fresh wineskin, the new wine just spills onto the floor (Matthew 9:17).

Understanding the contrasts between the prophetic and governmental graces can give us new appreciation for the necessity to become comrades and not competitors in this prophetic revolution. Help, Lord, we need each other!

The Cracked Pots at Antioch

In gazing at this complex subject of comrades or competitors, let's take a closer look at a familiar Scripture about a meeting of first-century leaders at Antioch. As we ponder, chew and digest these verses, we will find a gold mine at our fingertips just waiting to be excavated.

> There were at Antioch, in the church that was there, prophets and teachers: Barnabas, and Simeon who was called Niger, and Lucius of Cyrene, and Manaen who had been brought up with Herod the tetrarch, and Saul. While they were ministering to the Lord and fasting, the Holy Spirit said, "Set apart for Me Barnabas and Saul for the work to which I have called them." Then, when they had fasted and prayed and laid their hands on them, they sent them away.
>
> Acts 13:1–3

Who Were These Guys, Anyway?

For a moment I want to peer behind the scenes at these guys who got thrown together in this Antioch leadership prayer and fasting summit. You will be surprised at what we find.

BARNABAS, A MESSIANIC JEWISH PROPHET FROM CYPRUS

You say, "What did you say?" Yep, that's right! According to Acts 4:36, Barnabas' original name was Joseph. He was a Levite (that means he was a Jewish man preparing for the priesthood) who came from the island of Cyprus and met Jesus as his Messiah. The apostles called him Barnabas, which means "son of encouragement, exhortation or consolation." So here we have an islander Jew studying for the Levitical priesthood who met Jesus and became a messianic prophet.

SIMEON, A BLACK MAN

Next we find a convert named Niger. This term means "black man." Now imagine, we have a Jewish prophet and a black man whose national identity is not clearly revealed. But he was probably African, maybe Ethiopian. Interesting mix already!

LUCIUS, A LIBYAN ARAB?

Lucius came to this summit from Cyrene, which was probably modern-day Libya. We do not know for sure, but Lucius could have been Arab in descent, coming from that part of northern Africa. Now this is starting to get volatile—a Jew, a black man and a north African, possibly an Arab. There was probably a whole lot of iron sharpening iron (Proverbs 27:17) going on behind the scenes!

MANAEN, THE GREEK ARISTOCRAT

The name *Manaen* is Greek in origin. The text also says Manaen grew up with Herod the ruler—the king who imprisoned John the Baptist and later beheaded him (Matthew 14:1–12). So Manaen, as a Greek aristocrat, had grown up with a whole different educational and philosophical worldview. Talk about opposites being brought together!

SAUL, THE PERSECUTOR CONVERT FROM TARSUS

All the Acts passage says in identifying this man is "Saul." But by now all Luke's readers knew what this man had done—persecuted the Church, dragged men and women off to prison, carried out death threats. Was his zeal ever misdirected! We also know that Saul came from Tarsus, which would be in modern Turkey. Barnabas went on a mission to search out this revolutionary convert and bring him to Antioch to convene with the other leaders (Acts 11:19–26).

How Could They Get Along?

Talk about a cat fight—they could have been scratching one another's eyeballs out! After all, they were clay, cracked pots just like you and me. They might still have been carrying some of the extra baggage that came with all of their ethnic, cultural, religious, political, philosophical, educational, preconceived, prideful, prejudicial thinking. In fact, I am sure of it. I think they were excited about this historic summit and probably more than a bit apprehensive at the same time. How could they get along? Would they be comrades or competitors?

Realize, too, that the Scriptures indicate these five men even came with opposite giftings. Two or three of them were teachers and the other two or three were noted prophets. From my experience, that alone was a miracle, since it is extraordinary for prophets and teachers to complement, bless, honor and esteem one another. God had His work cut out for Him! They had their work cut out for themselves, too.

Chew on it a little more. What would they eat? When they played instruments, what ethnic style dominated? When they danced, did they do the Hebrew Horah together? It would have been complicated. I am positive there was some reconciliation ministry that went on in this leadership summit. What was the unifying factor?

The Cord That Binds Us Together

The Lord Himself was the unifying factor in the leadership meeting at Antioch. Follow with me on eight little points that turned potential chaos into a time of cooperation.

1. They celebrated their *diversification in unity* instead of *conformity of uniformity.*
2. They ministered to the Lord. This became the unifying factor. Everything else fades in the background when we center on Him.
3. Opposites attracted (school of the Spirit and school of the Word) and a new birth occurred: The ATM came into being!

4. They emphasized fasting as a lifestyle, not just as an issue of crisis intervention. They knew that sacrifice releases power.

5. The Holy Spirit moved in their midst with liberty to such an extent that the Scriptures record no nametags put on the prophecies. Awesome!

6. The jealousy of God came in their midst and God told them to "set apart for Me Barnabas and Saul." They had their priorities straight and gave Him first place.

7. After fresh consecration to the Lord first, then Barnabas and Saul gave themselves to "the work to which I have called them." They got the horse ahead of the cart, as it should be. It is not as much work when He is pulling the load!

8. Without competition, jealousy or strife, they laid hands on them with prayer and fasting and sent Barnabas and Saul on their missionary journey. After this point Saul was now called Paul (Acts 13:9) and they were referred to as the apostolic team.

That's Worth Dying For!

That is the kind of prophetic revolution we need to take place in the Body of the Messiah. Isn't it interesting that, according to Acts 11:26, it was in Antioch that the disciples were first called Christians? Such unity and testimony are worth praying for, fighting for and living for. And even more importantly, worth dying for!

Authentic, apostolic Christianity is being birthed in the Church once again. A call is going out for passionate, consecrated warriors. Will you answer the call?

OUR INTERCESSORY CRY

Father, for Jesus Christ's sake, we lift the cry to You that You would change the understanding and expression of Christianity across the earth in this generation. We want Jesus to receive the rewards of His suffering. We want to be ministers unto our Lord and His Christ.

Forgive us for our petty competition and help us see one another as You see us. Teach us that unity is the celebration of diversity under Your Lordship. Teach us new ways. Deliver us from our fears of one another, in Jesus' name. May we become such comrades in love, preferring one another, that the world will look on us and say, "Now there's a real Christian!" We pray this for the honor and glory of Jesus' great name in the earth. Amen.

POP QUIZ—KEEPING YOU ON YOUR TOES!

1. From your understanding, what transpired according to Acts 13:1–3?
2. What occurs when opposites attract?
3. In your life and ministry, how do you wed the "school of the Spirit" and the "school of the Word"?

FOR MORE, LORD!

Jack Deere, *Surprised by the Power of the Spirit* (Grand Rapids: Zondervan, 1993)

Ernest B. Gentile, *Your Sons and Your Daughters Shall Prophesy* (Grand Rapids: Chosen, 1999)

Eddie and Alice Smith, *Intercessors and Pastors* (Houston: SpiriTruth, 2000)

THE REVOLUTIONARY VISION

SETUP

John's Testimony of Jesus

> I fell at his feet to worship him. But he said to me, "Do not do that; I am a fellow servant of yours and your brethren who hold the testimony of Jesus; worship God. For the testimony of Jesus is the spirit of prophecy."
>
> Revelation 19:10

Reflect with me for a moment on the prophetic journey we have taken together. We have found this man named John who, as a "son of thunder," zealously wants to call down fire on others. He is changed as he learns to lean his head on the chest of his Beloved. This son of Zebedee becomes a messenger, not just a hotshot with a big gun ready to pop off whenever he gets an itchy finger. This same John, the beloved, becomes the friend of God. He is the only disciple of the original Twelve mentioned at the cross of our Lord Jesus Christ. He learns to walk the talk.

Then, as an aged man, exiled in solitude on the Isle of Patmos, John seems to have nothing left in his life. He is abandoned by men—but not by God. Not at all by God and His brilliant presence! God is now his constant companion.

First John 1:1 wonderfully states, "What was from the beginning, what we have heard, what we have seen with our eyes, what we have looked at and touched with our hands, concerning the Word of Life. . . ." Is this the same man? How did this transformation take place? The motivation seems different; the focus of the message is distinctly changed. This man is not talking about calling down judgment. He is not just teaching about gifts and ministries. He is speaking about a life consumed by the Person of God Himself.

In the midst of all of this, he gives us a revolutionary concept concerning the central issue of what authentic prophetic ministry is all about: *Worship God!* Worship God, and you will be walking in the opposite spirit from that of this world. And as you worship God, someone—no, the great Someone—will inhabit your praises, and the Holy Spirit's revelatory presence will be poured out. Yes, the true heart of the prophetic is the testimony not of how great you are, but of how awesome He is! The testimony of Jesus is the spirit of prophecy.

Do you want to become a true messenger of the Lord with fire burning in your bones? Then have the Man of fire dwelling in your heart. Abandon any attempts to build your own kingdom or ministry. Forget about building your own empire; build His instead. Worship God passionately. Consecrate yourself to Him to be His holy dwelling place.

This closing Track 4 is a passionate call for "The Revolutionary Vision" to come forth. What could that type of vision include? Instead of being competitors, we will now walk with others. Instead of having tunnel vision on what *our* callings alone might be, we want to help brothers and sisters seize their prophetic destinies. And then—oh yes, then, our of our own lives of worship, we will qualify to prophesy life to dry places, dry people and dry nations.

John, the "Son of Thunder," was changed. John the fisherman became a wisdom spout for the purposes of God. He taught people how to forgive, how to love, how to cover one another. In fact, his last writing is not as much a scenario of end-times cataclysmic things as it is a profound epistle concerning the revelation of Jesus Christ Himself.

Do you want to see an authentic prophetic revolution? Then worship God. Like John on the Isle of Patmos, speak of this wonderful Man, Christ Jesus. Let the holy revolution begin!

10

LET'S DO IT TOGETHER

In those days there was no king in Israel; everyone did what was right in his own eyes.

Judges 21:25

As we start the fourth and last track of our journey together, "The Revolutionary Vision," we gaze into the future with faith, hope and love that a new order will emerge. We will look at the vision of a revolutionary apostolic and prophetic Church arising in this new millennium. The vision is cast of diverse ministries in cooperation with one another.

As we see in the above verse from Judges, when there is no king or government in place, people are separated from one another by their own judgments of right and wrong. There are no guidelines for godly living. During those days in Israel's history, God raised up men and women from among the populace to serve as leaders, "judges," during times of chaos and unrest. It was during those times that unlikely leaders such as Gideon and Deborah came to the forefront to speak forth God's intent and bring His order to a disorderly people. Likewise, in the days ahead, God is going to use unlikely people in both prophetic and apostolic roles to facilitate a revolution in the Church that will usher in a powerful move of His Spirit on the earth. Let His glory fall!

My friend Tommy Tenney has some timeless words of wisdom that pound into us like well-driven nails:

> Nothing disheartens me more than the lack of unity and the prevalence of division in the church. It is enough to break my heart, and I am just a brother. It has already broken the Father's heart.
>
> The "game" being played out in the world today has high stakes for the church—the lost souls of men and women—and our "Coach" is calling us to act together in unity to win those souls for Him. Only when we become "one" and act in unity as Jesus prayed will we prove to be unstoppable, unbeatable and relentless in bringing down the gates of hell.
>
> It is time the one unanswered prayer of Jesus Christ—when He prayed that we become one—be answered by the church—God's Dream Team.[1]

We as God's people must cooperate, therefore, so we can move swiftly in response to His call. We must hum together like the parts of a well-tuned engine as He prepares our hearts and minds to overpower the kingdom of darkness with the light of His love.

We saw in the previous chapter that the prophetic and governmental roles, although they are quite different, complement each other. The prophetic role is to *hear* the instruction of God, and the governmental role is to *implement* that instruction. These roles represent a variety of gifts and ministry operations. Like facets of a diamond, they are different sides of the same sparkling gem. Now, in this new track on revolutionary vision—building on the wisdom we discussed in the last chapter—let's see how the prophetic and the governmental can cooperate in this great revolution.

Cooperation Brings Implementation

These two diverse roles are designed to act in harmony. "If two of you agree on earth about anything that they may ask, it shall be done for them by My Father who is in heaven" (Matthew 18:19). Harmony between the prophetic and the governmental will bring God's blessing and will to earth. What a marvel it will be to have pastors, teachers, administrators, elders, evangelists, visionary leaders and prophets all working together and creating concerts of God's will throughout the earth! Then true equipping will take place, and God's anointed men and women will make a profound impact for the Kingdom.

The prophetic and governmental ultimately serve the same purpose of God. These graces should work in unison, playing the same melody, and may even reside in and operate through the same person. But in reality, the way we often come into functional agreement is through conflict. Again, iron sharpens iron (Proverbs 27:17). This synchronizing of roles takes time, patience and numerous experiences of initial disagreement before the two are harmonized.

Presently the Church sounds like an orchestra warming up before a performance. Each instrument is practicing its skills apart from the others. I hope by the grace of God that we will come together soon under the divine Conductor and perform an incredible symphony that will electrify the world and glorify our King.

The people of God must move forward on two tracks running parallel to one another in order to ensure success and safety:

- *The revealed will of God* (guidance and revelation) is the prophetic track. Those on this track hear the word of God and present it with grace and humility so the whole Body can benefit from the revelation.
- *The cooperative response to the revealed will of God* is the governmental track. Those on this track receive the revealed word with grace and humility and, through prayer and skilled administration, bring a sound application of that word to the whole Body.

There must be cooperation between these two gifts so there can be implementation of God's guidance and revelation. First comes the revelation, then the processing of the revelation, and finally the application of the revelation. All the various giftings should work together cooperatively to produce forward motion in the life of the Church.

Unity and Progress

Neither unity nor progress can be achieved without the true knowledge of God's will. If some puffed-up, fantasy-type word comes forth and we run with it, we may end up in shipwreck because such a word cannot produce God's will. Without a true knowledge of His will clearly in place, we cannot become unified, nor will we make any noticeable progress.

Let's look at some Scriptures to see how this principle operates.

> In the second year of Darius the king, on the first day of the sixth month, the word of the LORD came by the prophet Haggai to Zerubbabel the son of Shealtiel, governor of Judah, and to Joshua the son of Jehozadak, the high priest, saying. . . .
>
> Haggai 1:1

Notice the action between the prophetic and the governmental in this passage. It is an Old Testament example of team ministry cooperation among the three offices of prophet (Haggai), priest (Joshua) and king (Zerubbabel).

> "Thus says the LORD of hosts, 'This people says, "The time has not come, even the time for the house of the Lord to be rebuilt."'" Then the word of the LORD came by Haggai the prophet, saying, "Is it time for you yourselves to dwell in your paneled houses while this house lies desolate?" Now therefore, thus says the LORD of hosts, "Consider your ways! You have sown much, but harvest little; you eat, but there is not enough to be satisfied; you drink, but there is not enough to become drunk; you put on clothing, but no one is warm enough; and he who earns, earns wages to put into a purse with holes." Thus says the LORD of hosts, "Consider your ways! Go up to the mountains, bring wood and rebuild the temple, that I may be pleased with it and be glorified," says the LORD.
>
> verses 2–8

This is a case of the people saying one thing and the Lord, coming to judge their hearts, saying something very different. God was admonishing them to "look at the condition of My house!" It was time to rise up, He said, even when they did not think it was the right time. The *true* will of the Lord came forth to dispel the *perceived* will of God in their minds. And when the true word came, it released an appropriate action:

> So the LORD stirred up the spirit of Zerubbabel the son of Shealtiel, governor of Judah, and the spirit of Joshua the son of Jehozadak, the high priest, and the spirit of all the remnant of the people; and they came and worked on the house of the LORD of hosts, their God.
>
> verse 14

The Holy Spirit stirred everyone up from leaders to lay people. They came together in unity and made progress.

Now I want to speak a word of appeal on this subject to prophetic types. In the past I have been a pastor as well as an itinerant prophetic speaker. I have been on both sides, prophetic and governmental. I have suffered wounds caused by both sides. Prophetic people must not come into a congregation or group, shoot off their guns and then leave the pastor with a bunch of wounded, bleeding people. The prophetically gifted must be sensitive to pastors and the problems they face within their bodies of believers. Prophetic words must come forth in a way that will encourage groups and congregations to heed the will of God and make changes, if needed. Prophetic types must not run off and leave the leaders without making sure that the word was presented with grace and humility, and that it was received in the same way.

In this word from Haggai, true correction came forth, but also instruction that encouraged the people to change their previous mindset and take hold of the vision to build. Every person, from the governor and high priest right on down to the remnant of the people, was stirred up and encouraged. Everyone took hold of the vision, because life was prophesied, not just the knowledge of their error.

A real prophetic word has the potential of releasing an impartation of encouragement to motivate people to life. "Surely the Lord GOD does nothing unless He reveals His secret counsel to His servants the prophets" (Amos 3:7).

Unity Outside God's Will

It is possible for unity to occur *outside* the will of God even when the true will of God has come forth—and this is not good. 1 Kings 22 is a complicated chapter that I don't completely understand, but I want to share some things in it that warrant our attention.

> Three years passed without war between Aram and Israel. In the third year Jehoshaphat the king of Judah came down to the king of Israel. Now the king of Israel said to his servants, "Do you know that Ramoth-gilead belongs to us, and we are still doing nothing to take it out of the hand of the king of Aram?" And he said to Jehoshaphat, "Will you go with me to battle at Ramoth-gilead?" And Jehoshaphat said to the king of Israel, "I am as you are, my people as your people, my horses as your horses." Moreover, Jehoshaphat said to the king of Israel, "Please inquire first for the word of the LORD."
> Then the king of Israel gathered the prophets together, about four hundred men, and said to them, "Shall I go against Ramoth-gilead to battle or shall I refrain?" And they said, "Go up, for the LORD will give it into the hand of the king." But Jehoshaphat said, "Is there not yet a prophet of the LORD here that we may inquire of him?"
>
> 1 Kings 22:1–7

Some interesting dynamics are taking place here. The kings of Judah and Israel have come together in unity to seek the Lord about making war on Syria to take back the territory of Ramoth-gilead. But King Jehoshaphat wants the king of Israel to "inquire first for the word of the LORD." Now does that mean pray and seek the Lord, or is Jehoshaphat asking him to get a directive word from a prophet? It is not clearly stated, but in any case there is no prayer going on here. So the king of Israel gathers up four hundred prophets (that's a bunch of prophets!)—and guess what? They all agree that Israel and Judah should go up to battle, and that the Lord "will give it into the hand of the king."

But Jehoshaphat is not sure about this word. Maybe he thinks all these four hundred prophets are just "yes men" to the king of Israel. He asks if there is another prophet available.

Let me insert a recommendation to pastoral and apostolic leaders: Don't be intimidated by the prophetic. If a particular prophetic word does not sit just right with you, pay attention. It is always good to check things out with God. A word of instruction or admonition must ring true with you in order for you to implement the word successfully for the people. Unity can be made outside the will of God, but it will not result in the right kind of progress. Sometimes we think we know what the will of God is, but zeal without wisdom can cause us to proceed in the wrong direction.

So we see King Jehoshaphat seeking more confirmation from God about the agreement to go to war.

> The king of Israel said to Jehoshaphat, "There is yet one man by whom we may inquire of the LORD, but I hate him, because he does not prophesy good concerning me, but evil. He is Micaiah son of Imlah." But Jehoshaphat said, "Let not the king say so." Then the king of Israel called an officer and said, "Bring quickly Micaiah son of Imlah." Now the king of Israel and Jehoshaphat king of Judah were sitting each on his throne, arrayed in their robes, at the threshing floor at the entrance of the gate of Samaria; and all the prophets were prophesying before them. . . .
>
> When he came to the king, the king said to him, "Micaiah, shall we go to Ramoth-gilead to battle, or shall we refrain?" And he answered him, "Go up and succeed, and the LORD will give it into the hand of the king."
>
> verses 8–10, 15

Things are looking pretty good here as the four hundred prophets are putting out these words before the two kings on their thrones, arrayed in all their finery. The words keep confirming that Israel and Judah should go to war.

What Is God's True Word?

Then Micaiah comes in—the prophet who usually says things the king of Israel does not like. At first he confirms the other prophetic words. Perhaps Micaiah is tired of being the only one who puts out disagreeable words, and he has decided to go along with the crowd. Micaiah wants to be accepted, and he acts accordingly. That is a familiar pitfall for prophets. Good governmental

leaders can pick up on that and bring some correction. The king of
Israel does just that as he addresses Micaiah:

> "How many times must I adjure you to speak to me nothing but
> the truth in the name of the LORD?" So [Micaiah] said, "I saw all Israel
> scattered on the mountains, like sheep which have no shepherd.
> And the LORD said, 'These have no master. Let each of them return
> to his house in peace.'" Then the king of Israel said to Jehoshaphat,
> "Did I not tell you that he would not prophesy good concerning me,
> but evil?" Micaiah said, "Therefore, hear the word of the LORD. I saw
> the LORD sitting on His throne, and all the host of heaven standing
> by Him on His right and on His left. The LORD said, 'Who will entice
> Ahab to go up and fall at Ramoth-gilead?' And one said this while
> another said that. Then a spirit came forward and stood before the
> LORD and said, 'I will entice him.' The LORD said to him, 'How?' And
> he said, 'I will go out and be a deceiving spirit in the mouth of all his
> prophets.' Then He said, 'You are to entice him and also prevail, Go
> and do so.' Now therefore, behold, the LORD has put a deceiving spirit
> in the mouth of all these your prophets; and the LORD has proclaimed
> disaster against you."
>
> verses 16–23

There are some important points to understand here. The governmental brings correction to the prophetic, and the prophetic
speaks the true word of the Lord. The true word is a corrective
toward the governmental leaders—a serious word of warning.

If the prophetic is to deliver corrective, warning words to the
Church, we must have hearts of genuine concern for the welfare
of the people we are addressing. God's heart is to bring merciful
correction to the Body, and the prophetic voice He uses must
deliver that correction with true love toward the people and in the
fear of the Lord.

We also see the possibilities for deception in the prophetic, even
when there appears to be agreement. This lesson primarily reflects
the issues of a backslidden people, not a God-fearing, passionate
community of believers. These kings had many issues of the heart
that needed correction. It takes the prophetic working along with
the governmental overseers in real cooperation, however, to search

out and find the true word of the Lord, even for those who passionately seek His will.

One of the apostolic networkers the Holy Spirit has raised up for this hour is Dr. C. Peter Wagner, who adds the following insight: "The prophet can err. Therefore he or she must be open to correction by the rest of the Body. True prophets are willing for this. They want their words to be tested, and when they are wrong they will admit it. They want their prophecies to be confirmed by the Word of God and by the Body as a whole."[2]

Through Whom Is the Will of God Revealed?

There are occasions when the will of God may come first through prophetic rather than governmental voices:

> At this time some prophets came down from Jerusalem to Antioch. One of them named Agabus stood up and began to indicate by the Spirit that there would certainly be a great famine all over the world. And this took place in the reign of Claudius. And in the proportion that any of the disciples had means, each of them determined to send a contribution for the relief of the brethren living in Judea. And this they did, sending it in charge of Barnabas and Saul to the elders.
>
> Acts 11:27–30

A prophet brought forth a revelatory word concerning a famine yet to come. In response to that word, the leaders (disciples) interpreted the word and then determined its correct application, giving birth to a missionary work in Judea. Through the ministry of helps and compassion, they began reaching out to this area even before the famine manifested itself. Also, note that Agabus did not work alone. He traveled in a company of prophets, and perhaps gave voice to their consensus (or they to his).

This kind of cooperation requires character, gifting and wisdom from both the prophetic and the governmental. Agabus obviously carried authority and credibility in his expression and delivery that were recognized by the apostolic or local leaders. They, in turn, wisely evaluated the word and responded in a way that exemplified the character of Jesus. Thus, the prophetic released the testimony of Jesus, and it worked in tandem with the other gifts.

There are also times when the will of God may come first through the apostolic, governmental voices. Such was the case in Acts 15–16, when there was major controversy among the Jewish believers about taking the Gospel to the Gentiles. In the context of this problem, the expression of God's will came through the governmental leadership of the Jewish Church, and the prophetic voice came as a confirmation of that expression:

> All the people kept silent, and they were listening to Barnabas and Paul as they were relating what signs and wonders God had done through them among the Gentiles. After they had stopped speaking, James [a governmental voice] answered, saying, "Brethren, listen to me. Simeon has related how God first concerned Himself about taking from among the Gentiles a people for His name. With this the words of the Prophets agree, just as it is written, 'After these things I will return, and I will rebuild the tabernacle of David which has fallen, and I will rebuild its ruins, and I will restore it, so that the rest of mankind may seek the LORD, and all the Gentiles who are called by My name,' says the LORD, who makes these things known from long ago. Therefore it is my judgment that we do not trouble those who are turning to God from among the Gentiles, but that we write to them that they abstain from things contaminated by idols and from fornication and from what is strangled and from blood. . . ."
>
> Then it seemed good to the apostles and the elders, with the whole church, to choose men from among them to send to Antioch with Paul and Barnabas—Judas called Barsabbas, and Silas, leading men among the brethren, and they sent this letter by them.
>
> Acts 15:12–20, 22–23

James, a governmental voice, was putting forth a directive from the Lord concerning the Gentiles, and he confirmed it with the written word of the prophet Amos. The other elders and church government leaders added their agreement to the word and applied it by setting apart men to deliver an encouraging letter to the Gentile believers in Antioch. Thus, another mission work was raised up and a commissioning took place to carry out the will of God.

The results: The messengers went down to Antioch, gathered the congregation and delivered the letter. "Judas and Silas, also being prophets themselves, encouraged and strengthened the brethren with a lengthy message" (verse 32). And the will of God—received by the governmental first and confirmed by the prophetic—continued to spread out into other places through the ministry of Paul and Timothy. "While they were passing through the cities, they were delivering the decrees which had been decided upon by the apostles and elders who were in Jerusalem, for them to observe" (Acts 16:4).

It is clear in these Scriptures that the governmental leadership did not move ahead without the *yes* and *amen* of the Holy Spirit through the elders, prophets and community of believers. This is a wonderful picture of the cooperation between the governmental and the prophetic as they received the will of God, assimilated it and applied it in a way that brought clarity to a controversial subject. Cooperation brings glorious implementation!

First to the Prophetic

In this section I want to give you some more scriptural accounts of the will of God coming first through the ministry of the prophetic. These examples can be considered typical and can be applied generally to the prophetic ministry. But they are not laws; they are just activities that can be helpful in identifying the ministry of the prophetic:

- *Foretelling events* (Acts 11:27–30).
- *Confirming personal ministry* (John 1:29; Acts 10:9–13; Acts 13:2). The prophetic is typically used in the area of confirming personal callings and ministry.
- *Delivering God's message* (Isaiah 40:1–8).
- *Edifying churches* (Acts 11:27; Acts 13:1).
- *Receiving revelation and delivering apostolic counsel* (Acts 15:32; Acts 16:4). In this instance the prophetic may not initiate but act as a response to the apostolic counsel.
- *Judging and discerning messages* (1 Corinthians 14:29–33, 37). The prophetic should not just be receiving and declaring,

but also working together to judge and discern each other's words. In some places prophetic councils are formed to act as watchdogs for the prophetic voices who want to participate.

- *Warning* (Acts 21:8–12).

First to the Governmental

These Scriptures are examples of revelatory words that come first to the governmental ministries. Again, remember that these are not laws, just typical kinds of revelation that would come first through governmental voices.

- *Theological revelation* (Acts 2:42; Acts 15). Typically revelation concerning doctrinal issues comes to pastors and teachers first. It brings clarity to the Body on these issues.
- *Revelation requiring management* (Acts 4:32–37). Governmental leaders are usually the first to receive revelation about managing the affairs and ministries within the local body.
- *Revelation requiring structural change* (Acts 6:1–7). When there is a need for administrative change in the functions of the church, the governmental leaders usually receive that revelation.
- *Revelation requiring overall changes in the condition of local congregations* (Revelation 1–3). John, an apostle (governmental), received incredible words to the seven churches about the changes God required of them.

Areas Addressed by the Prophetic

The following areas are not typically brought out in the public arena. Neither are they given to a novice prophetic person. Revelatory persons who have proved their authority and character through many experiences will bring these kinds of correctional words to the Church. Your job description is not to correct everyone; it is to declare life. But mature and seasoned prophetic voices do bring these kinds of revelation to the Church so that the leaders can move into the mainstream of God's will.

- Correctional judgment on governmental leadership
- Confirmation of what the leadership has already heard
- Mishandling or intrusion on the part of the prophetic person into an area or sphere of ministry that is not his or hers

Regardless of which ministry hears the Lord first, the governmental or the prophetic, progress cannot be made within local fellowships until the complementary gifting can say *yes* and *amen!* There will be no real cooperation between these two ministries without humility on both sides.

Daniel is an excellent example of a humble prophetic voice. He was prepared by God to deliver hard and demanding words to the evil secular governmental authority of Babylon. But he did not deliver those words in a defiant and arrogant manner. He addressed Nebuchadnezzar with respect and honesty (Daniel 5). King Nebuchadnezzar, in turn, was humbled by the Lord, and his life was eventually changed.

We do well to exercise great patience and grace toward one another as we learn to cooperate in the work of the Kingdom.

Tools for the Toolbox

What are the prerequisites for participation in the last-generation Church? Let's turn again to a veteran voice, that of Dr. Bill Hamon, to gain understanding:

> Those who will be participating in the great apostolic and prophetic companies of overcomers will not be there simply because of their faith, revelation and preaching. They will have to be absolutely Christlike and powerful in ministry. Participants and leaders of past restorational movements were mightily used even though they were immature and carnal in areas of their lives. But those days have come to an end for the last generation that will participate in these coming moves of God. The only Christians who will participate in these last activities of the mortal Church will be those who have fully died the death to sin and self. The declaration of Galatians 2:20 will have become a lifestyle reality to them. Every attitude

and action contrary to divine principle will have to be purged. Nothing short of conformity to the image of Jesus Christ will suffice.[3]

No one office alone can properly build the Church. There is more than one tool in a toolbox. The most important is the one needed at the time.

Understanding

Each gifted person must seek to understand the other. The requirements of building the Church and the Kingdom include knowing when to call in what parts of the team to assist. This takes humility, availability, understanding and cooperation. To dishonor another servant or position or gifting of God is to dishonor God Himself. To have a viable revolution, we must restore the honor code.

Recently I had the opportunity to be part of launching a new national youth prayer movement called The Cause, joining Cindy Jacobs, Lou Engle, Chuck Pierce, Dutch Sheets and others to form the adult prophetic advisory council to this new thrust. A wonderful young man from Connecticut named Billy Ostan was chosen to become the national director. At the United States Strategic Prayer Conference held in Boston in November 2000, we laid hands on Billy and set him apart "to the Lord and for the work for which God has chosen him."

The first thing this young man did was call his parents to the platform, kneel before them and ask them to forgive him for any rebellion, whether in his heart or by his actions. The place was a puddle of water as we all wept before the Lord! He then stated publicly to them that he wanted to honor them in all that he did. What an example!

Yes, there are Daniels and Josephs alive today. This kind of character is what is needed to join the generations in cooperation.

Honor

One of the keys to being in concert together is the art of honoring authority. Cindy Jacobs, co-founder of Generals of Intercession, addresses this needed area of spiritual protocol:

One little-understood concept in the church today is that of honoring those in authority over us. This is probably because a lack of respect for authority is becoming rampant in the youth of many cultures.... Of course, we are not to venerate leaders over us, but we do need to understand how to esteem and respect them. We honor them not just as people, but also for the positions in which the Lord has put them.[4]

Accountability

All governmental and prophetic vessels should be accountable to some kind of spiritual oversight, such as a denomination, fellowship, person, council, network of churches, or ministry. Even if you are in itinerant ministry, you need to be part of a functioning local church. Maybe you are a mature, seasoned prophetic veteran and feel called to live in a quiet, secluded place to be able to hear the voice of God more readily. You, too, need to be accountable to and work in cooperation with other leaders in the Body of Christ. Every person in every level of ministry needs community and friendship. We all need counsel and confirmation to operate in the fullness of the gifts God has placed within us. Our health and safety are at stake. Take heed to the plan of God and become accountable to a proven group of leaders.

Dialogue

The goal is to have regular dialogue between prophetic and governmental ministries in order to facilitate cooperation. Communication is the key to understanding.

Some time ago the Lord gave me this wisdom word concerning the importance of communication: *The lack of communication breeds misunderstanding. Misunderstanding brings accusation. And accusation always results in some form of alienation.*

Most divisions in the Church are not doctrinal in their foundation. Most deal with personal wounds. A personal hurt may have occurred and was never communicated through dialogue. Most divorces are not the result of people disliking each other; they come from wounding and failing to accurately dialogue about the hurt. We must experience the sacrifice of communication. Dialogue and communication are the keys to walking together, learning together and building together.

Planning and Spontaneity

In the wedding of the prophetic and the governmental, we must learn to love both these qualities. Pastors and governmental leaders must learn to appreciate the spontaneous combustion activity in which the prophetic operates so freely. Prophetic people must also embrace the importance of the steady planning methodology that many left-brained administrative people walk in. These elements together will bring balance to the Church and cause her to rise up as a glorious, healthy Bride.

Closing the Gender Gap

If we are to talk realistically about restoring authentic apostolic team ministry—my dream of ATM!— then sooner or later we must deal with the issue of women in ministry.

Women have been and are in ministry. That actually is not the issue. The issue is women in leadership. It is my firm conviction that great harm has been done to the Kingdom purposes of God because we have shot ourselves in our better foot. Believers are limping around in part because of the second-class status we men have relegated to many women.

Dr. Fuchsia Pickett, noted preacher, teacher and author, says it this way:

> It is difficult to estimate the damage that has been done to the Body of Christ because of prejudice against gender. What giftings, ministries, consolations, and virtues have been inadvertently robbed from the Church because of strong prejudicial discrimination against the female gender! And what overt harm has been perpetrated on the Church because of women's harsh reactions against the limitations placed upon them that frustrated their expression of the giftings of God in their lives.[5]

In the early days of Pentecostalism, the primary issue was not sex but anointing. Edith Blumhofer, in *Pentecostal Women in Min-*

istry, observes that "having the 'anointing' was far more important than one's sex. As evangelistic bands carried the full gospel across the country, women who were recognized as having the anointing of the Holy Spirit shared with men in preaching ministry. . . . A person's call—and how other believers viewed it—was far more important than [ministerial credentials]."[6]

What am I getting at? When we talk about apostolic teams emerging, let's remember the word *teams*. Teams have many players functioning in many roles. For a true revolution to take place in the Church, there must be an end to the overall attitudes and actions of the good ol' boys club.

> "And it shall be in the last days," God says, "that I will pour forth of My Spirit on all mankind; and your sons and your daughters shall prophesy, and your young men shall see visions, and your old men shall dream dreams; even on My bondslaves, both men and women, I will in those days pour forth of My Spirit and they shall prophesy."
> Acts 2:17–18

We cannot leave the subject of cooperation without acknowledging the larger portion of this revolutionary prophetic army. Did you know that statistics reveal that sixty percent of all church members are women, and that eighty percent of all intercessors are women? This figure reveals the staggering effect of women in the life of the Church. Yet in many places today there is still no room for women to come forward and utilize the prophetic gifting God has placed in them. What general of any army would only use half his forces? We need secure leaders who will graciously extend a biblical invitation to the women of our land to come alongside them and walk in wonderful prophetic anointing. The goal is not to make the exception the rule, but to produce liberty and equality.

So let the revolution begin. And watch who steps forward! There will be women on the frontlines.

Prophetic Women in the Bible

Throughout biblical history, women have held key prophetic roles and performed other important duties in God's army. Let's look at the impact women have had in the places of service God has entrusted to them.

Miriam. "Miriam the prophetess, Aaron's sister, took the timbrel in her hand, and all the women went out after her with timbrels and with dancing" (Exodus 15:20). Miriam, the prophetess, stood alongside Moses and Aaron as one of the three main leaders of the Israelite nation as they left Egypt.

Deborah. "Deborah, a prophetess, the wife of Lappidoth, was judging Israel at that time" (Judges 4:4). Deborah stood as judge before God on behalf of Israel during this time, and came alongside Barak, a military authority, to lead the Israelite army to victory against the Canaanites.

Huldah. "Hilkiah the priest, Ahikam, Achbor, Shaphan, and Asaiah went to Huldah the prophetess, . . . and they spoke to her" (2 Kings 22:14). Huldah was visited by the high priest, the scribe and a servant of the king so they could obtain the word of the Lord on behalf of young King Josiah. She must have been held in great regard by all of them.

Isaiah's wife. "I approached the prophetess, and she conceived and gave birth to a son. Then the LORD said to me, 'Name him Maher-shalal-hash-baz'" (Isaiah 8:3). We are not given her name, but the wife of Isaiah was a prophetess. What a team they must have made!

Elizabeth and Mary. "When Elizabeth heard Mary's greeting, the baby leaped in her womb; and Elizabeth was filled with the Holy Spirit. And she cried out with a loud voice and said, 'Blessed are you among women, and blessed is the fruit of your womb! . . .' And Mary said: 'My soul exalts the Lord, and my spirit has rejoiced in God my Savior'" (Luke 1:41–42, 46–47). This interchange between Elizabeth, the mother of John the Baptist, and Mary, the mother of Jesus, resulted in exuberant praise and prophesying concerning the destiny of Mary's Child within.

Anna. "There was a prophetess, Anna the daughter of Phanuel, of the tribe of Asher. . . . She never left the temple, serving night and day with fastings and prayers. . . . She came up and began giving thanks to God, and continued to speak of Him to all those who were looking for the redemption of Jerusalem" (Luke

2:36–38). Anna was the praying prophetess present with Simeon the seer at the dedication of Jesus by His parents on His eighth day of life.

A man, a woman; a seer, a prophetess: equal distribution with unique expressions of the same prophetic presence. As it was at the first coming of Jesus, so it will be at the Second Coming.

Philip's daughters. "Entering the house of Philip the evangelist, . . . we stayed with him. Now this man had four virgin daughters who were prophetesses" (Acts 21:8–9). Philip the evangelist had four daughters who prophesied. Four in one family!

Other Women Leaders in the Bible

Jael (Judges 4). She drove a tent peg into Sisera's head and delivered him into the hands of Barak. (Deborah had prophesied that the Lord would give Sisera to Barak. God did it through the hands of a woman.)

Abigail (1 Samuel 25). As an advocate, she pleaded the case of mercy to David (on the run from King Saul) on behalf of her wicked husband.

Esther. She was the godly queen who saved the Jewish race through her intercession.

Proverbs 31 woman. She was skillful in household and business issues, bought and sold real estate, ministered to the poor and more.

Woman at the well (John 4). She is considered by many the first evangelist in the Bible, as she went forth proclaiming the good news of the Christ.

Mary Magdalene (Matthew 28:1–10). She was one of the women who were first at the tomb, first to hear that "He is risen" and first to announce His resurrection.

Lydia (Acts 16:14–15). She is noted as the first convert in all of Europe.

Priscilla and Aquila (Romans 16:3–5). They were probably a husband and wife teaching team explaining the Word of God with accuracy.

Phoebe (Romans 16:1). She was a deaconess who washed the feet of the saints.

You can see through these many examples—if you needed any persuading!—that women have always been used by God to do exploits in His Kingdom work on the earth. Women carry the gifting of the prophetic with sincerity and excellence equal to that of men. We need women in the prophetic ministry, as well in as other areas of gifting, to bring balance and strength to the coming prophetic revolution.

> Women of the Church, you have been shackled long enough! As a man in the Church, I want to confess to you that we, the men of the Body of Christ, have feared you and have clung tightly to our rights, our positions, and our functions out of the fear that we would lose them to you. In our own insecurity and sin we have been unwilling to fully recognize your gifts, calling, and anointing in the Spirit or to accept you as full equals in the life and ministry of the Church. This might sound a bit brash, but in my opinion it is time for the "good old boys' club" to come to an end!
>
> Therefore, I ask you, the women, to forgive us for holding you back, for not being cheerleaders for you, for not helping to equip you, and for not releasing you to fulfill God's calling on your lives. Forgive us for paying only lip service to your value, your gifts, your call, and your anointing. Forgive us for treating you like second-class citizens of the Kingdom and for not recognizing your equal status with us.[7]

Let's Do It Together

We are coming to a time when we more clearly appreciate and understand the various ministries of Christ. Let none of us deceive ourselves into believing that understanding in itself is equal to achievement. Understanding must motivate us to humility and prayer for God to establish mature, functioning role models among us.

Let me share one more recent account with you to encourage your heart that a quick and sudden change is on the horizon. At the end of the World Congress on Revival in Guatemala City in October 2000, there was a stadium outreach in which Claudio Freidzon of Argentina ministered powerfully. This was followed by the public recognition of fourteen apostolic leaders of the nation of Guatemala.

Much prayer and interaction had gone before this process. John Kelly of the International Coalition of Apostles was present for the special consecration. It was a historic event. At the close of the ordination, I was asked to come and minister prophetically to each of these servants of the Lord. What an honor it was for me to be present and to see firsthand the prophetic serving the apostolic! The Lord confirmed their gifts and callings in a wonderful atmosphere where all were cheering for the other. Thank You, Lord! It can work and it is working.

So let's be grateful for each other. We need each other. Let's learn to defer to the gifts and ministries needed and approved for active service in the appropriate time. Let's seek and pray for divine cooperation so that a clear, rather than discordant, sound will be produced. Let's receive and honor the giftings of His most precious Holy Spirit in and through each other, so that the Church will be victorious and Jesus will be glorified. Let's do it together!

Our Intercessory Cry

Father, we thank You for the glorious, many-faceted manifestations of Your Holy Spirit in our midst. We thank You for the unique gifts You have placed within each member of the Body of Christ. We celebrate the diversity of many members of the Body under the singular authority of our Head, Christ Jesus. What a wonder it is, Lord!

Now, Father, we ask that You come and grace us with the understanding of cooperation that will move us into immediate action and cause us to advance with new strength and vitality. Take the blinders off our eyes and the plugs out of our ears, and soften our hearts so that we can see, hear and receive each other in the true spirit of unity. Heal us where we have been wounded, restore our confidence in Your graces and help us create a symphony that will resound to the testimony of Jesus! We praise You for these things, in His mighty name. Amen.

POP QUIZ—KEEPING YOU ON YOUR TOES!

1. When the apostolic is made personal, what will be the outcome?
2. Is there a biblical precedent for women in prophetic ministry? Give three examples.
3. State some examples of how the apostolic and pastoral may benefit from the prophetic. State some examples of how the prophetic can benefit from apostolic and pastoral input.

FOR MORE, LORD!

Bill Hamon, *Apostles, Prophets and the Coming Moves of God* (Shippensburg, Pa.: Destiny Image, 1997)

Tommy Tenney, *God's Dream Team* (Ventura, Calif.: Regal, 1999)

C. Peter Wagner, *Apostles and Prophets* (Ventura, Calif.: Regal, 2000)

11

SEIZING YOUR PROPHETIC DESTINY

God has a dream in His heart—and our God is a *big* dreamer. His revolutionary vision is large enough to encompass a universe. He wants to instill this infinite dream in the heart and mind of every believer, every family and every congregation in every city of every nation. But how can we, finite as we are, contain such a dream?

It takes a "corporate" heart to hold a vision from the God of this universe! It takes every believer working together in unified precision to grasp the totality of the dream proceeding from the heart of God. And the only way we can be formed together as one is to catch the vision God has for our individual lives.

Our individual prophetic destiny is to catch and hold and live the unique life God has prepared for us as we dare to enter into His incredibly big dream. Only He knows how to blend millions of separate and diverse people into a unified and glorious Bride for the Son of His love. Each person, family, congregation, city and nation daring to seek and search out its individual destiny within the heart of God will become flourishing members in the beloved Body of the glorified Church.

So while we hold onto our desire to share a corporate heart with other believers, let's dare to reach for our individual prophetic destiny. Let's seek and stretch and dare to dream big with our big God.

His plan for you is unique and specially tailored to fit your individual destiny.

God's Plan for You

Let's start our quest for our prophetic destiny by reviewing what God's individually tailored plan for each of us involves.

Vision. "Where there is no vision, the people are unrestrained, but happy is he who keeps the law" (Proverbs 29:18). In this Scripture we see that without vision there is no restraint, no personal direction, just aimless, wandering people. Conversely, where there is vision, people are channeled in a specific direction. The result: happy people! We will talk more about the connection between restraint and vision in a moment.

Knowledge of God's law. "My people are destroyed for lack of knowledge. Because you have rejected knowledge, I also will reject you from being My priest. Since you have forgotten the law of your God, I also will forget your children" (Hosea 4:6). God was saying that the people had no revelatory knowledge because they had rejected His standards, and that darkness would pass down to the next generation.

Knowledge of His will. "For this reason also, since the day we heard of it, we have not ceased to pray for you and to ask that you may be filled with the knowledge of His will in all spiritual wisdom and understanding, so that you will walk in a manner worthy of the Lord, to please Him in all respects, bearing fruit in every good work and increasing in the knowledge of God; strengthened with all power, according to His glorious might, for the attaining of all steadfastness and patience; joyously giving thanks to the Father, who has qualified us to share in the inheritance of the saints in Light" (Colossians 1:9–12). Paul prayed this apostolically as a father for the church of Colossae, and we can do the same, taking this Scripture and many others and turning them into devotional prayers for our lives and the lives of our families, congregations, cities and nations. Power resides in these words!

Once when I was away on one of my many travels, my wife was crying out to the Lord out of sheer exhaustion. She was just plain weary, and she called out to Him for strength. Then she had a dream. When she awoke she could not remember what it was, but she knew it was significant. She looked at the clock; it read 1:11 A.M. She knew the Lord was trying to say something to her, so she searched our Psalm 1:11 and Proverbs 1:11 trying to find a Scripture that might be meaningful, but nothing connected. So she went back to sleep.

Then, in another dream, the Lord came to her. She saw Mike Bickle, the founding pastor of Metro Christian Fellowship in Kansas City, with his Bible open, and he said, "It's Colossians 1:11."

She awoke from this dream and opened her Amplified Bible to Colossians 1:11: "[Be] invigorated and strengthened with all power, according to the might of His glory. . . ." Then the presence of the strength of God started coming on her with waves of strength and invigoration, and she knew God had answered her cry with "His glorious might." Glory to God!

Wisdom and revelation. "[I] do not cease giving thanks for you, while making mention of you in my prayers; that the God of our Lord Jesus Christ, the Father of glory, may give to you a spirit of wisdom and of revelation in the knowledge of Him. I pray that the eyes of your heart may be enlightened, so that you will know what is the hope of His calling, what are the riches of the glory of His inheritance in the saints, and what is the surpassing greatness of His power toward us who believe" (Ephesians 1:16–19). I have prayed these verses more often than any other set of verses I know. For about a ten-year period in my life, I prayed them almost daily, and then at least weekly for another decade–plus.

Paul prayed this for the church of Ephesus, which at that time was viewed as the model church. But Paul saw they needed their hearts opened up so they could have three important things: *The knowledge of the hope of God's calling in their lives; revelatory understanding of the glorious inheritance that is in the saints; and revelatory understanding of the surpassing greatness of His power toward those who believe.* If the church at Ephesus needed these things, surely we need to have our eyes filled with light so that we can have them, too.

I ask the Father to open the shutter of the camera lens of my heart so it will be flooded with shafts of revelatory light. How does vision happen? Just as light enters a camera, vision comes through the lenses of our hearts. A picture is taken and the vision of God's plan for our destinies begins to unfold within our spirits. May His light bring you vision!

Future and hope. "'I know the plans that I have for you,' declares the LORD, 'plans for welfare and not for calamity to give you a future and a hope. Then you will call upon Me and come and pray to Me, and I will listen to you. You will seek Me and find Me when you search for Me with all your heart'" (Jeremiah 29:11–13). We are a chosen people, and God has chosen plans, purposes, destinies and pursuits for each of us. The above passage is a promise given to Jeremiah and a city and a whole generation. It is with us today as it was with them. God also wants to give us a future filled with hope.

The word *vision* can be translated "revelation, mental sight, or a revealed word from God." Without a revealed word the people will be unrestrained. This indicates the absence of guidance or direction. But we are not to be aimless and without direction. A restraint is like a bit in a horse's mouth. The bit is used not to bind the horse but to give it direction. If you have no vision—a revelation of God's destiny for your life—you will be without direction, with no sense of His guidance. You will be perishing! If you have vision, on the other hand, He will guide you into your purpose, direction and destiny.

An anonymous writer penned these thoughts about the necessity of having a vision:

> A vision without a task is a dream.
>
> A task without a vision is drudgery.
>
> A vision with a task is the hope of the world.

10 "D's" to Help Us Dream

Can prophetically oriented people be of any earthly good? Absolutely! But while many people, leaders, congregations and cities aim at nothing and hit it, we must be a people who dare to dream God's dreams. God wants us to delight in Him, and He will put His desires, dreams and determinations for destiny within us.

The following one-word guidances are inspired (although not directly quoted) from my friend William Greenman of Purpose International, gleaned from his first book, *How to Find Your Purpose in Life.*[1]

1. **Delight.** "Delight yourself in the Lord . . ." (Psalm 37:4a). Opening your heart and soul to receive the knowledge of God's will is a prerequisite. There is nothing better than His will. It is wonderful, majestic, powerful! And as we delight in Him, something transpires: He changes us.

2. **Desire.** ". . . and He will give you the desires of your heart" (Psalm 37:4b). *Desire* means "to long for, crave, yearn or covet." We are to be passionate people motivated to pursue God's purposes for our generation. As we make Him our delight, He puts His passionate yearnings in our heart, "for it is God who is at work in you, both to will and to work for His good pleasure" (Philippians 2:13). God gives us the will, the desire and the ability to perform His good pleasure. The key here is *delight.*

One of the things I absolutely cannot stand is passionless Christianity! You can call it religion, but don't call it Christianity. If we want to be people who seize our prophetic destiny, we must become passion-filled—people on fire, hot with the love of God.

3. **Dream.** "Where there is no vision, the people are unrestrained" (Proverbs 29:18). People who have no dream are without direction. *Webster's Dictionary* says that a dream is "a fond hope or a vision."[2] Let's be people willing to dream.

4. **Destiny.** Your dream will guide you into your destiny. *Webster's* defines *destiny* as "an inevitable series of events or that which determines those events, that is a supernatural thing."[3] We must plan a dream to turn it into a destiny.

5. **Decision.** Deuteronomy 30:19 explains that God has given us the choice of "life and death, the blessing and the curse." When we choose to follow the dream that the Lord places in our heart, we are choosing life. When you make this quality decision of the heart, you start the sanctification process. This is part of delighting in Him and doing what delights Him, and it moves you out of self-motivation and selfish ambition. He will sanctify you (set you apart) as you choose His will and move toward it.

6. **Determination.** Once having decided to run with the vision that God has placed in your heart, you will then be forced to exercise determination. Resolve that nothing will stop you. "Run with endurance the race that is set before [you]" (Hebrews 12:1). It does not mean the road is without obstacles. In fact, the forces of hell and darkness will try to hinder and defeat you. But you must keep running and not look back.

7. **Dedication.** After you have determined in your heart that you will act on the vision God has given you, you must dedicate yourself to it. As you devote yourself to the vision, you are giving yourself to the Lord. Your dedication will be received by Him as an act of worship.

8. **Discipline.** "Discipline yourself for the purpose of godliness" (1 Timothy 4:7). Once you have dedicated yourself, you must exercise discipline. It takes discipline—the training that develops self-control, character, orderliness and efficiency—to devote yourself to your dream. Don't throw out spiritual disciplines, thinking they are too "religious." We do not discipline ourselves to earn points with God. That is performance-based acceptance. But we need to pray, read the Word, fast and be part of a committed people who will walk together toward the dreams God has placed in our hearts. Sometimes it may feel dry, boring and uneventful, but keep pressing on. This discipline will bring character formation to make you a vessel that can carry the glory of the Lord. (Read Matthew 25:23 and Luke 19:17 on the related subject of faithfulness.)

9. **Diligence.** "A righteous man falls seven times, and rises again" (Proverbs 24:16). That is diligence! Don't quit. Quitters never win and winners never quit. *Diligence* means "to be constant, to make careful and continual effort." Romans 12:11 encourages us not to "[lag] behind in diligence" but to be "fervent in spirit, serving the Lord."

10. **Death.** "Truly, truly, I say to you, unless a grain of wheat falls into the earth and dies, it remains alone; but if it dies, it bears much fruit" (John 12:24). At some point the Lord may ask you to give back to Him the vision you have received from Him. It is like Abraham giving up Isaac. It hurts like everything, and you wonder what in the world is going on. But God's purpose is to see how sticky and

gooey possessive you have become, and to make sure you know the vision is His.

Once I had a dream in which I was being introduced on a new platform, in a conference setting, by Dr. Don Finto of Nashville, whom I consider an apostolic father. In the dream the people I was addressing were a little antsy. Things did not seem to be going well. So I got up to speak and said, "I want to teach you about times of transition." All ears perked up now. And even though I was asleep, I, too, became attentive and perked up my own spiritual ears so I could hear what I was about to say!

In the dream I said, "There are three points you must always remember when going through a time of transition. First, you must always remember that it is God who is at work in your life, to will and to work for His good pleasure. Second, you must trust God's word that has been given to you, because it will not return void, but will accomplish the very purpose for which He sent it. And third, always remember that God wants you to do His will more than you want to. God will help you do it."

What an unusual dream—one filled with wonderful guidance from the Lord!

The Goal Is God Himself!

Kenneth W. Osbeck reminds us of the two shoe salesmen sent to a primitive island. The first salesman wired back, "Coming home immediately. No one here wears shoes." The second man wired, "Send a boatload of shoes immediately. The possibilities for selling shoes here are unlimited." Comments Osbeck, "May we as believers be characterized as people of vision—'looking unto Jesus, the author and finisher of our faith . . .' (Hebrews 12:2)."[4]

Ultimately it is not the vision, plan or purpose that is God's goal. *His goal is to be your delight.* When we put the cart before the horse, we give God's vision and purpose precedence over God Himself. We can become driven people who use God, instead of people who serve God. When this happens, God must oppose us and turn us around so we can be formed into the image of His Son. Jesus was never driven to fulfill a ministry or vision; He was compelled by love to do the will of the Father, whatever the cost. He was not purpose-driven but Person-driven.

Paul shared the same goal: "Forgetting what lies behind and reaching forward to what lies ahead, I press on toward the goal for the prize of the upward call of God in Christ Jesus" (Philippians 3:13–14). The upward call is not becoming a pastor or prophet or having a great healing ministry. The upward call is being conformed into the image of Jesus Christ.

I can tell you from experience that, at times, you must let the vision die so the Lord can help you die to self. This is the pattern of life that leads to multiplication. God is well able to resurrect any dream or vision He chooses. I heard once of a lost ax head that floated (2 Kings 6:5–7)! He will release grace to help us do what He desires most—become lovers of God and people of character and carriers of His glory.

Lessons from the Life of Joseph

We can learn valuable lessons from the life of Joseph as he walked into the destiny God designed for him. Take time to review his life for yourself. But here we will make some observations that, I hope, will help you seize your own destiny in God.

Dreams and a Lack of Wisdom

At the age of seventeen the favored son of Jacob had a dream from the Lord. Joseph responded to the revelation, zealously and ignorantly, by sharing it with his brothers, thinking they would be as thrilled about it as he was. "Please listen to this dream which I have had; for behold, we were binding sheaves in the field, and lo, my sheaf rose up and also stood erect; and behold, your sheaves gathered around and bowed down to my sheaf" (Genesis 37:6–7). Joseph's brothers were already jealous of him because their father had singled him out and given him that special coat of many colors. But when Joseph shared what was spoken to him privately by God, his brothers hated him even more.

At this stage of his life, Joseph had not developed much wisdom. Wisdom is not a gift (although a "word of wisdom" is). It must be developed and gained through teaching and experience. Joseph apparently lacked both.

Then he shared another dream indicating that even his father and mother would bow down to him. The whole family was aghast at this audacious dream, and he began to suffer severe persecution. Guess what? Persecution sometimes follows people of vision. Misunderstanding and jealousy often come with the territory, whether or not you are wise.

Joseph became the target of an evil plot devised by his brothers. You know the history lesson after that: They threw him into a pit, thinking to murder him, but instead sold him to Midianite traders, and he was taken to Egypt. At that point it did not look as if anybody was going to bow down to Joseph. It looked as though Joseph was doing all the bowing!

More Dreams and Learning Wisdom

After Joseph arrived in Egypt, he was sold into slavery and brought into the service of Potiphar, an Egyptian officer of Pharaoh. But the Lord was with Joseph and he found favor with his master. "So [Potiphar] left everything he owned in Joseph's charge; and with him there he did not concern himself with anything except the food which he ate" (Genesis 39:6).

Things did not stay rosy for long. Potiphar's manipulative wife unjustly accused Joseph of taking advantage of her after he refused her advances. This time, although Joseph was walking in wisdom, he was persecuted again. Off to prison he went. But even there the Lord was with Joseph and he found favor with the jailer. "The chief jailer did not supervise anything under Joseph's charge because the LORD was with him; and whatever he did, the LORD made to prosper" (Genesis 39:23).

Think of the discouragement Joseph must have faced in the darkness of the dungeon. He had finally gotten to a place of significance and honor in his life, and *wham!* More injustice, and he found himself in jail with some pretty rough characters.

But God did an awesome thing with Joseph in the midst of that hopeless-looking set of circumstances. While the Hebrew was seemingly wasting away in an Egyptian prison, God began to deepen his revelatory gifting, and he interpreted two other prisoners' dreams. As he practiced his gifting on these fellow inmates, his reputation within the prison grew. Eventually Pharaoh heard about the amazing young prisoner who could interpret dreams with astounding accuracy. Pharaoh called Joseph out of prison to help him with a set of perplexing dreams. None of Pharaoh's wise men and magicians had been able to interpret them, so out of desperation he turned to the Hebrew for answers.

After skillfully interpreting the Pharaoh's dreams and giving credit to the Lord, Joseph proceeded to give Pharaoh an action plan to prepare Egypt for the famine predicted in the dreams. Action must follow vision!

Joseph had learned well in the difficult place of trial and testing. He dreamed, interpreted, then implemented the dreams of God, and he was again promoted to a place of authority. Pharaoh declared, "See, I have set you over all the land of Egypt" (Genesis 41:41). God used what seemed like a nightmare to Joseph in order to prepare him for the manifestation of his own dream!

From Dreamer to Deliverer

Joseph was a man who had literally been brought out of the pit into a place of prominence, respect and authority. God's favor surrounded him and caused him and a whole nation to prosper, even in a time of famine. God did amazing things in and through Joseph, and continued to work out the dreams he had originally placed in Joseph's heart.

Because of severe famine that spread beyond the borders of Egypt into Canaan, Joseph's brothers came to Egypt seeking food that had been made available by the hand of God. Eventually Joseph revealed himself to his brothers, who had violated him horribly. Joseph stated with a forgiving heart, "God sent me before you to preserve for you a remnant in the earth, and to keep you alive by a great deliverance" (Genesis 45:7). This wisdom revelation is summed up in Genesis 50:20: "As for you, you meant evil against me, but God meant it for good in order to bring about this present result, to preserve many people alive."

God took a proud and haughty young dreamer and turned him into a man who carried the humility, wisdom and skill of his God. He dared to dream God's dreams, and God changed him into a deliverer.

Lessons to Learn from Joseph

Look at the lessons we can learn from Joseph:

1. Joseph did not know the proper ways of responding to revelation. Proverbs 14:33 suggests we must first ask permission to tell our revelation: "Wisdom rests quietly in the heart of him who has understanding, but what is in the heart of fools is made known" (NKJV). Others might not have the wisdom and maturity to handle the repercussions of the words we bring.
2. Joseph learned wisdom through his failures. Genesis 40:8 reveals that Joseph learned to inquire of the wisdom of God to properly interpret his revelations: "Do not interpretations belong to God?"
3. A right attitude will keep you going in the right direction in spite of your failures. Joseph held a respectful posture toward the Pharaoh although he was a difficult taskmaster. This attitude was visible to all, and it released favor from those in authority.
4. Ultimately Joseph did not let go of his dreams but saw them come to fruition. Do not harden yourself against your gift and calling. Do not curse your sensitivity; rather, embrace it and let it make you, like Joseph, one who weeps over his brothers.
5. Joseph's character was molded to carry the gift, and all flourished. Today God is looking for those who will embrace the cross of the prophetic lifestyle and be vessels who carry the prophetic message, instead of being crushed by it.

Lessons from the Life of Amos

Frankly, though Joseph learned great wisdom and grew in character to carry the gift, I wonder what might have happened if he had prayed before speaking about his dreams. Undoubtedly the end result was humility, brokenness and the fear of God. But in the life of Amos, we are shown the result of prayer as the *primary* response to revelation. Judgments were averted and mercy was purchased for the people. God took both these men and used them for His glory. But they took very different paths to get to the same place!

Amos 1:1 and 7:14–15 give some background about the prophet Amos. He was not from the school of the prophets, but rather was a keeper of flocks and a grower of figs. God put a seer anointing on a common man and commissioned him to prophesy to his own people before judgments and great trials were released.

The Proper Response to Revelation

One pivotal passage shows us a principle that governs the prophetic: "Surely the Lord GOD does nothing unless He reveals His secret counsel to His servants the prophets" (Amos 3:7).

Now we are given the antidote for times of crisis. "Thus says the LORD to the house of Israel, 'Seek Me that you may live!'" (Amos 5:4). Revelation came concerning pending judgment, yet the Lord granted an opportunity for change: "Perhaps the LORD God of hosts may be gracious to the remnant of Joseph" (verse 15). "If Your people. . . ."

God showed Amos that devastation on the farmland was imminent. In a vision Amos was shown a swarm of locusts come to destroy the vegetation. Amos cried out to the Lord in response to that prophetic word of judgment: "Lord GOD, please pardon!" (Amos 7:2). The Lord relented.

This was followed by a round of visions of fire destroying the land. Once again Amos responded to revelation with prayer. He did not just fold his arms and say, "What will be will be." Rather, he cried out, "Lord GOD, please stop! How can Jacob stand, for he is small?" (verse 5). Again the Lord stopped.

Lessons to Learn from Amos

1. God can put his prophetic graces on common people, not just the specially trained.

2. The Lord will always cue His people in before a major event transpires. His is looking for co-laborers, not puppets.
3. Remedies to problems are generally simple but often overlooked. Seek the Lord and live!
4. Amos revealed the secret of proper biblical response to revelation: *Pray before you act!* Prayer is your first act in response to revelation.
5. Your prayers can hold back God's judgment and evil from the enemy, and they can unlock the prophetic promise.

Discovering Your Prophetic Destiny

Negative influences must be removed through confession of sin, repentance, acts of spiritual warfare and deeds of retribution. As the obstacles are removed, the prophetic promises can be released.

The following principles lead to the unfolding destinies of individuals, families, congregations, denominations, cities and nations. Although the applications vary, these principles are held in common. I state them briefly, but more on each of these topics can be found in "Referral Reading for More Good Stuff" on p. 298 and in the books, tapes and study guides mentioned in "Other Equipping Tools" on p. 315.

The Value of Research

Many questions need to be asked: Who were the founders of your city, nation or church? What were their goals, visions, purposes and origins? What is your family's history, ethnic background, religious heritage and so on? Often we must research the foundations in order to build properly. Study to show yourself approved.[5]

The Meaning of a Name

What does your name mean? Is there a promise contained within it? What is the name of your city, church or denomination? Whom are you named after? What is the outstanding characteristic of your namesake? Redemptively turn names into promises as a tool of discovering your prophetic destiny. Claim your generational inheritance and call forth the blessing. Remember, the power of the blessing is greater than the power of the curse.

Picking Up the Baton

Not all promises have to be received directly by you or by your generation. Receive the inheritance of those who have gone before. Daniel 9:2 shows an example of receiving the baton of promise of a previous generation, the promise given in Jeremiah 29:10: "When seventy years have been completed for Babylon, I will visit you and fulfill My good word to you, to bring you back to this place." What are the unfulfilled promises that have gone before you? Research them, pick them up and seize them for your life and generation.

The Importance of Revelation

Particular gifts of the Spirit such as the discerning of spirits, the word of knowledge and the gift of prophecy are very valuable here. They will assist you in determining specific points the Lord wants you to know. Also consider the following questions: What are the intercessors discerning? What are the hindering powers of darkness? What are the current-day revelatory promises? What are the prophets saying? What is the voice of the Holy Spirit saying to you personally?[6]

Walking in Unity and Taking Counsel

Each person needs to walk in a committed relationship with a local expression of the Body of Christ. They will greatly assist you as you look for your specific destiny. What are your authorities saying? What does your leadership team have to say? Are the city leaders praying together? Are you walking in unity and counsel with others? We must each find confirmation, wisdom and counsel through the safety net of walking circumspectly with others.

Kneeling on the Promises

Now let's take those confirmed, authentic promises and remind God of His word: "On your walls, O Jerusalem, I have appointed watchmen; all day and all night they will never keep silent. You who remind the LORD, take no rest for yourselves; and give Him no rest until He establishes and makes Jerusalem a praise in the earth" (Isaiah 62:6–7). Pray those precious promises into being. Humbly yet boldly lay hold of God, and don't let Him go until you see His Kingdom come, His will done on earth (and in your life) as it is in heaven. Follow the examples of the revivalist of old, but don't just stand on the promises—kneel on them! Give birth to them, for Jesus' sake.

Proclaim the Promises

We are not called just to discern darkness; we are called to turn on the light. One of the powerful ways of doing this is through the power of proclamation. We can join praise with prayer and pronounce "to the rulers and the authorities in the heavenly places" (Ephesians 3:10) that the power of the blessing is greater than the power of the curse. By announcing God's word, we release individual and corporate declarations of the will of God. Watch faith ignite and destinies unfold.[7]

Acting in the Opposite Spirit

Another important tool to seize your destiny is that of "acting in the opposite spirit." What does this mean? If a curse or demonic presence is discerned, then begin to look for, teach and act out proper biblical expressions of the love of God that you and others can model. If the demonic power is greed and materialism, then look for opportunities to give and minister to the poor. If the resistance says hate, then sow deeds of love, forgiveness and kindness. Turn the tables on the enemy by doing the servant works of Christ.

Writing It Down

Habakkuk 2:2 gives us the details and reason for these activities: "Record the vision and inscribe it on tablets, that the one who reads it may run." Writing down God's promise ensures that it will be kept before your eyes and properly passed on to the next generation.[8]

Stepping Out

Nothing takes the place of stepping out of your comfort zone and out onto the end of the limb. Remember that faith is always spelled *r-i-s-k*. We must formulate practical plans of implementation, wait on God, get His mind and timing on the matter—and then get up and go, obey and step out.

Some people need to hear words like *wait, listen, pray,* and *slow down.* Others need words like g*et up, get going, rise up* and *do something.* Eventually we must add works, or corresponding actions, to our faith (James 2:14–26). So in order to seize your prophetic destiny, step out. God is not only good, but He will catch you if you fall and help you get up and try again.

We have explored much Scripture and many practical ways of seizing our prophetic destinies. This process takes time and patience. We are programmed in this culture of ours to expect instant results, so we must set our minds and hearts toward persistence and perseverance. Our prophetic destinies lie in knowing the God who designed them. Give yourself wholeheartedly to the pursuit of knowing Him in all His fullness; then He will surely reveal who He has created you to be in the midst of your pursuit. Our goal is not the plan, but the Man, Christ Jesus.

Let me round this chapter out by reminding you of the lyrics of the eighth-century Irish hymn "Be Thou My Vision":[9]

> Be Thou my vision, O Lord of my heart;
> Nought be all else to me, save that Thou art;
> Thou my best thought, by day or by night,
> Waking or sleeping, Thy presence my light.
>
> Be Thou my Wisdom, and Thou my true Word;
> I ever with Thee and Thou with me, Lord;
> Thou my great Father, I Thy true son,
> Thou in me dwelling, and I with Thee one.
>
> Riches I heed not, nor man's empty praise;
> Thou mine inheritance, now and always;
> Thou and Thou only, first in my heart;
> High King of heaven, my treasure Thou art.

Be Thou my breast-plate, my sword for the fight;
Be Thou my armour, and be Thou my might;
Thou my soul's shelter, and Thou my high tower;
Raise Thou me heavenward, O Power of my power.

High King of heaven, my victory won,
May I reach heaven's joys, O bright heaven's Sun!
Heart of my own heart, whatever befall,
Still be my vision, O Ruler of all.

OUR INTERCESSORY CRY

Father God, we are continually amazed and astounded at the grace and mercy You pour out on us as we stumble along the path of life. You have designed an incredible plan for each of us, and we desire with all our hearts to live the lives that Jesus died to give us, and walk securely on the paths You have designed for us.

Father, we ask for the power of Your Holy Spirit to come and assist us in this quest for our prophetic destinies. Speak again to our hearts the desire You have for each of us, and change our selfish desires into Your own perfect will. We ask for dreams, visions, words of knowledge and prophetic utterances to come forth and point the way toward Your purposes. The dreams You have given us that have been lost or forgotten or trampled on, we ask that You come by Your redemptive grace and restore them to us again.

We cry out for our destinies, O God! And may we come to know You more intimately and be changed into the likeness of Your dear Son and our dear Savior, in whose powerful name we pray. Amen.

POP QUIZ—KEEPING YOU ON YOUR TOES!

1. What were some of the lessons Joseph learned in order for his vision to be fulfilled?

2. Explain the steps we are to take according to Habakkuk 2:1–3.

3. What are some practical steps you can take to seize your prophetic destiny?

FOR MORE, LORD!

Terry Crist, *Warring According to Prophecy* (Springdale, Pa.: Whitaker, 1989)

William D. Greenman, *Purpose, Destiny, Achievement* (Shippensburg, Pa.: Destiny Image, 1998)

Chuck D. Pierce and Rebecca Wagner-Sytsema, *Possessing Your Inheritance* (Ventura, Calif.: Renew, 1999)

12

PROPHESY LIFE!

In this last chapter we are going to study a very familiar prophetic Scripture from the book of Ezekiel that demonstrates the subject of this chapter. If you have been a Christian for very long, you have probably heard this passage preached twenty different ways; but we will look at Ezekiel 37 with a New Testament set of lenses. I want to crash, bam, break up and annihilate some wrong Old Testament concepts that some of us have in our minds concerning the way we see prophets today, the way we look at the things prophets do and the messes they can leave behind.

Our concepts must change if we are to fully assume our appointments in God's end-time prophetic revolutionary army. We cannot operate from outdated and wrong interpretations of Old Covenant concepts of prophetic people and revelation. We must see with New Covenant vision in order to operate effectively in the revolution that will bring global change to the Body of Christ.

Give your present mindset to the Lord as we delve into this wonderful passage of God's Word.[1]

The Valley Through a New Testament Lens

Read it all the way through first. Then we will break it down and draw out some principles that may surprise you.

> The hand of the LORD was upon me, and He brought me out by the Spirit of the LORD and set me down in the middle of the valley;

and it was full of bones. He caused me to pass among them round about, and behold, there were very many on the surface of the valley; and lo, they were very dry. He said to me, "Son of man, can these bones live?" And I answered, "O Lord GOD, You know."

Again He said to me, "Prophesy over these bones and say to them, 'O dry bones, hear the word of the LORD.' Thus says the Lord GOD to these bones, 'Behold, I will cause breath to enter you that you may come to life. I will put sinews on you, make flesh grow back on you, cover you with skin and put breath in you that you may come alive; and you will know that I am the LORD.'"

So I prophesied as I was commanded; and as I prophesied, there was a noise, and behold, a rattling; and the bones came together, bone to its bone. And I looked, and behold, sinews were on them, and flesh grew and skin covered them; but there was no breath in them.

Then He said to me, "Prophesy to the breath, prophesy, son of man, and say to the breath, 'Thus says the Lord GOD, "Come from the four winds, O breath, and breathe on these slain, that they come to life."'" So I prophesied as He commanded me, and the breath came into them, and they came to life and stood on their feet, an exceedingly great army.

Ezekiel 37:1–10

The historical setting for the book of Ezekiel is Babylon during the early years of Israel's exile (593–571 B.C.). Ezekiel's prophetic ministry occurred during the darkest hour in Old Testament history—the seven years preceding the 586 B.C. destruction of Jerusalem and the fifteen years following it.

Ezekiel's prophetic ministry had a threefold purpose:

1. To deliver God's message of judgment to apostate Judah and Jerusalem and to the seven nations around her.
2. To sustain the faith of God's remnant in exile concerning the restoration of His covenant people and the final glory of His Kingdom.
3. To make each person aware of his or her own responsibility to God. The exilic judgment was not simply the result of their ancestors' sins.

We must look at these verses in Ezekiel 37 through lenses described by Paul in 1 Corinthians 14:3: "One who prophesies speaks to men for edification and exhortation and consolation." This is also the way we as Christians—who live with almighty God in the reality of the New Covenant—are to view the prophetic.

Yes, the office of the prophet does additionally move in the realms of declaring direction and correction, whereas the simple gift of prophecy does not include these dimensions. But for the time being let's tear this passage apart with the redemptive perspective that even tearing down is ultimately for the purpose of building up.

We are off to the races and are going to cover a lot of ground in a little bit of time. So hold onto your hat; we are about to go on one exhilarating ride!

The Temporary Condition: Are These Bones Dry!

> The hand of the LORD was upon me.
>
> verse 1

Too many people have the idea that God has a clenched fist and is ready to hammer us with words of judgment every chance He gets. Thus they view the prophetic lifestyle as one in which God continually pours out His wrath toward a wayward people through whoever is unfortunate enough to receive and convey His vengeful words.

No, no, a thousand times, no! That is not the connotation of the word *hand of God* in this Scripture. The word for "hand" here, in Hebrew, is *yad*, which means "the open hand of God." It was the *open* hand of God that was on Ezekiel—open to release a blessing, to "edify, exhort and console."

> And He brought me out by the Spirit of the LORD and set me down in the middle of the valley; and it was full of bones.
>
> verse 1

Dr. David Cho of South Korea has stated, "The American Church has a lot of talkie, talkie but not a lot of walkie, walkie." Sometimes we get overspiritualized notions of what it means to be "in the Spirit." If we are going to be in the Spirit, we must be so heavenly minded that we are definitely going to do some earthly good! We must release practical applications of God's Kingdom all around us. Here Ezekiel, led by God's Spirit, was given an "otherly" perspective. Let's walk in the Spirit by experiencing the Spirit to release the life of the Spirit in life-practical ways.

> He caused me to pass among them round about, and behold, there were very many on the surface of the valley; and lo, they were very dry.
>
> verse 2

Ezekiel was making an observation about the condition of these bones: They were very dry, fragmented and in great disarray. Many times we get words of knowledge about the present or even past conditions in a church, city, nation or in an individual's life, and it might not look too great. It might look dark and even hopeless. But God does not intend to leave us in that condition.

How would you like it if you were called out in front of a lot of people, told all about your problems and then asked to sit down? No word of encouragement, no solution, just an exposure of a raw soul! That is *not* what the prophetic is all about. God desires to give us remedies to our illnesses and evils. He has a solution for all our pollution. He wants to give the Church a hope-filled word so we can move out of the dry places we find ourselves in. That is the purpose of prophetic revelation.

When I was a young pastor, a nationally recognized leader came to our city to minister. We held the meetings on the local university campus in hopes of making it more of an outreach. The noted guest speaker detected that our fellowship was experiencing a difficult and dry time. He spoke from what he saw at present and not from our prophetic potential. Basically he told us to dig around the joint for a year, see if there was any life, and if not, to write *Ichabod* over it and shut it down. He really left me encouraged—*not!* I made a determination through that painful process that if the Lord ever released me to go minister at other churches and cities, my goal would be to encourage them, not to deflate them.

God has a word of wisdom (prescription) to go along with every word of knowledge (diagnosis). Jehovah Jireh, our Provider, is better than any physician on earth. Even a medical doctor follows up with a prescription after giving a diagnosis. Shouldn't we do the same—or even better?

> He said to me, "Son of man, can these bones live?" And I answered, "O Lord GOD, You know."
>
> verse 3

God's question to Ezekiel was an invitation to intervention. Ezekiel responded honestly by admitting he did not know, but that he was sure God did. To Ezekiel they looked dry and lifeless, but maybe God had a different perspective. He was right, God did. And prophetic revelations are invitations from God to bring change to situations, circumstances and temporary problem areas of life. We are invited into divine cooperation. Remember, God knows the answer—but He has predetermined to involve us in bringing His solution.

The Hebrew word for *live* in this passage is the same word used for *Eve*, and it means "to declare life." God wants to bring us remedies and teach us how to declare life. Ezekiel did not know about those bones, but God was fixing to show him something awesome. The prophetic is an invitation to see the open hand of God release His blessing on hopeless, helpless lives.

Can the dry bones of your life, family or city live?

Prophesy Over These Bones

> Again He said to me, "Prophesy over these bones and say to them, 'O dry bones, hear the word of the LORD.'"
>
> verse 4

This is the purpose of the prophetic—to speak the word of the Lord to dry bones. Leaders in the Church need to be speaking to the dry bones of the Body of Christ that they might rise up and live. Believers need to unite and declare life over the broken, fragmented structures of society. Let's not leave the inner cities to the dogs; let's get a higher vision. For Jesus' sake, let's transform the very darkest places into centers of revival and light.

"To prophesy" is simply to speak or sing, with inspiration, the current mind or heart of God. We need to be seeking God that we might excel in edifying the Body of Christ. "So also you, since you are zealous of spiritual gifts, seek to abound for the edification of the church" (1 Corinthians 14:12). We are to release God's life by declaring life to dry people, dry places, dry churches and dry cities.

Have you noticed that in the New Testament we do not find prophetic words given in the verbiage of "thus saith the Lord"? That is primarily an Old Testament model. I suggest that we need a more down-to-earth delivery to put the word of the Lord within reach of people. His message is coming not to make a grandiose display of flowery and exaggerated words, but to help people. Simple presentations delivered in a humble style can make a profound impact on another's life when it is the true word of the Lord.

Living in modern-day America, not in old England, I am not even sure what some of the King James language means, as poetically beautiful as it is. The Lord uses the words and expressions familiar in our day to communicate His heart. And when we visit another country, He often uses different expressions and language forms according to the culture of the people He is addressing.

At the London Prayer Summit in June 2000, I was speaking on the theme "Creating an Opening," but my attention kept being drawn toward a gentleman to my right. Every time I glanced his way, syllables kept running through my mind like *A-la-ha-bad*. It started becoming persistent, even a bit annoying.

I knew in my spirit it was name of a city, but my mind kept attempting to analyze as I was preaching: *Now that's either in Pakistan or Afghanistan.* I would look at the hungry gentleman and strong impressions would come, yet my natural mind would argue, *Don't make a fool of yourself. You don't know what nation he's from, and you can't even say it right, either!* All the while I was preaching away on the necessity of being a people of God's presence.

Finally I grew just plain tired of the inner debate, walked over to him and in proper British English, not Nashvillian slang, blurted out, "Conrad of Allahabad."

I was not even sure what I had said.

His reaction was startling; his eyes opened up really big.

I proceeded to announce that he had come from India to London to catch the spirit of prayer, and that he would return to his city and begin a 24-hour house of prayer.

The man looked both shaken and enlightened. It was obvious that life had been imparted.

Later he said to me, "You told me my name and what city I was from. How did you know those things?"

I looked at him and said, "I didn't."

He reacted quickly. "Yes, you did! My name is Conrad and I'm from the city of Allahabad on the Ganges River in India, where every year thirty to forty million Hindus come to wash themselves of their sin. I came here to get an impartation for prayer since I want to start a house of prayer in one of India's darkest cities."

Praise the Lord! Life had been spoken. Vision had been imparted. The "hope lights" had come on, and Conrad returned home to Allahabad, India, filled with faith.

One of the amazing things to *me* was that I had spoken in British English with the correct vowel pronunciation and emphasis on the right syllables. For a guy who grew up in Cowgill, Missouri, a town of 259 people, that is a cultural miracle!

But the real point is, God wants us to look deeply into His heart and breathe forth His blessings into and over the broken circumstances we see around us in a way people are able to receive. Build a bridge to carry your cargo, not a wall they cannot see over!

> "Thus says the Lord GOD to these bones, 'Behold, I will cause breath to enter you that you may come to life. I will put sinews on you, make flesh grow back on you, cover you with skin and put breath in you that you may come alive; and you will know that I am the LORD.'"
>
> verses 5–6

Prophecy calls forth the breath of God to enter difficult circumstances and situations. This "breath" is the Holy Spirit Himself being released. As His breath blows into the fragmented structures of people's lives, then families, churches, cities and nations can come together and live. God is the source of life, and prophecy acts as a refreshing wind that brings His life-giving oxygen to a stale and dry environment.

Breathe life, O God, into us, Your Church. Breathe upon the nations. Awaken us that we might truly know You!

So I Prophesied

Let's move to the next installment:

> So I prophesied as I was commanded; and as I prophesied, there was a noise, and behold, a rattling; and the bones came together, bone to its bone. And I looked, and behold, sinews were on them, and flesh grew and skin covered them; but there was no breath in them.
>
> verse 7–8

Who does the prophesying? We do. We just do it! Whatever God has called us to do, we are the ones who do it. The Holy Spirit does not fall on us and knock us down and pour things into us, and then push them out of us, by force. We begin by faith to speak out the small words we have received, and then God multiplies those words in our mouths. There are different levels of revelation, for sure. But you have to start somewhere.

Much of the time when I prophesy, I do not feel any special anointing or push from within; I just do it because I know God wants to speak. I yield my voice to Him and then I speak forth His word. We do not have to rely on some special feeling or manifestation to cause us to open our mouths. There is a sense in which we prophesy by faith. "Since we have gifts that differ according to the grace given to us, each of us is to exercise them accordingly: if prophecy, according to the proportion of his faith" (Romans 12:6). But please learn to stay in your measure of faith!

Nowhere in the Bible does it say the Holy Spirit speaks according to the gift of tongues. Nor does it say angels are to preach the everlasting Gospel for us. Guess what? Nowhere in the Bible does it say God prophesies, either! He gives the inspiration; we supply the perspiration. In other words, all vocal gifts are released through the vocal cords of a living being. All God is looking for is a donkey

He can come and sit on who will carry Him into the city. Hey, I qualify for that! Don't you?

Let Your breath enter my being, O Lord, and let me exhale words of life.

The word *command* means "to appoint" or "to be charged"—not so much by prompting but by commandment. This term denotes stewardship. Just as we are stewards of our money and give because God's Word tells us to, we are to be stewards of the word of the Lord. We should not act like children who have to be reminded continuously to do their daily chores. Maturity is doing what you are commanded without being told over and over to do it. Maturity and love emphasize obedience. Maturity is obeying even when you are not told to obey. "If anyone loves Me, he will keep My word; and My Father will love him, and We will come to him and make Our abode with him" (John 14:23).

As we begin to step out on that limb of faith called *r-i-s-k*, miraculous things happen. As Ezekiel stepped out and spoke to those dry bones, he heard a noise as those bones began rattling and moving together. Just imagine the word of the Lord coming through *you* and causing new life to spring up in a person or in a body of believers or even in a nation. It can happen!

At the wedding in Cana of Galilee, when Jesus turned the water to wine, do you know when it happened? Not when the servants filled the waterpots with water, but "when the headwaiter tasted the water which had become wine" and told the bridegroom, "You have kept the good wine until now" (John 2:9–10). The water was not wine as it was being poured into the vessels, but when it was drawn out of the vessels for tasting! It is the same with us. As we step out in faith, God turns the living water He has given us into wine for the thirsty.

Another Vocal Miracle

In October 2000 I was ministering in Guatemala City, Guatemala, to the leadership of El Shaddai Church. I felt directed at the end to have us pray in the Holy Spirit out loud together for the World Congress on Revival that was to begin the next day.

As we entered into corporate prayer, I began to intercede in the gift of tongues in a forceful, repetitive manner. It was obvious that I kept repeating particular phrases. Pastor Harold Caballeros came up to the platform and explained in Spanish to the people that I had been speaking in two languages that he recognized. He stated, and others confirmed, that I had spoken in Korean saying, "Lord, Lord, Lord," over and over. Then in Quiche, a native Guatemalan language, I had declared, "It's time for My people to enter in."

I opened wide my mouth, got into the river and God supplied the vocal miracle. But I did the speaking! It was encouraging and faith-building for me (let alone those who were listening) to see that happen.

At a general session of the World Congress that week, with people gathered from more than sixty nations, I recounted in a teaching on "Gatekeepers of His Presence" that I had spoken in the Quiche language. Then I called for all who were from that region or who spoke that language to come forward. They came literally running to the front—hungry native peoples, many dressed in their tribal clothing. I declared over them, "It's time for My people to enter in!" The power of God's presence came powerfully on those humble indigenous people as life was declared over their lives, hearts and villages. I was overwhelmed as the Lord's goodness moved among them. You see, it is not about us; it is really all about Him.

The psalmist said, "Open your mouth wide and I will fill it" (Psalm 81:10). You must open it and He will use you to declare a vocal miracle.

There Was a Noise!

When we step out in faith and do what we know to do, something happens. A noise begins to erupt from within people whose lives are being quickened by the word of the Lord. A rattling goes on in those dry bones as they come together, bone to bone, to form a structure for life. People get excited and start moving when prophecy touches their dry places and the wine begins to lift their spirits and they start to act like the people God created them to be. It is the noise of celebrating life. One thing I have learned from the births of our four children—life brings a lot of noise to the house!

Another kind of noise, too, often follows prophetic revelation: the noise of persecution. People get unsettled when the status quo is disturbed. Jesus was a master at disturbing the status quo of religious people. And if we speak the testimony of Jesus, we will rattle the religious and they will make an awful noise. But praise God for those who dare to disturb religion and bring forth life!

While in another nation recently, I heard God's voice one morning calling me to "change the equilibrium of the Church. What she calls balance, I call imbalance." But that raises some eyebrows. The voice of the Lord thunders and creates a sudden shift or change in history. It creates noise. Doesn't that sound like the work of a revolutionary? (Hey, this prophetic revolution is not my idea; it is His!)

Prophesy to the Breath

> Then He said to me, "Prophesy to the breath, prophesy, son of man, and say to the breath, 'Thus says the Lord GOD, "Come from the four winds, O breath, and breathe on these slain, that they come to life."'"
>
> verse 9

We see here God teaching Ezekiel prophetic intercession. He instructed Ezekiel in how to speak prophetic prayers, inviting the Spirit of God to bring life to the dead. Ezekiel was prophesying to the breath—to the wind!

You might say, "I don't know how to prophesy. I don't think I hear the word of the Lord." Well, listen to me with both ears: Just pick up your Bible and begin to declare the living Word over those whom you know to be dead. Anyone who can read can prophesy the Word of God. He has already told us what His will is, so declare it in prayer over those you know. Declare it over your families, your cities, your nation. Speak to the wind! Address the heavenlies and call for a new beginning to come forth. Declare life through the power of prophetic proclamation. Let life *be*, in Jesus' name!

"So that the manifold wisdom of God might now be made known through the church to the rulers and the authorities in the heavenly places. This was in accordance with the eternal purpose which He carried out in Christ Jesus our Lord, in whom we have boldness

and confident access through faith in Him" (Ephesians 3:10–12).
Hallelujah! We have boldness and confidence through our faith in
Jesus to access the heavenlies and declare life.

The Church has a powerful weapon in the area of prophetic intercession to unseat the enemy from his strongholds and to expand the
territory of the Kingdom of God in this earth. We ought to be pillag-
ing the forces of darkness. I exhort you to "prophesy to the breath"
and bring forth the Spirit of God where death has been ruling.

Calling Forth the Army

> So I prophesied as He commanded me, and the breath came into
> them, and they came to life and stood on their feet, an exceedingly
> great army.
>
> verse 10

We must prophesy out of God's bigger vision. Let God fill your
heart with a vision of His purposes. Out of the inspiration of Scripture and by the current daily operation of the revelatory inspiration of the Holy Spirit on our lives, we can declare that which is
not as though it already is (Romans 4:17). We can declare God's
plan for our generation.

But you say, "I don't know a word for my city or my generation."
Then prophesy one from another generation, as Daniel did. Daniel
took a prophecy from Jeremiah 29, more than a generation before
him, and prophesied what he read to his own generation, exiled in
Babylon.

Study your family history or your city's history and find promises of God that will lift your family or city out of death into life.
Apply yourself to the written Word of God, and inspiration will
spring forth into your prayer life and convert your everyday place
of living. Then you can go out into the streets and prophesy to the
lady at the grocery store, the man at the service station and your
next-door neighbor, and speak the living Word of God into their
lives. You will watch an exceedingly great army begin to arise out
of the throngs of death and take on the life of God. Don't wait for
a revolution; *be* the revolution!

You do not know whom you will have an impact on. That one you speak to just might end up influencing the world. You might see dry bones, but look deeper into the heart of God. Prophesy life!

My friend Mickey Robinson and I were doing a prophetic conference together in east Texas in March 1995. Mickey proceeded to bring a nice-looking, well-dressed gentleman before me and asked me to minister to him.

The man stood there a bit like a totem pole, straight, respectful and cautiously reserved. I look at him and thought, *Help!* Then I looked past the natural into the heart of God. As I did, I began to see pictures in the eye of my spirit—promises, purposes and destiny—and described to the man what I saw.

"I see a new national platform that will be built for you soon," I said. "You will become like a missile with a new fire lit under you." I saw some different Scriptures written on the missile and identified them to him. Then I said with a bit more unction, "Soon a new fire will be lit under your life, and you will be like a missile that will be shot forth, and that fire will go around the world seven times!"[2]

He did not bat an eye. And as he walked away I wondered, *Huh? What was that?* I thought I had hit the target but was left a bit puzzled. Later I learned that this man was already a seasoned evangelist and that he had lived in South America at one point.

Three months later, on Father's Day, June 1995, he went to do a one-time Sunday morning meeting at the Brownsville Assembly of God Church in Pensacola, Florida. Truly a fire *did* get lit under him that morning and a national platform was built. It began the Brownsville Revival, which is still going on today. That nice-looking, reserved man was Steve Hill, who is turning the world upside-down calling forth a new Jesus revolutionary army.

Paradigm Shifts for the Twenty-First Century

Now that we have taken a look at Ezekiel 37 and learned principles of declaring life over broken, fragmented structures, let's peek into the future to see part of what this prophetic revolution might look like. Remember that a revolution consists of a sudden shift or change in society and history.

Yes, as we cross the threshold of a new millennium, there will be a lot of shifting taking place in the Church and in the world. It will be a time of cleansing and preparing for a spiritual "churchquake" to transpire as we move full-steam ahead. With this view in mind, let me present some bullets on paradigm shifts for the twenty-first century.

- An apostolic relational mandate will be released, emphasizing networking as opposed to vertical authority structures. This fresh emphasis on cross-pollination will replace much of the inbred church associations that are rife with the spirit of competition and control.

- While in worship I was given the following phase: *When the Apostolic is Made Personal (AMP), there will be Mighty Authority in the Prophetic (MAP) in that day.* The Lord will amplify His voice in these relational renewal centers, and the Holy Spirit will put them on His map.

- Confrontation with the political spirit in the Church will come, and with it the ushering in of a post-sectarian era. Even as the prophetic movement exposed and confronted the religious spirit in the Church, so an apostolic movement of grace will expose and lay an ax to the historical root of the political spirit.

- The restoration of David's Tabernacle as prophesied in Amos 9:11–12 and Acts 15:16–18 will come forth, resulting in authentic 24-hour houses of prayer and praise, worship and intercession, sprinkled across the nations. New creative songs and sounds will emerge, as happened with the radical ministry of William and Catherine Booth's Salvation Army bands in the late nineteenth century. No longer will praise be confined within the four walls of the church, but it will spill out into the open air.

- The church world will continue to shift theologically away from the false theory of cessationism—that spiritual gifts passed away with the closing of the canon of Scriptures or with the second-generation apostles of the early Church. In other words, cessationism is going to cease!

- A new signs and wonders movement is emerging. Healing rooms and centers will be instituted in many cities, devoted to praying for the sick and the casting out of evil spirits (Luke 10). We will see parades of people healed of various diseases, as in the days of John G. Lake in the 1920s.

- There will be a great move of the Holy Spirit among women. Many women will be released into the fivefold ministry and used in the worldwide revival that is coming and that is already on us. Ultimately the issue will not primarily be doctrinal; it will be one of necessity, due to the need for laborers for the harvest. The coming period could easily be termed "the decade of women preachers."

- A renewed quietist movement will emerge, as believers in Christ find the secret place of the Most High truly to be their dwelling places (Psalm 91). A fresh revelation will come forth of intimacy with God and communion with our Lover, Husbandman and Master. A generation of Mary of Bethany's will arise and gladly "waste" their lives on the Lord!

- A fresh holiness movement will spring up in the Church worldwide. It will emphasize the Father's mercy mixed with an authentic spirit of conviction of sin (John 16:8–11), causing many to repent and have their stained garments experientially cleansed by the power and blood of the Lord Jesus Christ.

- The Body of Christ will awaken to her call and responsibilities to reach and lift up the poor and oppressed, as stated in Isaiah 58:6–12. Finances will be released to care for the widow and orphan, as declared in James 1:27. Orphanages will be started as the Church awakens from her self-centered lifestyle and restores hilarious, joyful giving (2 Corinthians 9:7).

- We will see tremendous transfers of wealth into the Kingdom of God through the ministry of "marketplace apostles and prophets." Those with anointings for business, administration and creativity shall be blessed, not resisted, by the Church. The walls between clergy and laity, between spiritual ministry and the secular marketplace, will come down.

- An extravagant youth movement will sweep over the global Body of Christ and rock the nations. Public events will be led by youth to encourage prayer and fasting for revival, which will spread rapidly around the nations. This will be a transgenerational anointing, in which the hearts of the fathers are turned to their children and the hearts of the children to their fathers (Malachi 4:5–6). Events such as The Call, which gathered hundreds of thousands of youth and adults in Washington D.C., on September 2, 2000, will multiply and ripple across the nations.

- A wave of identificational repentance will overwhelm a remnant of the Gentile Church, causing her to repent of historical wrongs against the Jewish people. In response, a revelation of the Sabbath rest will be released from the throne of grace that will be nonlegalistic and result in healing to many.

- A great harvest among the Jewish people will increase in this decade. This will affect the Russian Jews, in particular, around the world. There will be what some missiologists term "a people movement" among them. A parallel persecution of the Jews will also take place in "the land of the north," and potentially other lands as well. It is the devil's strategy to precipitate another holocaust—but God will raise up trumpeters like Mordecai who will prepare the corporate Esther, the Church, for such a time as this. Radical prayer will open a window of escape for those Jewish people who feel called to leave, and a hedge of protection for those temporarily called to stay (Jeremiah 16:14–16).

- A "convergence of the ages" will come upon us. The falling of Pentecostal fire, healing and deliverance crusades, the latter rain presence, the evangelical burden for the lost, the charismatic giftings, the zeal of the Jesus people movement, the credibility of the third wave, the revelation of the prophetic movement, and the relational networking of the apostolic reformation—all will swell into a tidal wave greater than the impact of the Reformation five hundred years ago and create what could be called the great revolution.

- The Lord will give the Church an opportunity to rewrite her stained and spotted history. Radical deeds of identificational repentance, acts of mercy to the poor and oppressed, presence and power encounters to the sick and demonized, warrior praise and intercession arising over cities—all these will mount as a revolution comes on the global Body of Christ, creating a great societal awakening. If a history book is written about the years that lie ahead, it might be termed *The Days of His Glorious Presence.*

I am sure much more will occur as these days unfold. We see in part, know in part and prophesy in part. But when we each bring our own part to the table, it creates a whole. This is a little bit of the part I perceive. The Holy Spirit will give other parts to other players as we cooperate together and the ATM—the Apostolic Team Ministry—comes forth.

Do You Want to Be Part?

Prophetic revelation is a key to bringing forth an end-time army of believers that will take the Gospel to the four corners of the earth and spread the testimony of Jesus from pole to pole. Can you hear the call? Can you feel the Spirit moving on your heart for you to arise and take your place in the prophetic revolutionary army God is forming? May we all join forces under the leadership of the Almighty, and move forward to meet our Bridegroom as He comes in the power of His might to claim His inheritance!

Remember my beginning thesis statement? *If there is to be a revolution in the prophetic, then there must be a prophetic revolution in the Church. And if there is a prophetic revolution in the Church, there will be the greatest global awakening of authentic Christianity that this world has ever seen.*

Do you believe this? I do, and am sold out to see it happen. Want to join me and a cast of thousands who will sign on for something radical to transpire? Hey, there's gonna be a revolution! Enlist as one of His passionate, consecrated warriors for a last-days invasion of planet earth, and be sold out to Jesus, to prophesy life wherever you go.

OUR CLOSING CONSECRATION

*Holy God, we submit ourselves to You and ask for the baptism
of fire to consecrate our very lives to You and Your will. We volunteer freely in the day of Your power, and we ask that You
empower us with a fresh baptism from on high.*

*Teach us to declare life wherever we go. Help us look on the tem-
poral, and then look up for the spiritual, and speak life to our valley of dry bones. Come, Holy Spirit, breathe on our lives. Breathe
on our families. Breathe on our churches and denominations.
Breathe on our cities. Breathe on our nations. May a revolution
take place in the Church, and the greatest outpouring of Your love,
power and conviction come streaming forth, in Jesus' name. Let
the revolution begin!*

POP QUIZ—KEEPING YOU ON YOUR TOES!

1. What did you learn from Ezekiel 37?
2. How can you declare life over your life, family, city and
   church?
3. What are some of the paradigm shifts for the 21st century?

FOR MORE, LORD!

Marc DuPont, *The Church of the Third Millennium* (Shippensburg, Pa.: Destiny Image, 1997)

Jim W. Goll, *Kneeling on the Promises* (Grand Rapids:
Chosen, 1999)

Barbara Wentroble, *Prophetic Intercession* (Ventura, Calif.:
Renew, 1999)

Scriptures That Deal with Prophecy

Following is a listing of Old and New Testament passages that demonstrate or address the area of the prophetic. (It is by no means exhaustive, since God speaks through human channels all the way through the Bible!)

Prophecy in the Old Testament

Gen. 5:29

Gen. 27:28–29
Gen. 27:39–40
Gen. 48:13–20
Gen. 49:1–27

Ex. 15:14–18
Ex. 16:6–7

Lev. 9:6

Num. 11:24–35
Num. 13:30
Num. 14:6–9
Num. 23:7–10

Num. 23:18–24
Num. 24:1–9
Num. 24:15–24

Deut. 32:1–47
Deut. 33:1–29

Joshua 10:25
Joshua 24:2–14

Judges 6:8–10

1 Sam. 2:1–10
1 Sam. 24:8–15

2 Sam. 3:18–19

2 Sam. 7:8–17
2 Sam. 23:1–7

2 Kings 3:16–19

1 Chron. 17:4–15
1 Chron. 22:8–13
1 Chron. 22:17–19

2 Chron. 15:2–7
2 Chron. 20:17

Ezra 9:6–15

Neh. 2:20
Neh. 9:5–37

Ps. 89:19–37

Is. 1:18–20
Is. 12:1–6
Is. 25:6–12
Is. 26:1–21
Is. 29:17–24
Is. 35:1–10
Is. 44:1–8
Is. 55:1–13
Is. 56:1–8
Is. 60:1–22

Ezek. 11:16–20
Ezek. 28:25–26
Ezek. 34:24–31

Hos. 2:14–20
Hos. 6:1–3
Hos. 11:8–9
Hos. 14:1–9

Joel 2:12–14
Joel 3:18–21

Amos 9:13–15

Obad. 15–18

Mic. 2:12–13
Mic. 4:1–8
Mic. 7:18–20

Nah. 2:2

Hab. 2:14

Zeph. 2:7
Zeph. 3:14–20

Haggai 2:4–9
Haggai 2:23

Zech. 8:1–23
Zech. 10:1–12

Mal. 1:11
Mal. 3:16–18
Mal. 4:1–6

Prophecy in the New Testament

Mark 10:29–30
Mark 14:8–9

Luke 1:41–55
Luke 1:67–79
Luke 2:25–38
Luke 11:9–13
Luke 22:31–32

John 6:35–40

Acts 1:4–8
Acts 2:14–36
Acts 11:28
Acts 13:2–3
Acts 15:30–35
Acts 20:28–31

Acts 21:10–11

Rom. 1:11
Rom. 12:4–8

1 Cor. 2:9
1 Cor. 3:10
1 Cor. 12:7–11
1 Cor. 12:14–26
1 Cor. 12:31
1 Cor. 14:1–5

Eph. 1:17–23
Eph. 4:11–16
Eph. 5:18

1 Thess. 5:19–21

1 Tim. 1:18
1 Tim. 4:14–15

Heb. 5:14

1 Pet. 4:10–11
2 Pet. 1:19–21

1 John 4:1

Jude 20–21

Rev. 1:17–19
Rev. 2:1–3:22
Rev. 19:10

MODELS OF PROPHETIC COMMUNICATION IN SCRIPTURE

Scripture mentions several different models of communication through which the prophetic spirit is released. The following teaching identifies seven distinct categories.

I. The Prophetic Oracle
A. The Form
The prophetic oracle is a declaration decreeing something into being. If this proclamation is authentic, it will be accompanied by a faith level, unction or anointing of God's presence.[1]

B. Effects
This style is often mocked by the world and mishandled by the Church. This form of delivery is the exception, not the rule, and can be abused. This type of expression implies that the Lord is speaking with authority.

C. Variety of Styles
There can be a great variety of styles and modes of delivery, which are usually learned and modeled more than most vessels often wish to admit (e.g., King James English, shouting, certain intonations, etc.).

D. Caution
Use wisdom here and don't tag God's name onto something He has not validated.

E. Scriptural Examples

A possible example is found in Acts 21:10–11, where Agabus warns Paul about what awaits him in Jerusalem. Also:

1. Isaiah 1:1–9
2. Isaiah 15:1–9
3. Isaiah 45:14–17
4. Isaiah 48:17–19
5. Isaiah 49:5–7
6. Isaiah 50:1–3
7. Isaiah 55:1–13
8. Isaiah 56:1–8
9. Jeremiah 2:1–3
10. Ezekiel 34:1–31
11. Acts 13:1–3
12. Acts 15:30–35

II. The Prophetic Exhortation

A. The Form

Its form is very similar to the prophetic oracle. It is more common in its usage as a tool to stir people up and urge them on in their faith and toward a particular goal.

B. Effects

The prophetic exhortation carries a tone of urgency for those to whom it is directed. It stimulates people into action and stirs up courage within them.

C. Variety of Styles

This can be an expression of the excitable, emotional realm of the gift of prophecy. There can be a variety of energetic expressions accompanying any of the categories of prophetic release.

D. Scriptural Examples

An example is Judas and Silas in Antioch, found in Acts 15:30–35. Also:

1. Isaiah 12:1–6
2. Isaiah 19:25
3. Isaiah 29:22–24
4. Isaiah 30:18
5. Isaiah 35:1–10
6. Isaiah 40:1–31
7. Isaiah 41:1–4
8. Isaiah 42:1–9
9. Isaiah 54:1–3

III. The Prophetic Prayer

A. The Form

Revelatory prayer is one of the most common expressions of the prophetic spirit. It is sometimes also referred to as prophetic intercession.[2]

B. God-Directed

This is not preaching directed at people but petitions filled with Holy Spirit illumination directed to God.

C. God-Inspired

This form of prophetic prayer takes place when we pray more than we know or understand on a given matter.

D. Scriptural Examples

1. Ezra 9:6–15
2. Nehemiah 9:6–37
3. Isaiah 25:1–12
4. Isaiah 38:9–20

5. Isaiah 64:1–12
6. Jeremiah 12:1–6

7. Jeremiah 20:7–18
8. Luke 1:67–69

IV. The Prophetic Song

A. The Form

This song is imparted or inspired spontaneously. Often it comes all at once to the person, complete and never to be repeated.

B. Expressing the Mood of God

The singer or instrumentalist is being used to express the current mind and mood of God through song. This can be an intercessory song from the heart of God or a more directed prophetic song from the Lord to His people.

C. Scriptural Examples

Among the many biblical expressions is Moses' poetic song found in Deuteronomy 32:1–43.[3] Also:

1. Isaiah 5:1–30
2. Isaiah 26:1–21
3. Isaiah 27:1–11

4. Isaiah 42:10–13
5 Ezekiel 19:1–14
6. Ezekiel 27:1–36

V. The Personal Prophecy

A. The Form

This is one of the most common and expected communication modes of the prophetic. It is referred to in Paul's first epistle to Timothy as "prophetic utterance with the laying on of hands by the presbytery" (1 Timothy 4:14).

B. Effects

1. It edifies, exhorts and comforts (1 Corinthians 14:3).
2. It may release conviction (2 Samuel 12:1–12 between Nathan and David).
3. It may provide information with specific direction, purpose or timing (Acts 21:10–11 between Agabus and Paul).

C. Caution

We must always test things that are brought forth (1 Thessalonians 5:19–21; 1 John 4:1). It is usually beneficial to wait and be patient when "words" come our way. Once again a word of caution is in order: Seek the God of the word and the Word of God more than a personal word through a gifted person.[4]

D. Scriptural Examples

1. 2 Samuel 12:1–12
2. Isaiah 37:21–35
3. Isaiah 38:1–8
4. Isaiah 45:1–7
5. Jeremiah 20:1–6

6. Jeremiah 21:1–14
7. Jeremiah 34:1–5
8. Jeremiah 45:1–5
9. Acts 21:10–11
10. 1 Timothy 4:14

VI. The Prophetic Vision
A. The Form
Many of the prophets in Scripture received prophecy through dreams and visions (e.g., Revelation 4:1–2). This is particularly true in Old Testament examples of prophetic ministry (e.g., Zechariah 4).
B. The Seer
The visionary person operates as the seer, versus the bubbling-up, *nabi*, prophetic type. They do not typically repeat phrases but rather describe pictures.[5]
C. Scriptural Examples
1. Jeremiah 1:11–19
2. Jeremiah 24:1–10
3. Ezekiel 1:1–28
4. Ezekiel 8:1–18
5. Ezekiel 9:1–11
6. Ezekiel 10:1–22
7. Ezekiel 11:1–13
8. Ezekiel 37:1–11
9. Ezekiel 40:1–49
10. Ezekiel 41:1–48:35
11. Daniel 2:19
12. Daniel 4:1–18
13. Daniel 7:1–28
14. Daniel 8:1–27
15. Acts 10:1–33
16. Acts 16:9–10

VII. The Prophetic Action
A. The Form
At times the parabolic prophetic person is moved on to physically demonstrate his or her word—to "live the word." The mode of communication, therefore, is that of gestures and actions. This form of prophecy is not the norm, nor should it be promoted as higher or more significant than another.
B. Contemporary Examples
There are numerous contemporary examples of this mode of prophetic communication. These can be both intercessory actions and words of declaration or inspiration.[6]
C. Scriptural Examples
Jeremiah and the yoke (Jeremiah 27:2–3); Ezekiel shaving his head with a sword (Ezekiel 5:1–4); Hosea marrying a prostitute (Hosea 1:2–3); Agabus and the belt (Acts 21:10–11). Also:
1. Isaiah 20:1–6
2. Jeremiah 13:1–11
3. Jeremiah 19:1–15
4. Ezekiel 4:1–17
5. Ezekiel 12:1–16
6. Ezekiel 12:17–25
7. Ezekiel 24:1–27
8. Ezekiel 37:15–23

RELATING TO VISIONARY LEADERS

The following material has been adapted from the teaching ministry of Michael Sullivant, pastor of the prophetic at Metro Christian Fellowship in Grandview, Missouri. Michael is also the author of the respected book *Prophetic Etiquette*. Permission has been granted to include this pertinent and insightful material.

Please note that in this appendix, a visionary leader is the head of a group or organization who has been entrusted with the vision for that group. This is often a "father mentor," one standing in an apostolic role.

1. Determine whether or not God has called you to work with a particular visionary leader and to support his or her vision. This is the basic and most important question. A major part of this decision is determining whether or not the visionary leader is a righteous person. Another factor: discerning if he wants you and trusts you as a partner.
2. One of the characteristics of God's visionary leaders is that they have extraordinary confidence in their judgment because God has gifted them with this to enable them to lead. This means they can be more susceptible to arrogance, so they need prayer in this area.
3. Visionary leaders often initiate in many areas with others who have differing gifts and capacities. This often causes them not to be able to think about the totality of the expanding work. This is exacerbated by the tendency we all have to act as if the whole work is that particular part of the work that is most important to us.
4. These visionary leaders also often experience loneliness in their work and vision because . . .

a. Their confidence leaves others with the impression that they do not need anyone else.

b. Their vision allows them to see ahead of others, so in things most important to them, rarely does the vision of someone else totally encompass theirs. The gap between their vision and that of others is where they often stand alone.

c. They are typically not good at functioning as partners. They are warm and affirming when they are recruiting, but often less so with those who have signed on for the long haul. The recruited person comes to feel demoted, while the leader thinks he is affirming the person's maturity and value simply by assuming his or her role on the team. In addition, the confidence that visionary leaders have in their own judgment can make it difficult for them to hear the Lord through others. They want others to be partners, but often the press of the vision and the many decisions that go along with it means there is not enough time to bring others in as "party of the first part," even though this may be a sincere desire. In some instances they want partnership in implementing the work but not in making the decisions about what should be done.

d. In the nature of their visionary work, they relate to greater numbers of people than most. This is a prime example of the principle that "the man with many friends comes to ruin." Relationally they often get spread out and overcommitted.

e. Because many people want to be close to them for selfish reasons, and they have gotten burned, they hold people at a safe distance. (This is sometimes the reaping of what they have sown, in that they have also drawn close to people for the sake of their own vision.) There is a pressure to be relationally utilitarian.

f. There can be a high turnover rate of subordinates who did not understand or tolerate these dynamics.

5. How do I relate to these gifted leaders?

a. Pray for them, especially when you are involved in a project with them.

b. Support wholeheartedly all that you hold in agreement with them.

c. When you have questions that leave you unsure, assume the best and trust their gift of vision.

d. When you think they may be misled, direct confrontation is rarely the best approach. Their God-given confidence makes it difficult to present differing points of view. Thinking of the right questions about issues is a more helpful way to move into discussions.

e. Encourage them to have contacts with other peer ministries and visionaries who can challenge and stimulate their thinking in ways that others cannot.

f. Encourage them to value the gifts of others rather than seeing the Body of Christ only as people who can be employed in their vision.

g. Walk with the Lord and be part of a team so you do not "need" the approval or blessing of the visionary leader. Having others in your life meets your need for equal partnership.

h. Make it a goal to consistently affirm these leaders because they need encouragement more than they appear to.

i. Be loyal! Guard against disloyal comments to others, especially to those who (for right or wrong reasons) have a grievance. Be careful when you "defend" them so as not to uncover the weaknesses you see so clearly, and thus defame their character. One way to deal with situations that arise is to agree with legitimate criticisms and show the criticizer how to cope, rather than denying that the visionary leader has a weakness.

j. Write your thoughts, concerns or thanks briefly, rather than initiating conversations. This can be an effective way to keep your "relational fire" burning.

k. Ask for appointments when you need them; they will probably not take initiative with the low-maintenance long-termers.

l. Don't expect a lot of socializing (or hang time) with them. Their need for this does not seem normal! Their vision is their entertainment.

m. Pressure them to take vacations. They will be grateful you did.

n. Protect them from administrative details. Encourage them to delegate.

o. Don't expect appreciation from them for figuring all this out!

10 M's for Maturing and Maintaining Manhood and Ministry

The following chart was prepared by Dr. Bill Hamon for his book *Prophets, Pitfalls and Principles* to help us determine the true or false status of prophetic ministers.[1] Although it is titled and starts with the terminology of "manhood," its emphasis is not gender but integrity, character and accountability. This chart is used gratefully with permission.

1. Manhood

Gen. 1:26–27	God makes a man before manifesting a mighty ministry
Rom. 8:29	Man—apart from position, message or ministry
Heb. 2:6–10	Personality = evaluating person, not performance
1 Tim. 2:5	Jesus: manhood 30 years, ministry 3 1/2 years; 10:1 ratio

2. Ministry

2 Cor. 6:3	No offense to ministry; 1 Cor. 2:4–5; power and demonstration
Matt. 7:15–20	By their fruits you shall know them; anointing and results
Deut. 18:22	Prophecies or preaching productive; proven, pure, positive

3. Message

Eph. 4:15	Speaking the truth in love; presenting truth; life-giving
2 Tim. 4:2	Message balanced, scriptural, doctrinally and spiritually right
Mark 16:20	God—not person, pride or reputation—confirms His Word

4. Maturity

Jas. 3:17	Attitude right; mature in human relations, heavenly wisdom
Gal. 5:22–23	Fruit of the Spirit; Christlike character; dependable and steadfast (Heb. 5:14)
1 Cor. 13	Not childish; not a novice; biblically knowledgeable and mature

5. Marriage

1 Tim. 3:2–5	Scripturally in order—personal family vs. God's family
1 Pet. 3:1–7	Priorities straight—God first, spouse and family next, then ministry
Eph. 5:22–33	Marriage to exemplify relationship of Christ and His Church

6. Methods

Titus 1:15–16	Righteous, ethical, honest, upright
Rom. 1:18	Not manipulating or deceptive; doesn't speak "evangelistically"
Rom. 3:7–8	Good end results do not justify unscriptural methods

7. Manners

Titus 1:7; 3:1–2	Unselfish, polite, kind, gentlemanly or ladylike, discreet
Eph. 4:29; 5:4	Using proper communication in words, mannerisms

8. Money

1 Tim. 3:3	Not craving wealth and resorting to ignoble and dishonest methods
1 Tim. 6:17	Not destroyed by love of money, materialism (Josh. 7; Luke 12:15)

9. Morality

1 Cor. 6:9–20	Virtuous, pure and proper relationships (Col. 3:5)
Eph. 5:3	Biblical sexual purity in attitude and action (1 Cor. 5:11)
Matt. 5:28	Wrong thoughts of desire even without the opportunity to act

10. Motive

Matt. 6:1	To serve or to be seen? Fulfill personal drive or God's desire?
1 Cor. 16:15	True motivation—to minister or to be a minister?
Prov. 16:2	To herald the truth or just to be heard by man?
1 Cor. 13:1–3	Motivated by God's love or lust for power, fame, name?

NOTES

Chapter 1: A Revolution of Intimacy

1. Edwin Hatch, "Breathe on Me, Breath of God" as printed in *The Methodist Hymnal* (Nashville: Methodist Publishing House, 1966), p. 133.

2. C. Austin Miles, "I Come to the Garden Alone," as printed in *Hymns for the Living Church* (Carol Stream, Ill.: Hope, 1974), #398.

3. Ed Silvoso, *That None Should Perish* (Ventura, Calif.: Regal, 1994), p. 154.

Chapter 2: Characteristics of a Prophetic People

1. Leonard Ravenhill, quoted by T. Austin Sparks in *Prophetic Ministry* (Shippensburg, Pa.: Destiny Image, 2000), p. vii.

2. Ernest B. Gentile, *Your Sons and Daughters Shall Prophesy* (Grand Rapids: Chosen, 1999), pp. 56–58.

3. Gentile, *Sons*, pp. 66–68.

4. Michael Sullivant, *Prophetic Etiquette* (Lake Mary, Fla.: Creation House, 2000), p. 200.

5. Sparks, *Prophetic*, pp. 7–8.

6. "Leaning on the Everlasting Arms," as printed in *The Baptist Hymnal* (Nashville: Elisha A. Hoffman, 1887), p. 254.

7. Michael L. Brown, *Revolution! The Call to Holy War* (Ventura, Calif.: Renew, 2000), p. 214.

Chapter 3: The Cross as Our Prophetic Lifestyle

1. Sparks, *Prophetic*, pp. 53–54.

2. Rick Joyner, *Prophetic Ministry* (Charlotte, N.C.: MorningStar, 1997), p. 28.

3. Bill Hamon, *Prophets, Pitfalls and Principles* (Shippensburg, Pa.: Destiny Image, 1991), p. 21.

4. John and Paula Sandford, *The Elijah Task: A Call to Today's Prophets* (Tulsa: Victory House, 1979), p. 29.

5. Ed Dufresne, *The Prophet: Friend of God* (Temecula, Calif.: Ed Dufresne Ministries, 1989), pp. 42–43.

6. Brown, *Revolution*, p. 224.

7. Thomas Shepherd, "Must Jesus Bear the Cross Alone?" *The Methodist Hymnal*, #183.

Chapter 4: Surrendering to the Commander

1. J. W. Van Deventer, "I Surrender All," from *101 More Hymn Stories* (Grand Rapids: Kregel, 1985), p. 135. It was first published in 1896 in the collection *Gospel Songs of Grace and Glory*.

2. Brown, *Revolution*, pp. 57–58.

3. Paul Cain, quoted by Mike Bickle in *Growing in the Prophetic* (Lake Mary, Fla.: Creation House, 1996), p. 124.

4. Larry Randolph, *User-Friendly Prophecy* (Shippensburg, Pa.: Destiny Image, 1998), p. 126.

5. Hamon, *Prophets*, pp. 9–10.

6. Leonard Ravenhill, *Picture of a Prophet* (Shippensburg, Pa.: Destiny Image, 2000), quoted in Sparks, *Prophetic*, p. vii.

7. Hamon, *Prophets*, p. 7.

8. Leonard Ravenhill quoted in Sparks, *Prophetic*, pp. vii–viii.

Chapter 5: Our Revelatory Arsenal

1. Kenneth Hagin, *Gifts of the Spirit* (Tulsa: Faith Library Publications, 1999), p. 53.

2. Dick Iverson, *The Holy Spirit Today* (Portland: Bible Temple, 1976), p. 155.

3. Derek Prince, "The Gift of Prophecy," *Teaching Tapes* (Ft. Lauderdale: Derek Prince Ministries, n.d.).

4. Gentile, *Sons*, p. 162.

5. Hamon, *Prophets*, pp. 196–197.

6. C. Peter Wagner, *Your Spiritual Gifts Can Help Your Church Grow* (Ventura, Calif.: Regal, 1994), p. 200.

7. Sullivant, *Etiquette*, pp. 131–132.

8. Adapted from Jim W. Goll, *Equipping the Saints* (Anaheim, Calif.: Vineyard, fall 1989).

9. Paraphrased from Derek Prince's tape "How to Judge Prophecy" (Charlotte, N.C.: Derek Prince Ministries, 1971).

Chapter 6: The Anatomy of a Prophetic Word

1. Steve Thompson, *You May All Prophesy* (Charlotte, N.C: MorningStar), pp. 74–75.

2. Frank Damazio, *Developing the Prophetic Ministry* (Portland: Bible Temple Publishing, 1983), p. 65.

3. Thompson, *Prophesy*, p. 73.

4. Hamon, *Prophets*, pp. 141–142.

Chapter 7: The Pits and Pinnacles of Prophetic Ministry

1. Jim W. Goll, *Kneeling on the Promises* (Grand Rapids: Chosen, 1999), p. 116.

2. Rex B. Andrews, *What the Bible Teaches about Mercy* (Zion Ill.: Zion Faith Homes, 1985), p. 2.

3. Ken Blue, *The Authority to Heal* (Downers Grove, Ill.: InterVarsity, 1987), p. 76.

4. Graham Cooke, *Developing Your Prophetic Gifting* (Kent, Sussex, U.K.: Sovereign World, 1994), p. 145.

5. Derek Prince, "How to Judge Prophecy," Part 1, *New Wine*, January 1977, p. 15.

Chapter 8: Too Hot to Handle?

1. David Guralnik, *Webster's New World Dictionary* (New York: Simon & Schuster, 1982), p. 42.

2. Gentile, *Sons*, p. 299.

3. Joyner, *Prophetic*, p. 103.

4. Rodney Howard Browne, *The Touch of God* (Louisville: R.H.B.E.A. Publications, 1992), p. 1.

Chapter 9: Comrades or Competitors?

1. Jack Deere, *Surprised by the Power of the Spirit* (Grand Rapids: Zondervan, 1993), p. 73.

2. Bryn Jones, "Apostles and Prophets: The Vital Role of these Foundational Ministry Gifts," *Issachar Journal*, Vol. 1, No. 2, 1995, pp. 13, 15–16.

3. Hamon, *Prophets*, pp. 121–122.

Chapter 10: Let's Do It Together

1. Tommy Tenney, *God's Dream Team* (Ventura, Calif.: Regal, 1999), p. 19.

2. Wagner, *Spiritual Gifts*, p. 229.

3. Bill Hamon, *Apostles, Prophets and the Coming Moves of God* (Shippensburg, Pa.: Destiny Image, 1997), pp. 223–224.

4. Cindy Jacobs, *The Voice of God* (Ventura, Calif.: Regal, 1995), pp. 157–158.

5. Fuchsia Pickett, quoted in Kelly Varner, *The Three Prejudices* (Shippensburg, Pa.: Destiny Image, 1997), p. 31.

6. Edith Blumhofer, *The Assemblies of God: A Popular History* (Springfield, Mo.: Gospel Publishing, 1985), p. 137, as quoted in Benvenuti, *Pentecostal Women in Ministry* (her journal).

7. Jim W. Goll, *Father Forgive Us!* (Shippensburg, Pa.: Destiny Image, 1999), p. 109.

Chapter 11: Seizing Your Prophetic Destiny

1. This section is inspired from the writing and teaching of William Greenman, *How to Find Your Purpose in Life* (Pittsburgh: Whitaker, 1987), pp. 163–176.

2. *Webster's New World Dictionary* (New York: Simon & Schuster, 1982), p. 141.

3. Ibid., p. 127.

4. Kenneth W. Osbeck, "Be Thou My Vision," *101 More Hymn Stories* (Grand Rapids: Kregel, 1985), p. 44.

5. See my study guides *War in the Heavenlies* and *Strategies of Intercession* for more on this subject.

6. See my study guide *Releasing Spiritual Gifts* for more on this subject.

7. See "The Power of Proclamation" in my study guide *Compassionate Prophetic Intercession* for more on this subject.

8. See my study guide *Experiencing Dreams and Visions* for more on this subject.

9. Ancient Irish hymn translated by Mary E. Byrne (1880–1931), versed by Eleanor H. Hull (1860–1935), *The Methodist Hymnal*, #256.

Chapter 12: Prophesy Life!

1. The inspiration for this section of the book came as I listened to the piercing yet humorous message by Larry Randolph, an author and prophetic minister of many years from Southern California. His message was entitled "The Anatomy of a Prophetic Word." He is the author of the book *User-Friendly Prophecy* (Destiny Image, 1998).

2. Recently I had the privilege of being with Steve Hill in Guatemala City, Guatemala. He began his public presentation by commenting on the impact that word had on his life and the launching of the Brownsville Revival in Pensacola, Florida. Today Steve has moved back to Texas as his base and travels the world spreading the fire of holy passion and evangelism.

Appendix 2: Models of Prophetic Communication in Scripture

1. See "The Power of Proclamation" in the study guide *Compassionate Prophetic Intercession*.

2. See the study guide *Compassionate Prophetic Intercession*.

3. See "The Prophetic Song of the Lord" in the study guide *Prophetic Foundations*.

4. See "Receiving and Releasing the Gift of Prophecy" in the study guide *Prophetic Foundations*, as well as "Judging Revelation" in the study guide *Experiencing Dreams and Visions*.

5. See "Visionary Revelation" in the study guide *Experiencing Dreams and Visions* and "The Seer and the Prophet: Similarities and Differences" in the study guide *Prophetic Maturation*.

6. See "Prophetic Gestures and Actions" in the study guide *Understanding Supernatural Encounters*

Appendix 4: 10 M's for Maturing and Maintaining Manhood and Ministry

1. Hamon, *Prophets*, pp. 19–20.

Defining Our Terms: A Contemporary Glossary

I hope this simple section will help clarify the meaning of terms used throughout this book or related terms. By no means is it a thorough and comprehensive professional dictionary. Rather, I have simply defined these terms in my own words to help build a bridge with my readers. I trust it will be of help to you.

Achilles' heel. A term denoting a blind spot or place of weakness, vulnerability in a person's life.

Angelic visitation. A time in which heavenly ambassadors or messengers are released into the earthly realm and individuals experience their appearing. At times their presence can be felt and seen as well as heard. See *Angels, Visitation.*

Angels. These heavenly messengers are created beings for the primary purpose of worshiping God. They also may go forth obeying the voice of His word (Psalm 103:20–21) to declare the message of the Lord and to release displays of God's power, judgment or manifested presence. See *Angelic visitation.*

Anointing. The presence and power of God manifested—or the manifested presence of God—working in, on or through an individual or group, enabling them to do the works of Christ. See *Manifested presence of God.*

Apostle. One called and sent by Christ to have the spiritual authority, character, gifts and abilities to reach and establish people in Kingdom truth and order, especially through founding and overseeing local churches.

290

Awakening. A historic intervention of God's presence that revives the Church to such an extent that it affects society and brings it back to the moral values of God. North America has experienced two Great Awakenings, and some believe the greatest awakening is about to be released on a worldwide level.

Baptism in the Holy Spirit. The receiving and continued infilling of the power and life of the Holy Spirit, enduing believers in Christ with power and life to be His witnesses.

Breakers. Those called to break open the way for the Lord to come forth (Micah 2:13). Like John the Baptist, they are forerunners preparing the way for the coming of the King. See *Forerunner.*

Cessationism. A theological belief system stating that the gifts of the Holy Spirit ceased when the canon of Scripture was closed or with the second-generation apostles of the early Church. Cessationists do not accept that the gifts of the Spirit are valid or necessary for today.

Character. The moral fiber of a person life proceeding from a heart commitment to the Lord Jesus Christ producing the fruit of the Spirit. See *Fruit of the Spirit.*

Charismatic. Coming from the Greek word *charis* for "grace," a term coined in the 1960s to describe those who believe that the gifts of the Holy Spirit are still active today.

Cross. The common wooden structure reserved for criminals on which the Lord Jesus Christ was crucified. Though without sin, He identified on the cross with our sinful condition and carried the judgment or penalty of the sin of all mankind. Believers, in turn, are called to die to self, pick up their crosses and follow Him.

Day of Atonement. The most holy day for the Jews, an annual day of fasting, penitence and sacrifice for sin. Before the destruction of the Temple, the High Priest would enter the Holy of Holies on the tenth day of the seventh month of the Hebrew calendar and offer sacrifices for the sanctuary, the priests and the people. This foreshadowed the entrance of Jesus, the great High Priest, who offered Himself as our eternal sacrifice once for all, having purchased for us eternal salvation. This holiday, also known as Yom Kippur, is observed today with fasting and confession of sins.

Deliverance. A Holy Spirit encounter by which an individual is set free in the name of Jesus from the oppression of evil spirits, and also from circumstances that oppress from without.

Demonization. The state of being under the influence or control of a demonic power.

Dream. The inspired pictures and impressions given to the heart while one is sleeping. These are given by the Holy Spirit in order to teach, exhort, reveal, warn, cleanse or heal.

Encounter. A personal experience in which an individual or group is confronted with the living reality of the Lord Jesus Christ by the present-day work of the Holy Spirit.

Evangelicals. Christians who believe in the inerrancy of Scripture and the classic doctrines of the Church—including the deity of Jesus Christ, His atoning death and His bodily ascension and return—with evangelistic zeal.

Forerunner. One who goes before so as to prepare the way for another. This term is commonly used today of the prophetic (e.g., John the Baptist) preceding the apostolic (e.g., Jesus Christ). See also *Breakers*.

Fruit of the Spirit. A reference to Galatians 5:22–23 concerning love, joy, peace, patience, kindness, goodness, faithfulness, gentleness and self control. These are the qualities in a person's life that make up their godly character. See *Character*.

Gatekeepers. The elders of a city or church who have the authority to open or close the gates of a city as alerted by the watchmen. See *Watchmen*.

Gift of discerning of spirits. Supernatural perception given by God to enable believers to distinguish the motivating spirits behind words or deeds, and to discern the source of operation as human, demonic or the Holy Spirit.

Gift of prophecy. The supernatural ability to hear the voice of the Holy Spirit and speak God's mind or counsel. Given for the purpose of edifying, exhorting, comforting, convicting, instructing, imparting and testifying of and from Jesus.

Gift of tongues. The supernatural ability given by God to enable believers to speak in a language, whether earthly or heavenly, that they have not learned. This gift is used in prayer, in communion with God, to edify the one speaking and to communicate a message supernaturally in a language known by those listening.

Gifts of the Spirit. The expression of God's power at work, given by the Holy Spirit, to be used at special times for special occasions. Such gifts as recorded in 1 Corinthians 12:4–11 are the attestation of the empowering of the Holy Spirit and are vital in the signs and wonders ministry.

Healing evangelist. One who heralds the Good News with signs, wonders, miracles and healings following.

Humility. A true knowledge of God and oneself. It means to declare and confess that the Lord is great and exceedingly to be praised, and to declare that before Him we are nothing.

Intercession. The act of making a request to a superior, or expressing a deep-seated yearning to our one and only Superior, God.

Intercessor. One who reminds God of His promises and appointments yet to be fulfilled; who takes up a case of injustice before God on behalf of another; who makes up the "hedge" (that is, builds up the wall in time of battle); and who stands in the gap between God's righteous judgments and the people's need for mercy.

Jesus people/movement. A movement in which thousands of young people came to know the Lord Jesus Christ in the late 1960s and early '70s.

Jezebel spirit. A demonic presence after the character and nature of Queen Jezebel (1 Kings 16:31; 21:25; 2 Kings 9:7; Revelation 2:20), married to King Ahab, who hated the prophets of God and whose aim was to destroy them. This is a domineering spirit that emasculates spiritual authority by manipulation, witchcraft and sexual immorality.

Latter rain movement. A historic move of the Holy Spirit in the late 1940s and early '50s in which the prophetic gifts, healing, the laying on of hands and singing in the Spirit were restored to the Body of Christ. See *Laying on of hands*.

Laying on of hands. A method of ministering to individuals for consecration, ordination, gift impartation, healing and blessing. This was a practice of both Old and New Testaments and the early Church, and it was restored to the Body of Christ in the last century as an accepted model.

Manifested presence of God. While God is omnipresent, or everywhere, He nevertheless reveals or manifests His presence strategically and locationally.

No common ground. Every spiritual warrior must allow the Holy Spirit to prepare him before battle through purification. The reason Jesus could stand in such power and authority, and deal so effectively with the wicked oppressor, was that He had no ground in common with His adversary.

Open heaven or portal. A hole, opening or portal between heaven and earth through which the manifested presence of God is poured forth over those in that vicinity.

Open vision. A kind of vision in which the natural eyes are open and the believer sees and perceives realities in the spiritual world.

Paradigm. A model or pattern in society or thought. The term is commonly used to describe new trends or facets that are creating a new way of viewing things (a paradigm shift).

Pentecostal. A Christian who emphasizes the baptism in the Holy Spirit with the accompanying gift of speaking in tongues; generally connected with one of several Pentecostal denominations.

Political spirit. A term used to describe a demonic spirit that comes against leadership (governmental authorities) to persuade them with strategic thinking and plans in order to come into alignment with the ways of darkness.

Power evangelism. The response to the spontaneous direction of the Holy Spirit to minister the power of the Gospel for salvation (as opposed to following a planned program to evangelize).

Power healing. Holy Spirit demonstrations in which one is set free and healed physically, emotionally or spiritually from the chains of captivity.

Presbytery. A group of elders or leaders in the Church; overseers set to watch over and care for the congregation.

Priest. One who pleads the needs of the people before God. In the Old Testament a special tribe, the Levites, was set apart for this purpose. In the New Testament each believer in Christ is a priest unto the Lord.

Priestly intercession. An intercessory task in which the priest not only represents himself before the Lord but, like priests of old, carries the twelve stones of Israel—the burdens, needs and cares of others—on his heart before the great High Priest.

Prophet/prophetess. A man or woman who represents the interests of God to the people. Having stood in the council of God, the prophet releases a clarion call to the people of what is in God's heart at the moment. Some refer to this as one of the fivefold ministry gifts listed in Ephesians 4:11.

Prophetic destiny. The revelatory promise of God portraying His purposes, plans and pursuits for an individual, group, city or nation.

Prophetic intercession. The act of waiting before God in order to hear or receive His burden—His word, concern, warning, condition, vision or promise—and responding back to Him and the people with appropriate actions.

Prophetic presbytery. A selected group of seasoned, mature, revelatory-gifted believers ministering together over individuals or congregations, often with the laying on of hands. See *Laying on of hands.*

Prophetic priests. Individuals in whom are united the Old Testament offices of prophet and priest with New Testament applications for today. They not only hear from the Father the pronouncements from His throne, but they pray the promises back to Him.

Prophetic song of the Lord. An inspired revelatory song sung by an individual or group declaring the heart of the Lord for that specific setting. It is hearing the voice of God and singing His heart.

Prophetic unction/anointing. When one is impressed by the Holy Spirit to speak, sing or act out what has been revealed by a special enduement of grace.

Radical. Someone seeking to change the current status of the Church, calling it back to its original roots. The kind of basic change that alters society.

Refreshing. To make a person or congregation feel replenished, renewed or stimulated to be made strong. A reference used today to refer to a move of the Holy Spirit called "the refreshing" (Acts 3:19–21). See *Renewal, Restoration, Revival.*

Renewal. To renew something that has been growing stale. This is a term used in the context of the Church, such as "the charismatic renewal." See *Charismatic, Refreshing, Restoration, Revival.*

Repentance. A turning around to go the opposite direction; a 180-degree turn. A change of heart that alters outward behavior. A turning away from sin and turning toward the Lord and His ways.

Restoration. To recover or return to an original state or condition. The progressive pattern of recalling a person, church or community to its former place of influence and impact (Acts 3:19–21). See *Renewal, Refreshing, Revival.*

Revival. To revive, to bring back to life. In Church history, it is a term used to call the Church back to a place of vigor and life and renew her call to evangelism and to be salt and light in the world. See *Renewal, Refreshing, Restoration.*

Revolution. A sudden shift or change in society that effects history, such as a call to return to radical, authentic Christianity.

Seer. An individual gifted as a "receptor" of God, operating in visions and revelatory gifts to "see" and describe what is received from the Lord.

Seven Spirits of God. The fullness of the expression of the ministry of the Holy Spirit as demonstrated by the Spirit of the Lord and the spirits of wisdom, knowledge, counsel, understanding, strength and fear of the Lord (Isaiah 11:1–3; Revelation 1:4; 5:6).

Spirit of revelation. The unfolding or unveiling of God's will to the eyes of the heart. The revelation of truth, otherwise unknown, can come through impressions, prophecy, dreams, visions, trances and messages from the Lord.

Spiritual warfare. The confrontation of the kingdom of darkness by the power of the Kingdom of God to displace the works of darkness and elevate God's Son Jesus.

Stronghold. A lie we believe that is not in alignment with the will and Word of God and that is transmitted into our minds from the enemy's camp (2 Corinthians 10:4–6).

Supplication. To entreat, seek, implore or beseech God in earnest prayer.

Trance. A visionary state in which revelation is received from God. In this rapturous state, an individual is no longer limited to natural consciousness and volition. He is "in the Spirit," where full consciousness of the natural may be temporarily transcended.

Travail. An intense form of prayer that brings forth a birthing in the spirit, which creates or enlarges an opening for an increased dimension of the Kingdom of God.

Vision. A sight disclosed supernaturally to the spiritual eyes. There are various levels of visions—with eyes both open and closed, panoramic (moving) and still-frame shots.

Visionary revelation. The grace of the Holy Spirit enabling a Christian to experience such manifestations as visions, dreams and trances.

Visitation. A supernatural experience in which a distinct sense of the presence of God is accompanied by fear of the Lord. This may come in the form of an angelic visitation, as in the book of Acts, or by other biblical means. See *Angels, Angelic visitation.*

Waiting. A posture of stillness before the Lord but attentiveness to His Spirit moving.

Watch of the Lord. A gathering in Jesus' name to watch, pray and be vigilant for the life of a church, city or nation (Matthew 24:42–44; Mark 13:35–37; Luke 21:36). A watch is also a position on the wall of the Lord in order to see outside the city and alert the gatekeepers of approaching enemies or envoys from the King; and to see inside the city to recognize and confront disorderly, unlawful activity of the enemy.

Watchmen. Those who serve in the position of watching. See *Watch of the Lord.*

Wisdom. An understanding of what is true and right; having good judgment and sound, prudent counsel.

Witchcraft. Any spirit other than the Holy Spirit in which people operate to manipulate and control others. See *Jezebel, Spiritual warfare.*

Word of knowledge. Supernatural revelation by the Holy Spirit disclosing the truth or a fact He wishes to make known about a person or situation.

Word of wisdom. Supernatural revelation by the Holy Spirit disclosing the remedy, solution or way of God that He wishes to make known for that particular situation. See *Wisdom.*

Worship. Posturing one's heart in awe and reverence before God; bowing down before Him. We worship God for who He is and we praise Him for what He has done.

REFERRAL READING
FOR MORE
GOOD STUFF

Alves, Elizabeth. *The Mighty Warrior*. Bulverde, Tex.: Intercessors International, 1987.

Andrews, Rex B. *What the Bible Teaches about Mercy*. Zion: Zion Faith Homes, 1985.

Anna Marie of Mar del Plata, Argentina, as told to R. Edward Miller. *I Looked and I Saw Mysteries*. College Park, Ga.: Peniel, 1971.

Anna Marie of Mar del Plata, Argentina, as told to R. Edward Miller. *I Looked and I Saw the Lord*. College Park, Ga.: Peniel, 1971.

Aune, David E. *Prophecy in Early Christianity*. Grand Rapids: Eerdmans, 1983.

Austin, Dorothea. *The Name Book*. Minneapolis: Bethany, 1982.

Bacovcin, Helen, trans. *The Way of a Pilgrim and The Pilgrim Continues His Way: Spiritual Classics from Russia*. New York: Doubleday/Image, 1992.

Baker, H. A. *Visions Beyond the Veil*. Minneapolis: Osterhus, 12th edition in English, 1973.

Bennett, Ramon. *When Day and Night Cease*. Jerusalem: Arm of Salvation, 1992.

Bickle, Mike. *Passion for Jesus*. Lake Mary, Fla.: Creation House, 1993.

———. *A Personal Prayer List*. Kansas City, Mo.: Metro Christian Fellowship, 1988.

——— with Michael Sullivant. *Growing in the Prophetic*. Lake Mary, Fla.: Creation House, 1996.

Billheimer, Paul E. *Destined for the Throne*. Minneapolis: Bethany, 1975.

Blomgren, David. *Prophetic Gatherings in the Church: The Laying on of Hands and Prophecy*. Portland: BT Publications, 1979.

———. *Song of the Lord*. Portland: BT Publications, 1978.

Bounds, E. M. *The Complete Works of E. M. Bounds on Prayer.* Grand Rapids: Baker, 1990.

Bradshaw, Paul F. *Two Ways of Praying.* Nashville: Abingdon, 1995.

Bright, Bill. *The Coming Revival.* Orlando: New Life, 1995.

Brown, Michael L. *Revolution! The Call to Holy War.* Ventura, Calif.: Renew, 2000.

Buck, Roland, as told to Charles and Frances Hunter. *Angels On Assignment.* Houston: Hunter, 1979.

Bullinger, Ethelbert W. *Numbers in Scripture.* Grand Rapids: Kregel, 1967.

Cain, Paul. *The Gift of Tears.* Kansas City, Mo.: Shiloh, 1997.

Campbell, Wesley. *Welcoming a Visitation of the Holy Spirit.* Lake Mary, Fla.: Creation House, 1996.

Capps, Charles and Annette. *Angels.* Tulsa: Harrison House, 1984.

Castro, David A. *Understanding Supernatural Dreams according to the Bible.* Brooklyn: Anointed Publications, 1994.

Chavda, Mahesh. *Only Love Can Make a Miracle.* Ann Arbor, Mich.: Vine, 1990.

Chevreau, Guy. *Pray with Fire: Interceding in the Spirit.* Toronto: Harper-Perennial/HarperCollins, 1995.

Clement, Kim. *The Sound of His Voice.* Lake Mary, Fla.: Creation House 1993.

Conner, Kevin J. *Interpreting Symbols and Types.* Portland: BT Publications, 1980.

———. *Today's Prophets.* Portland: BT Publications, 1989.

——— and Ken Malmin. *Interpreting the Scriptures.* Portland: BT Publications, 1983.

Cooke, Graham. *Developing Your Prophetic Gifting.* Kent, Sussex, U.K.: Sovereign World, 1994.

Cornwall, Judson. *Praying the Scriptures.* Lake Mary, Fla.: Creation House, 1990.

Crist, Terry. *Warring According to Prophecy.* Springdale, Pa.: Whitaker, 1989.

———. *Interceding against the Powers of Darkness.* Tulsa: Terry Crist Ministries, 1990.

Dahle, Anker G., publisher. *Visions of Sadhu Sundar Singh of India.* Minneapolis: Osterhus.

Damazio, Frank. *Developing the Prophetic Ministry.* Portland: Trilogy, 1983.

Dawson, Joy. *Intimate Friendship with God.* Old Tappan, N.J.: Chosen, 1986.

Deere, Jack. *Surprised by the Power of the Spirit.* Grand Rapids: Zondervan, 1993.

———. *Surprised by the Voice of God.* Grand Rapids: Zondervan, 1996.

Duewel, Wesley L. *Mighty, Prevailing Prayer.* Grand Rapids: Francis Asbury/Zondervan, 1990.

———. *Revival Fire.* Grand Rapids: Zondervan, 1995.

———. *Touch the World through Prayer.* Grand Rapids: Zondervan, 1986.

Dufresne, Ed. *The Prophet: Friend of God*. Temecula, Calif.: Ed Dufresne Ministries, 1989.

DuPont, Marc. *The Church of the Third Millennium*. Shippensburg, Pa.: Destiny Image, 1997.

Eastman, Dick. *Change the World School of Prayer*. Studio City, Calif.: World Literature Crusade, 1976.

———. *The Hour That Changes the World: A Practical Plan for Personal Prayer*. Grand Rapids: Baker, 1978.

———. *Love on Its Knees*. Old Tappan, N.J.: Chosen, 1989.

———. *No Easy Road: Inspirational Thoughts on Prayer*. Grand Rapids: Baker, 1971.

Engle, Lou. *Digging the Wells of Revival*. Shippensburg, Pa.: Destiny Image, 1998.

de Fénelon, François. *The Seeking Heart*. Beaumont, Tex.: SeedSowers, 1992.

Finney, Charles G. *Lectures on Revival*. Minneapolis: Bethany, 1988.

Forsyth, P. T. *The Soul of Prayer*. Salem, Oh.: Schmul, 1986.

Foster, Glenn. *The Purpose and Use of Prophecy*. Glendale, Calif.: Sweetwater, 1988.

Foster, Richard J. *Prayer: Finding the Heart's True Home*. San Francisco: HarperSanFrancisco, 1992.

——— and James Bryant Smith. *Devotional Classics: Selected Readings for Individuals and Groups*. San Francisco: HarperSanFrancisco, 1993.

Frangipane, Francis. *The House of the Lord*. Lake Mary, Fla.: Creation House, 1991.

Gardiner, Gordon P. *Radiant Glory: The Life of Martha Wing Robinson*. Brooklyn: Bread of Life, 1962.

Gastineau, Pat. *Modes of Prayer*. Roswell, Ga.: Word of Love, 1997.

———. *The Spiritual Fight*. Roswell, Ga.: Word of Love, 1997.

Gentile, Ernest B. *Your Sons and Daughters Shall Prophesy*. Grand Rapids: Chosen, 1999.

Goll, Jim W. *The Lost Art of Intercession*. Shippensburg, Pa.: Destiny Image, 1997.

———. *Father, Forgive Us!* Shippensburg, Pa.: Destiny Image, 1999.

———. *Kneeling on the Promises*. Grand Rapids: Chosen, 1999.

———. *Wasted on Jesus*. Shippensburg, Pa.: Destiny Image, 2000.

——— and Michal Ann Goll. *Encounters with a Supernatural God*. Shippensburg, Pa.: Destiny Image, 1998.

Graham, Billy. *Angels: God's Secret Agents*. Garden City, N.Y.: Doubleday, 1975.

Greenman, William D. *Purpose, Destiny, Achievement*. Shippensburg, Pa.: Destiny Image, 1998.

Grubb, Norman. *Rees Howells, Intercessor*. Fort Washington, Pa.: Christian Literature Crusade, 1987.

Grudem, Wayne. *The Gift of Prophecy in the New Testament Church and Today.* Westchester, Ill.: Crossway, 1988.

Guyon, Jeanne. *Experiencing God through Prayer.* Donna C. Arthur, ed. Springdale, Pa.: Whitaker, 1984.

Hagin, Kenneth E. *The Art of Intercession: Handbook on How to Intercede.* Tulsa: Kenneth Hagin Ministries, 1987.

———. *Concerning Spiritual Gifts.* Tulsa: Faith Library, 1974.

———. *The Gift of Prophecy.* Tulsa: Faith Library, 1982.

———. *The Holy Spirit and His Gifts.* Tulsa: Faith Library, 1974.

———. *I Believe in Visions.* Tulsa: Faith Library, 1984.

———. *The Ministry of a Prophet.* Tulsa: Faith Library, 1981.

Hamon, Bill. *Apostles, Prophets and the Coming Moves of God.* Shippensburg, Pa.: Destiny Image, 1997.

———. *The Eternal Church.* Point Washington, Fla.: Christian International, 1981.

———. *Prophets and Personal Prophecy, Vol. 1, God's Prophetic Voice Today.* Shippensburg, Pa.: Destiny Image, 1987.

———. *Prophets and the Prophetic Movement.* Point Washington, Fla.: Christian International, 1990.

———. *Prophets, Pitfalls and Principles.* Shippensburg, Pa.: Destiny Image, 1991.

Hamon, Jane. *Dreams and Visions.* Ventura, Calif.: Regal, 2000.

Hawthorne, Steve, and Graham Kendrick. *Prayer-Walking: Praying on Site with Insight.* Lake Mary, Fla.: Creation House, 1993.

Hayford, Jack W. *Prayer Is Invading the Impossible.* S. Plainfield, N.J.: Bridge, 1995.

———. *Did God Not Spare Nineveh?* Van Nuys, Calif.: Church On The Way, 1980.

Heschel, Abraham. *The Prophets.* Peabody, Mass.: Hendrickson, 1962.

Hess, Tom. *The Watchmen.* Charlotte, N.C.: MorningStar, 1998.

Hill, Clifford. *Prophecy Past and Present.* Ann Arbor, Mich.: Servant, 1991.

Hicks, Dr. Roy H. *Guardian Angels: How to Activate Their Ministry in Your Life.* Tulsa: Harrison House, 1991.

Hill, Stephen. *Time to Weep.* Foley, Ala.: Harvest, 1996.

Houston, Graham. *Prophecy: A Gift for Today?* Downers Grove, Ill.: InterVarsity, 1989.

Howard, Philip E. *The Life and Diary of David Brainerd.* Jonathan Edwards, ed. Chicago: Moody Bible Institute, 1949, 1995.

Intercessors for America. *USA Pray! Training Manual.* Reston, Va.: Intercessors for America, 1989.

Isleib, Mary Alice. *Effective, Fervent Prayer.* Minneapolis: Mary Alice Isleib Ministries, 1991.

———. *The Holy Spirit Today.* Portland: BT Publications, 1976.

Iverson, Dick. *Being a Prophetic People*. Portland: BT Publications, 1989.

———. *The Holy Spirit Today*. Portland: BT Publications, 1976.

Jacobs, Cindy. *Hearing the Voice of God*. Ventura, Calif.: Regal, 1995.

———. *Possessing the Gates of the Enemy*. Tarrytown, N.Y.: Chosen, 1991.

Jacobsen, Wayne. *A Passion for God's Presence*. Eugene, Ore.: Harvest House, 1991.

Johnson, Nita. *Prepare for the Winds of Change*. Omaha, Neb.: Eagle's Nest, 1991.

Joyner, Rick. *The Prophetic Ministry*. Charlotte, N.C.: MorningStar, 1997.

———. *The World Aflame: The Welsh Revival and Its Lessons for Our Time*. Charlotte, N.C.: MorningStar, 1993.

Keating, Thomas. *Open Mind, Open Heart*. New York: Continuum, 1986.

Kendall, R. T. *The Anointing*. London: Hodder & Stoughton, 1998.

Kenney, Carlton. *Standing in the Council of the Lord*. Hampton, N.Y.: Master-Builder Ministries, 1992.

Kelsey, Morton T. *Companions on the Inner Way: The Art of Spiritual Guidance*. New York: Crossroad, 1983.

———. *God, Dreams, and Revelation*. Minneapolis: Augsburg, 1974.

Lawrence, Brother, and Frank Laubach. *Practicing His Presence*. Auburn, Mass.: Christian, 1973.

Lindsay, Gordon. *Prayer and Fasting: The Master Key to the Impossible*. Dallas: Christ for the Nations, 1979.

Lloyd-Jones, Martyn. *Enjoying the Presence of God*. Ann Arbor, Mich.: Servant, 1991.

Meeks, Steve. *The Last Great Revival*. Houston: Calvary, 1994.

Mumford, Bob. *Take Another Look at Guidance*. S. Plainfield, N.J.: Logos, 1971.

Murray, Andrew. *Absolute Surrender*. Springdale, Pa.: Whitaker, 1982.

———. *Like Christ*. Springdale, Pa.: Whitaker, 1981.

———. *Waiting on God*. Springdale, Pa.: Whitaker, 1981.

———. *With Christ in the School of Prayer*. Springdale, Pa.: Whitaker, 1981.

Nori, Don Sr. *The Power of Brokenness*. Shippensburg, Pa.: Destiny Image, 1997.

———. *Secrets of the Most Holy Place*. Shippensburg, Pa.: Destiny Image, 1992.

Nouwen, Henri J. M. *The Way of the Heart*. New York: Ballantine, 1983.

———. *Making All Things New*. New York: Ballantine, 1983.

Patterson, Ben. *Waiting: Finding Hope When God Seems Silent*. Downers Grove, Ill.: InterVarsity, 1989.

Penn-Lewis, Jessie. *Opened Heavens*. Poole, Dorset, U.K.: Overcomer Publications (part of Overcomer Literature Trust), 1900.

Pierce, Chuck D. and Rebecca Wagner-Sytsema. *Possessing Your Inheritance*. Ventura, Calif.: Renew, 1999.

Prince, Derek. *Blessing or Curse: You Can Choose!* Old Tappan, N.J.: Chosen, 1990.

———. *Fasting.* Fort Lauderdale: Derek Prince Ministries, 1986.

———. *How to Fast Successfully.* Fort Lauderdale: Derek Prince Ministries, 1976.

———. *How to Judge Prophecy.* Fort Lauderdale: Derek Prince Ministries, 1971.

———. *The Last Word on the Middle East.* Lincoln, Va.: Chosen, 1978.

———. *Praying for the Government.* Fort Lauderdale: Derek Prince Ministries, 1970.

———. *Shaping History through Prayer and Fasting.* Old Tappan, N.J.: Spire, 1973.

——— and Ruth Prince. *Prayers and Proclamations.* Fort Lauderdale: Derek Prince Ministries, 1990.

Pytches, David. *Prophecy in the Local Church: A Practical Handbook and Historical Overview.* London: Hodder & Stoughton, 1993.

———. *Spiritual Gifts in the Local Church.* Minneapolis: Bethany, 1985.

Randolph, Larry. *User-Friendly Prophecy.* Shippensburg, Pa.: Destiny Image, 1998.

Ravenhill, David. *For God's Sake Grow Up!* Shippensburg, Pa.: Destiny Image, 1998.

Ravenhill, Leonard. *Revival Praying.* Minneapolis: Bethany, 1962.

———. *A Treasury of Prayer: The Best of E. M. Bounds on Prayer in a Single Volume.* Minneapolis: Bethany, 1981.

———. *Why Revival Tarries.* Minneapolis: Bethany, 1959, 1982.

Riffel, Herman H. *Dream Interpretation: A Biblical Understanding.* Shippensburg, Pa.: Destiny Image, 1993.

———. *Dreams: Wisdom Within.* Shippensburg, Pa.: Destiny Image, 1989.

Roundtree, Anna. *The Heavens Opened.* Lake Mary, Fla.: Creation House, 1999.

Runcorn, David. *A Center of Quiet: Hearing God When Life Is Noisy.* Downers Grove, Ill.: InterVarsity, 1990.

Ruscoe, Doris M. *The Intercession of Rees Howells.* Fort Washington, Pa.: Christian Literature Crusade, 1983.

Ryle, James. *Hearing the Voice of God* (seminar notes). Boulder, Col.: Boulder Valley Vineyard, 1992.

———. *Hippo in the Garden: A Non-Religious Approach to Having a Conversation with God.* Lake Mary: Creation House, 1993.

———. *A Dream Come True.* Lake Mary: Creation House 1995.

St. Teresa of Avila. *Interior Castle.* E. Allison Peers, trans. and ed. New York: Image/Doubleday, 1961, 1989.

Sandford, John and Paula. *The Elijah Task: A Call to Today's Prophets.* Tulsa: Victory House, 1977.

Scott, Martin. *Prophecy in the Church.* Altamonte Springs, Fla.: Creation House, 1993.

Shaw, Gwen. *Redeeming the Land.* Jasper, Ark.: Engeltal, 1987.

Sheets, Dutch. *Intercessory Prayer.* Ventura, Calif.: Regal, 1996.

Silvoso, Ed. *That None Should Perish: How to Reach Entire Cities for Christ through Prayer Evangelism.* Ventura, Calif.: Regal, 1994.

Simpson, A. B. *The Life of Prayer.* Camp Hill, Pa.: Christian Publications, 1989.

Sjoberg, Kjell. *Winning the Prayer War.* Chichester, W. Sussex, U.K.: New Wine, 1991.

Smith, Eddie and Alice. *Intercessors and Pastors.* Houston: SpiriTruth, 2000.

Sorge, Bob. *In His Face.* Canandaigua, N.Y.: Oasis, 1994.

Sparks, T. Austin. *Prophetic Ministry.* Shippensburg, Pa.. Destiny Image, 2000.

Stearns, Robert. *Preparing the Way.* Lake Mary, Fla.: Creation House, 1999.

Sullivant, Michael. *Prophetic Etiquette.* Lake Mary, Fla.: Creation House, 2000.

Swope, Mary Ruth. *Listening Prayer.* Springdale, Pa.: Whitaker, 1987.

Tenney, Tommy. *The God Chasers: My Soul Follows Hard After Thee.* Shippensburg, Pa.. Destiny Image, 1998.

———. *God's Dream Team.* Ventura, Calif.: Regal, 1999.

Thomas, Benny. *Exploring the World of Dreams.* Springdale, Pa.: Whitaker, 1990.

Thompson, Steve. *You May All Prophesy!* Charlotte, N.C.: MorningStar, 2000.

Tompkins, Iverna, with Judson Cornwall. *On the Ash Heap with No Answers.* Altamonte Springs, Fla.: Creation House, 1992.

Thompson, Steve. *You May All Prophesy.* Charlotte, N.C.: MorningStar, 2000.

Traylor, Ellen Gunderson. *John, Son of Thunder.* Wheaton, Ill.: Tyndale, 1979.

Virkler, Mark and Patti. *Communion with God.* Shippensburg, Pa.: Destiny Image, 1990.

———. *Counseled by God.* Woy, Australia: Peacemakers, 1986.

———. *Dialogue with God.* S. Plainfield, N.J.: Bridge, 1986.

Wagner, C. Peter. *Apostles and Prophets.* Ventura, Calif.: Regal, 2000.

———. *Engaging the Enemy: How to Fight and Defeat Territorial Spirits.* Ventura, Calif.: Regal, 1991.

———. *Warfare Prayer.* Ventura, Calif.: Regal, 1992.

———. *Your Spiritual Gifts Can Help Your Church Grow.* Ventura, Calif.: Regal, 1994.

Wallis, Arthur. *God's Chosen Fast.* Fort Washington, Pa.: Christian Literature Crusade, 1968.

Wentroble, Barbara. *Prophetic Intercession.* Ventura, Calif.: Renew, 1999.

Willard, Dallas. *The Spirit of the Disciplines.* San Francisco: HarperSanFrancisco, 1991.

Wilson, Walter. *Wilson's Dictionary of Bible Types.* Grand Rapids: Eerdmans, 1950.

Wilkinson, Bruce. *The Prayer of Jabez Sisters.* Sisters, Ore.: Multnomah, 2000.

Willhite, B. J. *Why Pray?* Lake Mary, Fla.: Creation House, 1988.

Wimber, John. *Power Healing.* San Francisco: Harper & Row, 1987.

Yocum, Bruce. *Prophecy.* Ann Arbor, Mich.: Servant, 1976.

SUBJECT INDEX

SCRIPTURE INDEX

Books by Jim and Michal Ann Goll

Fire on the Altar
The Lost Art of Intercession (also in audio condensed book)
Encounters with a Supernatural God
Kneeling on the Promises
Women on the Frontlines
Father, Forgive Us!
Wasted on Jesus
Exodus Cry
The Coming Prophetic Revolution

Other Resources

Prayers for Israel (CD and cassette), *Invitation to Intimacy* (CD) and *Restoring David's Tabernacle* (worship CD)

13 complete study guides on subjects such as *Equipping in the Prophetic*, *Empower Ministry Training* and *Blueprints for Prayer*, with corresponding tape albums

Hundreds of audio teaching tapes and numerous videotapes

For ordering or more information contact:

Ministry to the Nations
P.O. Box 1653
Franklin, TN 37065
Phone: (615) 599-5552
Fax: (615) 599-5554

www.mttnweb.com
www.jimgoll.com

Jim and Michal Ann Goll are the founders of Ministry to the Nations, a covering agency for twelve missions, prophetic and intercessory expressions around the globe, and home base for the prophetic teaching and intercessory ministry of Jim and Michal Ann.

Both came to the Lord at an early age. They have traveled extensively across North and South America, Europe, Asia, the former Soviet Union, Israel and the Caribbean, teaching and imparting the power of intercession, prophetic ministry and life in the Holy Spirit. After pastoring for thirteen years, Jim was thrust in 1987 into an itinerant role of equipping leaders and churches.

He is a prolific author on a variety of subjects. The author of eight books, including *Kneeling on the Promises* (Chosen, 1999), he and Michal Ann have co-authored another book, *Encounters with a Supernatural God.* He is a member of the Council of Prophetic Elders under Dr. C. Peter Wagner; an instructor in the Wagner Leadership Institute; and a prophetic advisor for several regional and national ministries. He has also taught in the School of the Spirit of the Grace Training Center of Kansas City and been a dean of Christian Leadership University, Buffalo, New York.

Jim and Michal Ann have been married for 25 years. Since the Lord healed them from barrenness, the Golls have four lovely children, ages eleven to seventeen. They presently live in Franklin, Tennessee. Michal Ann shares out of the depths of her own prophetic experiences in the supernatural and is an accomplished vocalist.

Jim and Michal Ann's passion is to see Christ Jesus receive the rewards for His sufferings and to help ignite fires of revival throughout the nations.